P9-CME-431

OLD TESTAMENT MESSAGE

A Biblical-Theological Commentary

Carroll Stuhlmueller, C.P. and Martin McNamara, M.S.C.

EDITORS

Old Testament Message, Volume 21

PSALMS 1

(Psalms 1-72)

Carroll Stuhlmueller, C.P.

 Michael Glazier, Inc.
Wilmington, Delaware

First published in 1983 by: MICHAEL GLAZIER, INC. 1723 Delaware Avenue, Wilmington, Delaware 19806
Distributed outside U.S., Canada & Philippines by: GILL & MACMILLAN, LTD., Goldenbridge, Inchicore, Dublin 8 Ireland

©1983 by Carroll Stuhlmueller, C.P. All rights reserved.

Library of Congress Catalog Card Number: 82-83727
International Standard Book Number
  Old Testament Message series: 0-89453-235-9
  PSALMS 1
    0-89453-255-3 (Michael Glazier, Inc.)
    7171-1185-7 (Gill & MacMillan, Ltd.)

The Bible text in this publication is from the Revised Standard Version of the Bible, copyrighted 1946, 1952, ©1971, 1973 by the Division of Christian Education of the National Council of the Churches of Christ in the U.S.A., and used by permission.

Cover design by Lillian Brulc

Typography by Susan Pickett
Cartography by Lucille Dragovan
Printed in the United States of America

To
my sister Louise
on her fiftieth anniversary as a
Sister of Notre Dame de Namur
and to another sister Mary also with the same community
on the tenth anniversary
of her going home to God

TABLE OF CONTENTS

COMMENTARY

Editors' Preface

Old Testament Message brings into our life and religion today the ancient word of God to Israel. This word, according to the book of the prophet Isaiah, had soaked the earth like "rain and snow coming gently down from heaven" and had returned to God fruitfully in all forms of human life (Isa 55:10). The authors of this series remain true to this ancient Israelite heritage and draw us into the home, the temple and the marketplace of God's chosen people. Although they rely upon the tools of modern scholarship to uncover the distant places and culture of the biblical world, yet they also refocus these insights in a language clear and understandable for any interested reader today. They enable us, even if this be our first acquaintance with the Old Testament, to become sister and brother, or at least good neighbor, to our religious ancestors. In this way we begin to hear God's word ever more forcefully in our own times and across our world, within our prayer and worship, in our secular needs and perplexing problems.

Because life is complex and our world includes, at times in a single large city, vastly different styles of living, we have much to learn from the Israelite Scriptures. The Old Testament spans forty-six biblical books and almost nineteen hundred years of life. It extends through desert, agricultural and urban ways of human existence. The literary style embraces a world of literature and human emotions. Its history began with Moses and the birth-pangs of a new people, it came of age politically and economically under David and Solomon, it reeled under the fiery threats of prophets like Amos and Jeremiah. The people despaired and yet were re-created with new hope during the Babylonian exile. Later reconstruction in the homeland and then the trauma of apocalyptic movements prepared for the revelation of "the mystery hidden for ages in God who created all things" (Eph 3:9).

While the Old Testament telescopes twelve to nineteen hundred years of human existence within the small country of Israel, any single moment of time today witnesses to the reenactment of this entire history across the wide expanse of planet earth. Each verse of the Old Testament is being relived somewhere in our world today. We need, therefore, the *entire* Old Testament and all twenty-three volumes of this new set, in order to be totally a "Bible person" within today's widely diverse society.

The subtitle of this series—"A Biblical-Theological Commentary"—clarifies what these twenty-three volumes intend to do.

Their *purpose* is theological: to feel the pulse of God's word for its *religious* impact and direction.

Their *method* is biblical: to establish the scriptural word firmly within the life and culture of ancient Israel.

Their *style* is commentary: not to explain verse by verse but to follow a presentation of the message that is easily understandable to any serious reader, even if this person is untrained in ancient history and biblical languages.

Old Testament Message—like its predecessor, *New Testament Message*—is aimed at the entire English-speaking world and so is a collaborative effort of an international team. The twenty-one contributors are women and men drawn from North America, Ireland, Britain and Australia. They are scholars who have published in scientific journals, but they have been chosen equally as well for their proven ability to communicate on a popular level. This twenty-three book set comes from Roman Catholic writers, yet, like the Bible itself, it reaches beyond interpretations restricted to an individual church and so enables men and women rooted in biblical faith to unite and so to appreciate their own traditions more fully and more adequately.

Most of all, through the word of God, we seek the blessedness and joy of those

who walk in the law of the Lord!...

who seek God with their whole heart (Ps. 119:1-2).

Carroll Stuhlmueller, C.P.   Martin McNamara, M.S.C.

Author's Preface

The goal of this commentary is to enable the reader to pray the psalms ever more devoutly, to hear the voice of God ever more distinctly within each syllable. Yet this is not a devotional work. It is primarily a study manual. Hopefully the exposition will stand on its own, even if a reader does not check out all the cross references to other parts of the Bible. Generally the most representative of these citations is quoted in full. Yet, to read the others within one's Bible will not only enrich greatly one's appreciation of the psalm in question, but it will also locate the psalm and one's own devotional life within Israel's long tradition of faith and prayer. Our own prayer today, to be authentic, must absorb the spirit of our ancestors in the faith.

The goals then of this commentary determined the style of presentation. Each psalm is here studied:

first, according to the *origin* of the psalm in the social-religious background of ancient Israel and its *absorption of later modifications* from the life and worship of Israel;

second, according to the *literary form and structure* of the psalm;

third, according to *key words or phrases* and other important or difficult items within the psalm;

fourth, according to the *impact of the psalm today* in public worship, private devotion and social-moral questions.

This four-stage procedure appears very similar to that within the German commentary of A. Deissler. Yet this manuscript was well along its way to completion before the resemblance became apparent.

Although this method is generally followed, still there are exceptions. Lest this commentary become too bulky and forbidding, we have occasionally dropped the text of the psalms or printed only representative verses. At times too we have short-circuited the four steps of the presentation, combining I and II and even III, or blending all four stages into a single explanation.

The following method is recommended for using this commentary:

first, always read the text of the psalm before turning to this or any other commentary, in order a) to focus one's attention upon the word of God in the Bible rather than upon any human explanation; and b) to hear that word within the immediacy of life and community today;

second, after reading sections I and II of the commentary, reread the text of the psalm, so as a) to appreciate better the word of God in the Bible; and b) to know that word in the context of its origin in biblical times;

third, after studying section III of the commentary, a) to reread the psalm in the light of the key words or phrases as explained here; and b) to check references to other parts of the Bible, so as to see how the psalm and its key phrases are supported and enriched by the larger patterns of biblical theology;

fourth, after reflecting upon section IV and its application of the psalm within today's world, it is crucial that each person a) seek the relevance of the psalm according to his or her needs and inspirations; and b) reread the psalm again: "Today, if you hear God's voice, harden not your heart" (Ps 95:7-8).

At the end of this commentary there is found a list of popular books for additional study by the reader and also the names of a few, more scholarly works which offered more continuous assistance in preparing this work. Many other books and articles, consciously and often enough unconsciously, aided me in my studies over the years; these are too numerous to cite in a popular exposition like the *Old Testament Message,* or else they are lost to my memory. I am grateful for this family of scholarship which reaches ecumenically in many directions. Occasionally I have cited a scholar by name whose investigations have been incorporated into the commentary. Because some readers may want to study these sources more carefully, full information is provided at the end of the second volume.

There is nothing creative about this commentary. Its goal is the modest one of summarizing the best of scholarship or that which seems the most enduring. We seek most of all to put this scholarship to the service of one's faith in a personal God, one's fuller participation in church life and worship, one's outreach in devotional piety and daily contemplation. All these goals are mirrored with contagious inspiration in the lives of my two oldest sisters, Mary and Louise, who have spent themselves in the service of the Lord as Sisters of Notre Dame de Namur, Mary till her death in 1972, Louise for fifty golden years and more! All of my family are grateful to them and to all the Sisters of Notre Dame de Namur who have exerted a strong formation upon our spiritual and intellectual life.

I acknowledge the work of Sister Cathy Katoski, O.S.F., alumna of the Catholic Theological Union at Chicago, now engaged in pastoral ministry in the diocese of Joliet, for quickly and expertly typing a difficult manuscript. The participants of the Israel Study Program, Ein Karim, 1982, helped generously in proof-reading. There are many others, like Kenneth O'Malley, C.P., the librarian at the Catholic Theological Union, and the editors at Michael Glazier, Inc., who assisted graciously behind the scenes. To each and everyone I extend my gratitude.

Abbreviations

ANET   *Ancient Near Eastern Texts Relating to the Old Testament.* James B. Pritchard, editor. 3 ed. with supplement. Princeton University: 1969.

JB   Jerusalem Bible

NAB   New American Bible

RSV   Revised Standard Version

chap(s). chapter(s)

v(v).   verse(s)

5(6)x   five (or six) times

All biblical references follow the chapter and verse arrangement in the RSV.

Hebrew, RSV, NAB, JB	Greek, Vulgate, Rheims-Douay
Pss 1-8	1-8
9-10	9
11-113	10-112
114-115	113
116	114-115
117-146	116-145
147	146-147
148-150	148-150

As an example of versification:

Hebrew, NAB, JB (French)	RSV, JB (English)	Rheims-Douay
51:1-2, title	title	title
51:3-21	51:1-19	50:1-19

Introduction

The psalms are perhaps the most significant and influential collection of religious poems ever written. Thomas Aquinas wrote in the prologue to his exposition of the Epistles of St. Paul: "Just as among the Scriptures of the Old Testament those most frequently used are the psalms of David, who after sin received pardon, likewise in the New Testament those most frequently read are the epistles of Paul, who was the object of divine mercy, so that from these examples sinners also rise to new hope." Thomas Aquinas is echoing the attitude of an early collector and editor of psalms who appended titles to many psalms that linked the poems to David in his human weakness, fleeing from enemies (Pss 18; 54; 56-57) or drawn into sin (Ps 51). The psalms, as we shall see repeatedly in this introduction and commentary, are close to the earthly side of our existence, even to the point that we can shout defiantly to our God, "Wake up!" (Ps 44:23), and this is a psalm that opens solemnly within the ancient tradition of Israel!

The psalms also reflect the heavenly side of our existence! Thomas Merton declared: "Those whose vocation in the Church is prayer, find that they live on the psalms, for the psalms enter into every department of their life." Jesus quoted more often from the psalms than from any other book of the Sacred Scriptures. The Church's liturgy calls upon the psalms more often than any other Old Testament book. Somehow or other, all the Scriptures reach us in their quintessence and compact strength in the psalms. André Robert, a well known French scholar, put it this way: "The Book of Psalms enables us to hear an echo of the entire Bible whose doctrine it expresses in prayer." Centuries earlier, St. Basil declared, while commenting on Ps 1, "The Book of Psalms contains a complete theology."

I
Seeking the Old Testament Message

To unlock the riches of the psalms we need to be formed in the ways of Israelite prayer. This formation tells us to be more humanly relaxed in God's presence, but to appreciate the full scope of this recommendation we may require further information about the human setting of each psalm. The *first section* of each psalm's commentary in this book attempts to summarize when and why the psalm came into existence and how it evolved in later ages. Out of the original setting flowed Israel's various types of prayer and worship. The *second section* in each commentary types the psalm from its literary or rhetorical qualities as a hymn of praise or a prayer of supplication, etc., and divides it into strophes or stanzas. As already inferred in this introduction, the psalms are a mine rich with doctrinal ore; at times the gold may be right on the surface, easily available; at other times it may be hidden within ancient patterns of speech. The *third section* of each commentary treats this ore so that we of the twentieth century after Christ can appreciate its full value and rich essence; here important phrases are explained in the light of the larger religious setting of the entire Bible. Finally, a *fourth section* is added, explicitly to point out how each psalm impacts our lives, our styles of prayer, our theology. This final section may be devoted to the New Testament incorporation of the ancient psalm. At times we branch out into a specialized question, like the problem of the curse psalms with Ps 69.

These commentaries in *Old Testament Message* are primarily an exposition of the Sacred Scriptures; we remain most of the time within the centuries before Christ, confident that the reality of the Israelite spirit and its interaction with a compassionate and creative God will mirror our reality today. Human nature hardly changes that much! We want to know and appreciate the heart and soul of our ancestors in the faith, thereby to know ourselves better. We seek that understanding which St. Paul considered very necessary: "I will pray with the spirit and *I will pray with the mind also*; I will sing with the spirit *and I will sing with the mind also*" (1 Cor 14:15).

II
Rereading the Psalms for Today's Inspiration

Although the fourth section of each commentary is the least developed, nonetheless, we firmly believe that the contemporary setting of today's world is an essential ingredient for the correct and full appreciation of God's inspired word within the Bible. We emphasize the importance of setting each psalm within our contemporary church and world, not only for accurate biblical interpretation, but also for indicating how the Bible itself frequently reinterpreted the psalms. The majority of the psalms, it would seem, were never left in their original historical setting but were transplanted and re-transplanted again: see the commentary on Pss 2 or 68. The Titles, frequently found at the beginning of a psalm, seldom locate the author's purpose in writing the psalm; rather, as when they refer to relatively minor episodes in the life of David — minor compared to his major accomplishments as warrior, king and reorganizer of Israelite life —they may be inviting us to relocate the psalms into our own relatively unimportant lives, actually into the details of our daily existence where we struggle against temptation and discouragement and where we sing our hymns of personal triumph, very important in our family or community, yet again insignificant for world politics and theological doctrine!

This process of adapting preexisting hymns and prayers to family settings or individual problems is what we find with the Scriptures. Many examples come to mind, but here we concentrate on one, the psalm of thanksgiving in the prophecy of Jonah. Granted that the psalm has been carefully integrated into the larger Book of Jonah, we still sense a highly strung tension between the larger setting of Jonah and the particular scope of the psalm. While Jonah was fleeing by sea as a way to save himself from God's command to go by land in the opposite direction to save the Ninevites, the psalm looks upon the sea as a place of destruction:

> I called the Lord, out of my distress,...
> out of the belly of Sheol I cried....
> all thy waves and thy billows passed over me....
> the deep was round about me (Jon 2:2-3, 5).

As a matter of fact, the waters protected and saved Jonah in ways never to be anticipated: in the depths he was swallowed by a whale and taken eastward in the direction of the Ninevites. Still another seeming contradiction strikes us. While the psalm locates the presence of the Lord "in your holy temple" at Jerusalem where vows are fulfilled and deliverance granted from the Lord (*cf.,* Jon 2:7-9), the Book of Jonah proclaims that the Ninevites are to be saved by their obedience, right there in their "unclean" land (*cf.,* Amos 7:17). The Book of Jonah imparts a dramatically new, universal interpretation to an ancient, liturgical psalm of restricted application.

This example shows a biblical readiness to re-read the psalms according to a new setting and a new set of problems; the latter are an essential ingredient, as already stated, in the proper interpretation of the psalm and in our arriving at the inspired message in the word of God. As a matter of fact, the New Testament will even reverse the original meaning of a psalm: see Ps 68:18 as quoted in Eph 4:8. In this as in other cases the New Testament is often relying upon a precedent among the rabbis. Such reversals of meaning, of course, are rare; they rely upon doctrinal developments within Israel which would make the original sense of the psalm appear at least inadequate, if not false. Re-reading or actualization of ancient Scripture within a new set of circumstances is always undertaken with continuity in the faith of the ancestors, a lively sense of their traditions, a grasp of traditions and practises from other directions and a sense of continuity with the body of believers in the church.

These reflections on biblical interpretation, we believe, will apply to all parts of the Holy Scriptures — *mutatis mutandis*, give or take what must be changed in particular circumstances. Yet the observations seem most in place for the psalms. Of any part of the Bible, the psalms are the least rooted in their original setting. Often enough each psalm begins, in a sense, a new book of the Bible; we cannot rely upon a larger environment as with the 52 chapters of Jeremiah or the 14 chapters of Hosea, not even the 2 of Haggai. The psalms have been deliberately uprooted, but still pulsing with life; they wait for us to replant them in our own community of prayer and reflection. Out of this new setting of prayer will come the most authentic doctrine, according to the ancient proverb: from the law of prayer we derive the law of doctrine: *lex orandi, lex credendi.*

III
The Canonical Shape: The Five Books of Psalms

The Name

Our word, *psalm*, simply transliterates a Greek word, *psalmos*, which in turn translated the Hebrew *mizmor*, a song to be sung with musical accompaniment, as in Ps 71:22 where the verb form reads: *"I will sing praises to thee with the lyre"* or in Dan 3:5 where the Aramaic language continues with the same meaning: "when you hear the sound of the horn, pipe, lyre, trigon, harp, bagpipe and every kind of *music*, you are to fall down and worship..." *Mizmor* is included in the title of 57 psalms. Certainly not all the psalms were intended to be orchestrated with musical instruments:

i.e., Ps 119. As a matter of fact, the Hebrew name for the Book of Psalms is *tehillim*, a plural masculine gender noun, derived from the verb, *halal* — "to praise." The English word, Hallelujah, comes from this same root; it means literally, "Praise Yah[weh]." Again it must be admitted that not all the psalms are hymns of praise. The name, "Psalms," instead of "Hymns," seems the preferred one already in the New Testament. Jesus is quoted as saying to the distraught apostles on Easter Sunday night: "'Everything written about me in the law of Moses and the prophets and the psalms must be fulfilled.' Then he opened their minds to understand the scriptures" (Luke 24:44-45).

This last quotation also indicates the place of the Book of Psalms within the Hebrew Scriptures. The third section began with psalms. Even though the Jewish Scriptures were not yet gathered into a single book (a most important discovery to come very soon as a way of collating and preserving documents), nonetheless, the Jews divided their sacred writings into three principal sections: *the law* or five books of Moses, *the prophets* which included the earliers ones of Joshua, Judges, Samuel and Kings and the later ones which embraced the three major (Isaiah, Jeremiah & Ezekiel) and the twelve minor prophets, and *the writings* which began with Psalms. The Greek Septuagint, the Old Latin and the Vulgate also placed the psalms at the beginning of its section, The Sapiential Books, even though it distributed these books somewhat differently from the Hebrew Scriptures. In fact, in the early centuries of Christianity, there existed many different arrangements of books within the Bible.

The Five Books Of Psalms

The Hebrew text and all later translations contain 150 psalms, divided into five books. The Greek Septuagint contains a final Ps 151 but notes in the title: "an authentic psalm of David but outside the number [of 150 inspired psalms]." The number of 150 has been reached somewhat arbitrarily — and mysteriously. We are left in the dark at this point! At times both the Hebrew and the Greek break a single psalm into two (Pss 42-43). The Hebrew does the same to Pss 9-10, while the Greek mistakenly combines Pss 114 and 115 as a single psalm, called Ps 113 in the Greek division. (See below for the enumeration of the psalms). Ps 13 is repeated as Ps 52 in both the Greek and the Hebrew. (Throughout this commentary we are following the Hebrew and RSV enumeration of the psalms; this question will be discussed again towards the end of this introduction.) One hundred and fifty, however, as a derivative of five, remains a sacred number, corresponding to the five books of Moses in the Torah. It is possible that an early arrangement of the psalms, dating from the time of Ezra (ca. 428 B.C.), corresponds to a three-year cycle for reading the five books of Moses. Both the five Books of Moses and the one hundred and fifty psalms could have been read according to a three year "cursus."

In presenting the arrangement of the psalms in five books, we add an interesting detail about the distribution of the divine name:

Book I	Pss	1-41	Yahweh, 272 times	Elohim, 15 times
Book II		42-72	Yahweh, 30 times	Elohim, 164 times
Book III		73-89	almost equally divided: 44 against 43	
Book IV		90-106	Yahweh, 103 times	Elohim, never
Book V		107-150	Yahweh, 236 times	Elohim, 7 times

One or two verses are added at the end of each book as a doxology of praise, even though it may break the spirit, as it does in the case of Ps 89 (Pss 41:13; 72:18-19; 89:52; 106:48). A final doxology for the entire psalter is found in Ps 150. These doxologies defend the Hebrew title for the entire series of psalms: *tehillim* or *Praises.*

Beginning with Ps 42, an endeavor was made generally to substitute Elohim for Yahweh as the divine name; the project got as far as Ps 83; for this reason Pss 42-83 are sometimes referred to as the "Elohist Psalter." Two forces seem to have been at work here, almost counterpoint. The divine name Yahweh had been used more consistently in southern traditions that centered in Jerusalem; the word Elohim is associated with northern traditions that centered in the kingdom of Israel — at least so far as studies on the Pentateuch reveal. Jerusalem, where the psalter was eventually collected and preserved, would favor Yahweh. Yet, it was also at Jerusalem in the postexilic age that the divine name Yahweh was suppressed out of reverence in public recitation. A substitute, *'adonai* (Our Lord) was used in the temple and synagogue, *ha-shem* (the name) outside of these holy places. The preponderant use of Yahweh in the psalms would witness to the antiquity of the psalms; the change to Elohim to the role of the Jerusalem temple in their preservation.

Earlier Collections

How the five books of the psalter were put together is lost in the sands of time, but some general observations can be made on the basis of earlier collections. From glancing at the table of content for this two volume commentary, the "named" psalms belong principally to David (73 altogether in the Hebrew; 82 in the Septuagint), to Korah (12 psalms) and to Asaph (12 psalms). These 97 named psalms, about 2/3rd's of the total, congregate mostly in the first three books. Those of David principally in the first book, those of Korah and Asaph in the next two books. The second and third books, as mentioned just above, also underwent the effort to switch the divine name from Yahweh to Elohim, constituting a separate collection, the Elohist Psalter (Pss 42-83). The David psalms, therefore, constituted the first cluster of psalms, those of Korah and Asaph were added to the former. The David psalms, moreover, seemed to have had a controlling influence in the first two books, in that a psalm concerned with the coronation of a Davidic king (Ps 2) was placed at the beginning of the first book (Ps 1 is a later addition to introduce the entire psalter of 150 songs) and the second book is concluded with the remark: "The prayers of

David the son of Jesse are ended" (Ps 72:20). Book Three ends with a lament over the Davidic loss of royalty (Ps 89).

Because the David psalms do not *generally* center around great moments of royal power (the conclusion of Book Three already indicates such a loss) but seem to stress sorrow and lament, the arrangement that stresses David in sorrow and in eclipse may indicate one of two things: either, as Brevard V. Childs claims, that a new David was expected to emerge out of the loss and therefore an eschatological age will again dawn, or else that true Israelite religion is not restricted to royal functions or to temple ceremonies, but reaches into personal needs and the strong devotional life of family and neighborhood. This latter would result from antagonism against the ruling Sadducaic priesthood at the Jerusalem temple during the postexilic age.

Psalms in the fourth and fifth books of the psalter are mostly unnamed, although minor collections of David psalms reappear especially in the last book (Pss 108-110; 138-145). Particularly in the last book we find two major collections: the songs of ascent (Pss 120-134) for pilgrimages to and from Jerusalem; and the Hallelujah or Hallel psalms (Pss 111-118; 135-136; 146-150). The latter collections were supplied from the temple liturgy.

In conclusion it would seem that the first major collection of psalms were under the patronage of David and consisted mostly of supplicatory prayers, spoken from an individual viewpoint and possibly used for services when no temple existed during a time of sorrow; two levitical collections were then added, of Korah and Asaph, from a sanctuary setting. At this point the first three books came into existence. Book Four was then added, the shortest of all the books; here the psalms are almost entirely anonymous (Pss 90-106). Book Four is somewhat like an appendix to the first three books, similar to other appendices to biblical books (2 Sam 21-24; Isa 36-39). Finally, a series of temple psalms of praise, the Hallel or Hallelujah collection, were attached and clustered with a few others to form Book Five. Within this complicated, uncertain history we sense a tension between private piety and official liturgy.

The Titles of the Psalms

All but thirty-four psalms (or all but nineteen in the Greek Septuagint) have titles or labels at the beginning; those without titles are frequently dubbed "orphan psalms." These titles are probably among the most obscure elements of the entire Bible, particularly those which designate musical instruments or melodies. In general the titles can be subdivided among: 1) indications of literary form; 2) musical accompaniment; and 3) patronage or author. As will be noted at the end of this introduction, all of the ancient texts and versions include the title under the versification system, counting it v. 1 or sometimes vv. 1-2. The Hebrew text prints them with the same shape and size of letters as the rest of the psalm, not in small italics as in most English editions and certainly not as in the RSV as separate from the psalm. The Hebrew tradition then considers the title an integral part of each psalm. Or to put the matter in another way, the style of composing, singing or celebrating a psalm was considered an essential ingredient in the inspired message of the psalm. Praying the psalm became the catalyst for communicating the message of the psalm. This fact reinforces the position taken earlier in this introduction that the contemporary context for praying or singing the psalm contributes an all-important element in the psalm's interpretation.

Yet the difficulty remains. The Pontifical Biblical Commission, even in the days when it was issuing very cautionary decrees, admitted that the titles are not necessarily from the authors of the psalms. Although the Septuagint took titles seriously enough as to add titles to five orphan psalms, nonetheless it also changed the wording of other titles. The ancient Syriac version called the Peshitta, substituted new titles, completely different from the Hebrew and Greek.

Literary Form

These titles include: *mizmor* (57x in the psalter; as a noun it does not reappear outside the psalter) calls for an accompaniment with musical instrument(s); *shir* (30x) indicates a "song," to be sung publicly; the distinction from *mizmor* is lost to us; *maskil* (13x) from a verb meaning "to be wise, careful or skillful," denotes either a song requiring a skillful or artistic rendition or a song that is didactic (see Ps 47:7, commentary); *prayer* (*tephillah*, 5x), a supplication or petition; *miktam* (Pss 16; 56-60) from an Akkadian verb, "to cover," implies atonement or reconciliation. Interestingly enough, the title *tehillah*, very close to the Hebrew name for the entire Book of Psalms (*tehillim*) occurs only once as a title (Ps 145)!

Musical Notations

A second series of titles, still more difficult to identify, center on musical instruments, melodies or public performance. The most frequent of all, "to the choirmaster" (in Hebrew, *lammenasseah* - 55x) comes from a Hebrew word, "to be preeminent" and refers to the one directing or leading the singing (*cf.,* 1 Chron 15:21) or supervising the liturgy (*cf.,* 1 Chron 23:4). The title leaves us in the dark about the exact duties of this person. One hypothesis explains the title as a north Israelite equivalent to "David" as patron of psalm writing. Other musical titles would be: *sheminith*, from a Hebrew word that means "eight," and possibly referring to an instrument of eight strings or chords (Pss 6; 12); *mahalath* or *mahalath leannoth* (possibly meaning "flute"), used for singing sorrowful laments — Pss 5; 53; 88. Still other phrases like *gittith, do not destroy, lilies* may refer to a well known melody according to which the psalm was to be sung, or *gittith* to a musical instrument from the Philistine city of Gath.

Closely aligned to this second series of titles is the enigmatic *selah*, found often at the end of a stanza or strophe. It occurs 71x in 39 psalms, especially in the Elohistic Psalter (Pss 42-83). It occurs elsewhere in the Bible only in chap. 3 of Habakkuk. It may be derived from a Hebrew word *salal* (to lift up voice or eyes) or from the Aramaic *salah* (to turn, bend or pray, similar to the Akkadian to bow or pray). It may indicate a pause for private prayer or for a musical interlude; the Septuagint favors the latter proposal.

Looking back over this second series of words in the titles we realize how little we know of ancient Hebrew music and liturgy. We can complete this series by adding that Ps 30 was to be sung for dedication; Ps 92 for the sabbath; Ps 100 for a thank-offering. Ps 45, according to its title, was "a love song" for a marriage. The listing of psalms for various days of the week was completed by the Septuagint, Vulgate and Mishnah (latter is a collection of Jewish legal interpretations). For the days after Sabbath, Ps 24 for the first day; Ps 48 for the second; Pss 82 & 94 for the third; Ps 81 for the fifth; and Ps 93 for the sixth.

Patronage

A third series of titles deals with the author, honorary or real. The three principal groups are: David (73x; 82x in the Septuagint); Korah (12x); and Asaph (12x). Once or twice a psalm is attributed to Solomon (Pss 72 & 127); Moses (Ps 90); Jeduthun (Ps 39); Heman the Ezrahite (Ps 88); and Ethan the Ezrahite (Ps 89). The last three are named in the Books of Chronicles as singers or musicians (1 Chron 16:38, 42; 15:17-18). It is possible that "Ezrahite" can mean "Canaanite" or more properly "aborigine," and shows the foreign source of some psalms.

As to David's role in the composition of the psalms, we certainly cannot deny his authorship of some, but we cannot affirm it for all, not even for those explicitly named David psalms according to the titles, like Ps 24 which presumes that the temple built by Solomon is already the center of devotion. Beyond a doubt David has gone down in history as a musician (1 Sam 16:18; Amos 6:5) and organizer of liturgical worship (2 Chron 29:30; Ezr 3:10). As is his wont, Sirach expresses it eloquently:

> He sang with all his heart,
>   and he loved his Maker.
> He placed singers before the altar,

to make sweet melody with their voices.
He gave beauty to the feasts,
and arranged their times throughout the year
(Sir 47:8b-10a).

It is most sensible and probably more scholarly to state that David's name became associated with the psalms in the way that Solomon's was with wisdom, Moses' with the Torah or Law, and Joshua's with conquest and settlement in the land. Each acted vigorously in the area of his competency, each released a tradition that developed under his patronage, each remained the norm and model for future ages. As a matter of fact, the Hebrew phrase, often repeated in the titles, *leDawid* — *of David*, can mean equally "by" or "to," that is, composed by or composed in homage to, or placed under the patronage of David.

IV
Texts and Versions

Of the books in the Hebrew Bible, textually psalms ranks among the worst. The divergences come easily to light by comparing the Hebrew text of identical psalms: *i.e.,* Pss 14 & 53; Pss 40 & 70; or Pss 96, 105 & 1 Chron 16. There are more than a hundred variants between Ps 18 and 2 Sam 22 which present the same psalm of David. Even important Davidic psalms like Pss 2 & 110 have serious textual problems. The Hebrew of Ps 141:5-7 is almost untranslatable. Perhaps the psalms are simply worst for wear, and the ragged condition of the text is due principally to frequent use in liturgical congregation and among private assemblies of prayer. The condition is by no means hopeless, only much more difficult than is usually the case with the Hebrew Bible. Unfortunately, the state of the ancient Greek version, the Septuagint, is even worse than the Hebrew text.

The Latin versions of the psalter are caught in a quagmire of liturgical tradition. The "Old Latin" version, taken freely from the Greek Septuagint, was both popular among early

Christians and very defective textually. Jerome attempted two corrections of it from the Greek text, the first endeavor became known as the "Roman Psalter" because of its popularity at Rome, the second is called the "Gallican Psalter" on account of its use in France. Then around A.D. 400 Jerome turned his attention to translating the entire Old Testament immediately from the Hebrew (*Veritas Hebraica*) and completed an entirely new psalter. This version, however, departed too radically from what people normally used at worship and was never accepted by the church at large. The Latin Vulgate consists of Jerome's work from the Hebrew except for the Psalter which was the "Gallican" version!

V
Hebrew Poetry

Before introducing the major literary forms, we summarize some general conclusions about Hebrew poetry. More information is available in Vol. 17 of *Old Testament Message*, which introduces the Sapiential Books, particularly Proverbs.

Hebrew poetry is structured basically on the principle of parallelism, in which the second line repeats or develops the thought of the first, and together they produce a quasi-independent statement. This procedure is sometimes called rhythm of thought. Rhyme is seldom found, and the system of accented and unaccented syllables is far more complicated than in English poetry.

Two major forms of parallelism show up in Hebrew poetry: synonymous and antithetical. As an example of synonymous form we cite Ps 2:1,

> Why do the nations conspire
> and the peoples plot in vain?

The antithetical type of parallelism reverses the meaning of the first line:

The Lord knows the way of the righteous,
but the way of the wicked will perish (Ps 1:6).

Further embellishments can be woven into the lines of Hebrew poetry. One is called chiasm in which the second line reverses the sequence of words (a-b b-a). Often this poetic device is difficult to communicate in translations from the Hebrew. We cite the example of Ps 19:1 and adapt the second line more closely to the Hebrew order of words:

(a) The heavens	(b) are telling	(c) the glory of God
(c) his handiwork	(b) is being announced by	(a) the firmament.

Parallelism can also be enriched by a system of repetition and enrichment, as in the case of Ps 29:1-2a, which can be diagrammed as follows: a-b-c a-b-d a-b-de,

(a) Ascribe	(b) to the Lord,	(c) O heavenly beings,
(a) Ascribe	(b) to the Lord,	(d) glory and strength,
(a) Ascribe	(b) to the Lord,	(d+e) the glory of his name.

There are several more instances of this stylistic flourish in Ps 29.

Accented syllables impart a rhythm or momentum to Hebrew, but the problem arises from the seeming indifference of Hebrew poetry to the number of unaccented syllables. Hebrew is to be read orally and in this case words naturally group together in clusters. Poetry in the Bible tends to eliminate minor words like relative pronouns, articles and other particles like the unpronounced indication of a definite accusative (*'eth*). The more normal beat of accented syllables is considered 3 + 3; more rarely 2 + 2. There is a fair amount of agreement that the mournful elegy consists of 3 + 2, the second part of the parallelism thus appearing unfinished, typical of sorrow and loss.

The division of a psalm into stanzas or strophes is also uncertain. There are times, of course, when the separation from one strophe to the next is clear enough, as in the use of a refrain (*cf.,* Pss 42-43; 46) or in the acrostic or alphabetic arrangement (*cf.,* Ps 119, where each strophe of eight lines is dedicated to a single letter of the alphabet; each line begins with it). At times the particle *selah* is found and it may be a clue to a pause in the recitation or singing of a psalm and therefore the transition from one strophe to the next. Evode Beaucamp favors this explanation.

Before approaching the individual literary forms conspicuous in the psalter, an initial *caveat* is in order. When literature and its literary form are involved in continuous, frequent use, a counterpoint movement can be noticed. If this material is associated closely with the cult, then there is a staying power to preserve the ancient wording and style. These in turn contribute to important symbols that can reflect any number of religious responses through the ages. For instance, the symbol of the exodus remains important, even after the people are settled in the land, because Israel is continually called to undertake a moral or spiritual exodus out of sin or bondage (*cf.,* Ps 95). Again, the symbol of the Davidic dynasty remained in Israel's cult, even after the royal family had been swept from power by the Babylonians in 587 B.C. No longer visible in the political and religious life of Israel, the Davidic dynasty as a symbol sustained the people's faith that God will bring a savior in the most mysterious and wonderful way, one far beyond the expectations of the moment. Therefore, the sense of a "divine birth" was enhanced as Ps 110 passed from the Hebrew into the Greek tradition. The Hebrew states, "From the womb, from the dawn, yours is the dew of your youth"; the Greek reads: "From the womb before the morning star I have begotten you." See commentary.

While individual symbols maintained a strong adherence to antiquity, nonetheless a notable evolution took place. The exodus could apply to many journeys, so that the people may be geographically in the promised land, yet spiritually back in Egypt (Hos 11). This same counterpoint action is observable in the use of literary forms. The most ancient form of all, the hymn of praise, manifests the most pronounced influence of non-Israelite polytheism (Ps 29); it continues into the late postexilic age in the hymns to Yahweh-king (Pss 96-99).

The pure form of the hymn can be mixed with other styles, like the didactic (Pss 19 & 24) and the prophetic threat (Ps 95). Of all types the hymn was most closely associated with the cult; the evolution of the cult was to influence profoundly the shape of the hymn, so that the hymn modulates into forms of thanksgiving to accompany the temple thank-offering and into enthronement psalms for Yahweh with little or no admixture of polytheism.

VI
Literary Forms

Basically we follow the investigations of Hermann Gunkel who turned the focus of psalm study away from the topical or subject approach to that of their literary forms. Gunkel's division of forms has been challenged and adapted by other scholars, notably of late by Claus Westermann, but not to the satisfaction of all scholars. Serious attempts have been made, especially by Sigmund Mowinckel, to reconstruct the liturgical background of the psalms, but this area remains one of the most illusive, not only because our knowledge of Old Testament temple ritual must be unscrambled from scattered evidence in and out of the Bible, but also because many of the final editorial touches, visible in the titles of the first three books of psalms, do not explicitly revolve around feasts and ritual actions.

Hymns Of Praise

This type of psalm centers on life and joy. Because Israel's God was a living God who offered to the people not only life but life with dignity, compassion and appreciation, the hymn was the most natural response to Yahweh.

Praise we define as the wondrous acclamation of God's redemptive acts as these continue among the people. According to this definition, praise gives nothing to God but joyfully manifests what God has done and continues to do for the people. If praise should give anything to God, this gift is provided by God's earlier initiative. God acted first, in hearing the people's cry of pain in Egypt and in sending Moses to deliver them; and as the tradition was to develop much later, whether in the Priestly account of creation in Gen 1:1-2:4a or in the sapiential poem of Prov 8:22-31, the initiative of God reached back to the first moment of creation. Before Israel existed, God was already at work for their sake.

Israel's religion derived its initial motivation from Yahweh's intervention in their history with Abraham and especially with Moses. The hymns, however, like Pss 19A and 29, or Ps 8 in its early or original form, do not center upon these great moments of Israel's history (exodus, covenant, journey, settlement) but upon creation. They also reflect polytheism. Quite likely, when Israel entered the Promised Land of Canaan and began to establish their religion in an organized way, with ritual, laws, personnel, sacred narratives and song, Israel was required to accept much from the highly cultured Canaanites. Quite likely too, these hymns with motivation from nature remained popular with the people at large. David probably gave a new impetus to Canaanite forms; his background was not so much rooted in the Mosaic traditions of the north but in a more Canaanite style of the south.

Israel's hymns emerge distinctly different from non-Israelite religious hymns in the sense that Yahweh was not to be placated, cajoled or charmed. The hymns give nothing to God but recognize what God is already accomplishing wondrously among his people in continuity with the ancient moments of their history. The hymns do not placate God; they do not demean either God or Israel. By means of the hymns Israel in fact grew in maturity by recognizing the wondrous possibilities of life.

Hymns, moreover, as already mentioned, acclaimed the God of life. Therefore, in the earliest hymns suffering, death or loss are not mentioned, except as victories over one's enemies. This attitude can be linked with the cultic requirement for priests. In Lev 21 the rules for the priests become all the more rigid in the case of the high priest: "he shall not go in to any dead body, nor defile himself, even for his father or for his mother; neither shall he go out of the sanctuary nor profane the sanctuary of his God" (Lev 21:11-12). This prescription, similar to that for the Nazirite (Num 6:6-7), reflects the nomadic origins of Israel when people had little time for mourning the dead but were obliged to move onward. Ancient forms of warfare are also lurking behind this practise. Returning to the hymns of praise, the early origins of Israel's religion insisted upon a living God; death, sin and disease were to have no place in the ritual and the hymnology.

In the later songs in honor of Yahweh King and Re-Creator (Pss 96-99), the hymns of praise could easily open up to an eschatological vista about the magnificent final age of Israel or of the universe.

We note in passing a different viewpoint or attitude in most forms of Christianity. Christianity stresses death and suffering as central, at least in the western church; sorrow for sin occupies an important role in one's approach to God. Today most Christians are moved to turn to God when circumstances in their life are difficult and painful; seldom do people come to their religious minister and seek to discuss and pray because anything is going very well!

The hymns of praise, again typical of biblical religion, acclaim Yahweh's goodness and majesty for what the Lord is doing *now*. In this connection it is helpful to point out that Hebrew grammar does not stress "time," present, past or future, different, therefore, from European languages. Time is secondary in the grammar of the Hebrew verb; the primary focus lies in the modality of the action or the involvement of the speaker or actor. Hebrew grammar answers the question *how*, not so much *when*. The hymn of praise then acclaims Yahweh, not for what the Lord did, but for the earlier event as it is happening now. Praise does not result from studying ancient traditions nor from one's exploration of the world of nature, as though praise is deduced from our own study and investigation. Praise is our involvement in God's actions now.

This same modality of seeing everything according to present interaction can also be deduced from the biblical name for God, *Yahweh*. We adopt the explanation that it comes from the root, *hayah*, the verb "to be," in its simple, incomplete form. Transferring this modality to Yahweh, the name signifies: "He who is always there," each moment, interacting with the circumstances of one's life. The name Yahweh, consequently, says nothing too definite about God's presence; details must be supplied by the set of circumstances and the attitude of the Israelite(s). Yahweh simply declares that God is *there*, wherever and whatever that be. As Albert Gelin concluded: Yahweh, as spoken by God, is a promise: "I will be always there"; as spoken by Israel, the sacred name becomes a confident prayer, "God, be there with us." The hymns of praise acclaim the ever present God, doing now what had been done for the ancestors and involving the worshipping community in that great redemptive act.

The literary form of the hymn is simple enough. An introduction summons the community to praise, wonder and adoration. The body of the hymn is often introduced by the Hebrew particle, *ki*. This word originally was more like an exclamation mark in English, to announce the wondrous action. As such, *ki* was not so much to be translated into a precise word as into an excited style of speech. Because something of importance took place, the word *ki* gradually came to take on the subsequent sense of "when" or "because." A great action leads to something else, is a cause why something happens, is a signal when it happens. We suggest that in the hymn of praise, *ki* maintains its original sense of exclamation!

As a result, the body of the hymn does not offer the reason for praise; as though we praise God after studying the reasons sufficiently. The purpose of the central section of the hymn is more to sustain wonder and adoration in God's presence, to involve the worshipping community in God's glorious action. The body of the hymn, therefore, will teem with activity: questions, invitations, exclamations, shouts, prostration, dance, etc.

The conclusion of the hymn generally turns out to be a more enthusiastic restatement of the introductory call for praise.

As the outline of the psalms at the close of this introduction indicates, the motivation of praise is found either in nature, acclaiming Yahweh as creator, or in Israel's sacred history and priceless possession of the torah or law. The hymn was extended, in postexilic Israel, to include the eschatological praise of Yahweh as king. Psalms like 47, 93, 96-99 may have existed in the preexilic period, but their present form shows the influence particularly of Deutero-Isaiah. Once the Davidic dynasty had disappeared, then exclusive attention could be directed to Yahweh as king. See the commentary on Ps 8 for a similar development.

Another extended form of the hymn would be the Canticles of Zion: Pss 46-48, 76, 84, 122, 132. These psalms are mixed in genre for they fold other literary forms into the pure style of the hymn.

Prayers

This type of psalm, particularly of supplication and lament, is most numerous in the first three books of the psalter. It is conspicuous among the psalms of David, the first major collection of psalms chronologically. While the hymns of praise, especially those with motivation from nature and creation, seem to have the deepest roots in early Israel's Canaanite origin, the prayers of supplication were more representative in the first major effort of the temple to gather and arrange its psalmody. This development came several centuries after David and represented a major prophetical influence upon psalmody. The impact of the prophet Jeremiah is particularly noticeable.

We divide the prayers between: supplication or lament, confidence and thanksgiving. Elements of confidence and thanksgiving enter almost every supplication, just as some account of sorrow and misfortune lies within the scope of the psalmist's confidence and thanksgiving — confidence for overcoming obstacles, thanksgiving once this deliverance takes place.

The style of piety found within the psalms of supplication or lament seems akin to spontaneous non-liturgical manifestations of religious feeling in Israel's early history. During the period of Moses and Joshua, the religious basis and principal ingredients of religion already existed but structure and organization had not yet evolved. Roland deVaux has called this the pre-religion period of Israelite history.

The action of Joshua after a military defeat at Ai represents a form of devotion, not legislated for in the Torah and therefore outside the later, more orthodox and organized forms of devotion. We read:

> Then Joshua rent his clothes, and fell to the earth upon his face before the ark of the Lord until the evening, he and the elders of Israel; and they put dust upon their heads. And Joshua said, "Alas, O Lord God, why hast thou brought this people over the Jordan at all, to give us into the hands of the Amorites, to destroy us?" (Josh 7:6-7; *cf.*, Judg 20:23, 26; 1 Sam 7:6).

Death and mourning did not properly belong to Israel's religion, neither did sin.

Although the Bible speaks of "sin offering," these sacrifices concerned faults of inadvertence, not willful offenses. Such sins sometimes happened unintentionally, as in the case of accidentally touching a corpse or contacting a skin disease; at other times, the "sin" was intentional but nonetheless the action was considered important like sexual activity among married people or the birth of children (*cf.*, Lev 12, 13, 15). If sin offering is made for willful offenses, then it is necessary that the sin be first confessed and recompense given to the injured party; only then could the guilty person proceed with the temple ritual of sacrifice (*cf.,* Num 5:5-10). In this regard it is important that in the popular penitential feast of Yom Kippur, the ceremony with the scapegoat actually followed the liturgical function in the temple; driving the scapegoat out into the desert and hurling it over the precipice for Azazel probably constituted the most important part of the ceremony for the people and so could not be eliminated, despite its strange liturgy and weird theology. Therefore, it was maintained as a non-liturgical conclusion, hopefully to control thereby some of the excesses.

Another reason why laments and prayers of supplication emerged only slowly within Israel's organized and accepted ritual lies in the belief in one God, at least for the people of Israel. Unlike the Canaanites, Israel could not attribute sin, suffering and death to a god *muth* or *moth* (semitic name for death). God, as we saw already, was the God of life and peace, not of death and chaos. Israel honored no gods of the underworld; Israel's Yahweh did not die and rise again. Therefore, the negative side of life was unaccounted for in the official religion of Israel — at least as this religion is represented in the Bible. Death remained the supreme mystery outside of God's presence (Pss 6:5; 16; Isa 38:18-19).

These assertions are further corroborated by another aspect of Israel's liturgy. The killing of the animal was not an official part of the liturgy. In the first chapters of Leviticus the sacrificial animal was to be slaughtered by the lay person, not by the priest; only after the blood had been separated from the animal and its body skinned, cleansed and properly divided, did the sacred ceremony begin. These consisted of the blood ritual or sprinkling, the holocaust burnt upon the altar and the sacred meal (*cf.,* Exod 24:3-11). Holocaust did not include our contemporary meaning of wholesale slaughter; rather it meant the total gift of one's life, symbolized by the smoke that went up towards God with sweet fragrance.

Yet people continued to suffer and die; sooner or later the ritual of the sanctuary had to take these facts into its arms of compassion and devotion. First, suffering had to be accepted as an act of God against sinful Israel. Beginning with Amos, the classical prophets announced the presence of God's hand in the foreign invaders that would level Samaria and Jerusalem and inflict untold suffering upon the populace. No one wept more over such sorrows than Jeremiah, "that our eyes may run with tears, and our eyelids gush with water. For a sound of wailing is heard over Zion: 'How we are ruined'" (Jer 9:18-19). Jeremiah, as Tournay-Schwab remarked, became the "parent of Jewish piety and of sacred lamentation." Pierre E. Bonnard wrote a book, entitled "The Psalter According to Jeremiah" (French edition, 1960) in which he ascribed 12 psalms to Jeremiah by way of literary influence, 21 more by way of spirituality.

Gradually a collection of laments came together. Perhaps they developed out of religious services during the exile, without temple or sacred place, or at the desecrated temple site in Jerusalem (Jer 41:5). Many of the collective laments in the plural can be associated with the fall of Jerusalem (*cf.,* Pss 60; 129; 137). A much larger number of psalms are the individual laments, grammatically in the singular, yet generally intended for community services of sorrow and lamentation. Because these individual laments constitute the largest single block in the psalter, Hermann Gunkel declared them to be the backbone of the psalter. Neither type, collective nor individual lament, attempted to explain suffering; their goal was more simple: to sustain in God's presence the devout Israelite, discouraged and religiously baffled by the turn of events, hounded by tragic memories, stricken with pain physically and emotionally.

The structure of the prayers of supplication or lament is not nearly as visible and neatly arranged as was the case with the hymns of praise. Can we expect good order amid chaos and tragedy? These psalms usually begin with a call for help and may expand this call by dwelling upon God's past favors. This initial section is generally very brief, just the opposite from Babylonian supplications in which the deity was charmed into good favor by multitudinous praise. The body of the psalm is explicit, personal, tense, honest. The attitude of the psalmist will vary from a prayer for help, to a lament or description of the misfortune, expressions of confidence, a confession of sin, the curse of the enemy. Towards the end the psalm of supplication generally modulates into a prayer of thanksgiving or confidence (Ps 22:22-31).

Another type of prayer is that of *confidence*, very similar to the preceding psalm of lament, yet emphasizing the aspect of trust in God's willingness to help and rescue the afflicted person. These psalms can stress a reflective peace and quiet (Ps 62) or God's gentle solicitude (Pss 23; 27). They offer a pledge of happiness and safety (Ps 16) and insist upon God's justice in remembering the innocent (Ps 11).

Finally we turn to the *prayer of thanksgiving*. Typical of human nature, these are the least numerous of all the prayers. They are found in Mesopotamia and Egypt and in ancient Israel (*cf.,* Exod 15; Judg 5). They are usually in the domain of individual piety, so far as grammar is concerned ("I") — *cf.,* Pss 18; 30. The structure of these psalms combines hymns and supplication. God is being thanked for delivering one from sorrow and danger. The introduction may resemble the first part of a hymn; it is addressed either to God, the object of gratitude, or to the community who witness the ceremony of thanksgiving or even join in it. The body of the psalm is developed in narrative style: dangers, attacks, persecution, confession of faults, expressions of weakness or innocence. Finally, the psalmist recounts God's saving intervention. Because salvation and its attendant blessings are stressed, Claus Westermann prefers to classify these psalms as "declarative praise." In conclusion the psalm looks towards the future with confidence. Often enough a formula of liturgical blessing can occur here.

Psalms of thanksgiving accompanied the liturgical *todah* or thanksgiving sacrifice. At this time part of the sacrificial animal was burned in adoration, symbolizing one's total dedication to God, and the remaining part of the food contributed to the sacred meal, to be consumed by the offerer and entire family (Lev 7:12; 22:29-30). These psalms are frequently enough associated with vows made during a time of misfortune (Pss 66:13; 116:17-19).

Wisdom Psalms

Wisdom was associated very early with royalty in Israel (*cf.,* 1 Kgs 4:29-34, a section which concludes, "They came from all peoples to hear the wisdom of Solomon, and from all the kings of the earth, who had heard of his wisdom"). As in other countries, finishing schools for noble youth must have existed at the royal capital and in the postexilic age the synagogues must have served as places both of worship and of instruction. The clearest reference to such schools occurs in Sir 51:23, "Draw near to me, you who are untaught, and lodge in my school."

The attitude of school and instruction can be characterized as traditional, reflective, moderate and refined. "Traditional" does not necessarily mean an attachment to covenant theology, or to the great religious symbols of Israel like the exodus out of Egypt, settlement of the land or establishment of the Davidic dynasty. In fact, these essential ingredients of Israel's religion seldom if ever enter the classic piece of wisdom literature, The Book of Proverbs. Only the very late books of Sirach (ca. 190 B.C.) and the Wisdom of Solomon (ca. 50 B.C.) blend these aspects of Israel's sacred history with instruction. Wisdom literature is traditional in the sense of incorporating age-old common sense, family loyalty, conscientious work, dependability, keen insight, well tested prudence, long experience. Therefore, the attitude tended to be reflective and rational. The positions have been thought out, even over generations of time, and further refinement has come from each new reexperience of the problem or situation. People formed in this background tend to be moderate, calm and self-controlled. The radical threats of the prophets do not echo in wisdom literature, nor do we find the stern laws of the Torah about clean and unclean. Wisdom received its authority in the community from human experience; generation after generation have testified that "it works." When all is said and done, this type of authority is probably more demanding and unbending than any other, be this other priestly or prophetical.

Wisdom literature seeks the harmonious, stable order of

life. It stands against chaos and violence. While the hymns, especially those that derive their motivation from God's creative action over the universe, portray Yahweh as supreme victor over the angry sea and the roaring storms of the winter season (Pss 29; 89:9-13), wisdom finds itself in the presence of the creator "like a master workman...daily his delight, rejoicing before him always" (Prov 8:30). Despite this attitude of being reflective and "rational," nonetheless wisdom always implies ultimate mystery, secretly in God's control. In Prov 8:22-31 wisdom rests with the Lord before creation; the same is found to be the case in Sirach chap. 24. The same aspect of mystery will show up in sapiential aspects of Ps 139, "Even before a word is on my tongue, lo, O Lord, thou knowest it altogether....Such knowledge is too wonderful for me; it is high, I cannot attain it."

In content, the sapiential psalms will tend to contrast the just and the wicked; one of its ways of inculcating wisdom is to stress the inevitability that the wicked are punished and the just rewarded. The dedicatory psalm for the entire psalter stresses this iron law of retribution (Ps 1). These psalms will offer solid advice about one's conduct, yet frequently lead the discussion to the "fear of the Lord."

Rhetorical elements are shared with the other sapiential literature of the Bible. In the wisdom psalms we find such features as:

1) the "better" sayings:

> Better is a little that the righteous has
> than the abundance of many wicked.
> For the arm of the wicked shall be broken;
> but the Lord upholds the righteous (Ps 37:16-17; also
> Pss 63:3; 84:10; 118:8-9; 119:72).

2) numerical sayings:

> Once God has spoken;
> twice I heard this:

> that power belongs to God;...
> For thou doest requite a man
>   according to his work (Ps 62:12-13; also 27:4).

3) the "*'ashre* or happy" sayings:

> Happy is the one
> who walks not in the counsel of the wicked
>   (Ps 1:1; also Pss 34:8; 112:1; 119:1).

4) the acrostic or alphabetic psalms (Pss 34; 37; 111; 112; 119; 145).

When we compare the sapiential psalms with the wisdom literature generally in the Bible, we find the psalms to be more conscious of God's presence in daily life. One would presume that the schools and synagogues developed an attitude of prayer and produced their own standard prayers. While the hymns of praise and the prayers of supplication respond more with adoration and stunned silence, with excitement and outrage, the wisdom psalms reply with reflection and calm strength, with moderation and appreciation for the learning experience.

The fact that a wisdom psalm not only inaugurates the entire series of psalms but also that it was placed here at the beginning of the psalter in the final stages of the formation of the canonical text, shows that the sages exercised more than their share of influence over the Book of Psalms.

Prophetical Psalms

These psalms are more difficult to distinguish. One of the more important guilds of levitical psalm-writers was described as prophets in 1 Chron 25:1, "David and the chiefs of the service also set apart for the service certain of the sons of Asaph, and of Heman, and of Jeduthun, *who should prophesy* with lyres, with harps, and with cymbals." In fact, the author of 1-2 Chronicles seemed to consider "prophet" and "levite" more or less synonyms. "Prophets" in the original source of 2 Kgs 23 was replaced by "levites" in 2 Chron 34:30.

The psalms manifest features of both charismatic and classical prophecy. The charismatic or ecstatic form had appeared early in Israel and was associated with shrines and prophetical communities as in 1 Sam 10:5 and 2 Kgs 2:3; classical prophecy, which began with Amos and eventually arrived at books to its name, spoke independently of any cultic association or group authority.

Classical prophets, well known for their threats and anger because of social injustices and religious formalism, seem to have exerted their influence upon such psalms as Pss 50; 82; 95:7d-11. The "oracle formula" shows up prominently among the classical prophets and the prophetical psalms like 2:6; 12:6; 50:1, 7, 16; 60:8-10.

Charismatic prophets became established fixtures next to kings and in temple ritual. Prophets such as Samuel and Nathan played an important role in the choice and anointing of kings (1 Sam 10:1; 15:1; 16:13; 2 Sam 7:1-7); Samuel and Elisha defrocked and destroyed monarchs (1 Sam 15:26; 2 Kgs 9). From this prophetical background may have evolved the series of Davidic royal psalms, especially for the anointing of the kings (Pss 2; 110).

This commentary does not accept S. Mowinckel's hypothesis of a preexilic feast for Yahweh's enthronement. Occasionally, however, Yahweh would be extolled as king in the preexilic period, not only according to widespread Semitic custom but also as a support to the Davidic dynasty. See the commentary on Ps 93.

Postexilic prophecy began to emphasize more and more the royalty of Yahweh. The Davidic dynasty had disappeared and attention could be given exclusively to the Lord. These later prophets came as a further development out of classical prophecy. Prophets like Zechariah and Malachi placed the hope of Israel in the ever more distant future. Amos already had spoken of the Day of the Lord as one of darkness (Amos 5:18), Isaiah had seen the tree or dynasty of

David cut down to the ground with only the roots of father Jesse in the ground (Isa 11:1). From this seemingly dead, certainly invisible source will come the new messianic king and savior. Sections of prophecy like Isa 24-27 and Zech 9-14 tend to stress the role of Yahweh-king after catastrophic suffering and world convulsion. Somewhere in between the first rumblings of this eschatological reaction in Second Isaiah and its full development in Zech 9-14 and Dan 7-12, we place the final form of those psalms honoring the eschatological domain of Yahweh: Pss 93; 96-99.

Prophetic influence, a mixture of the charismatic and the classical, shows up again in the canticles of Zion. Initial eschatological features also appear here; a better word would be cultic rather than eschatological, the wondrous anticipation now of God's power and promises through the divine presence in the temple ritual. We think of Pss 46; 48; 76.

The prophetic psalms, therefore, are not as clearly distinguishable as the other types; they blend much more easily into the previous categories, like the canticles of Zion and those honoring Yahweh as king which can take their place with the hymns of praise. Others, like the royal psalms, are not that easily at home with the other types and need a separate category.

VII
Origin and History of the Psalms

Many serious reasons prompt us to accept the great antiquity of the psalms. Despite later modification and additions, many psalms reach back into the pre-exilic period, approaching even the period of David and Solomon, and on rare occasions reaching even further back (Ps 68).

Wherever sacred ceremonies were held, songs were necessary; in fact, they would have been taken for granted. Singing is one of the most ancient and the most universal modes of community worship. At such ancient shrines as Gilgal (1 Sam 7:16; 11:15), Shiloh (Josh 18:1; 1 Sam 1:3), Shechem

(Josh 8:30), Bethel (Judg 20:18), Tabor (Ps 68, see commentary) and Dan (Judg 18:29-31), would have had collections of sacred melodies. On the same score, traditional songs would have been sung in community gatherings around the camp fire. In the early biblical narratives we encounter the song of Deborah (Judg 5), the blessing of Moses (Deut 33), the song of Moses (Deut 32), and the refrain of Exod 15:21.

Canaan was a cornucopia so far as music was concerned. She supplied Egypt and Assyria with both instruments and artists over a long period, according to R. Tournay and R. Schwab. Some of the heads of levitical guilds — Ethan, Heman and Korah — had names of Canaanite origin. The first two are called "ezrahites," which means "natives" or "aborigines." The Amarna Letters, written from Canaan to the Egyptian pharaoh in the fourteenth century, have phrases and sentences similar to those in the psalms: *i.e.,* "When shall I see the face of my lord and king" (Letter 144; Pss 17:15; 42:2); "If we mount to the sky or if we go down to the earth, yet our head is in your hands" (Letter 264; Ps 139:8). It is generally admitted that Ps 29 resonates many Canaanite expressions, even to the point that some scholars claim that it was written for Canaanite worship and slightly adapted for Israelite adoration of Yahweh. That the adaptation was not sufficient for later, postexilic psalmists, can be seen by comparing Ps 29:1 with the theological correction in Ps 96:7; the latter drops the reference to lesser gods around the throne of Yahweh.

An investigation of psalmic vocabulary has led M. Tsevat to the age of the conquest when the Hebrews adopted the cultic language of the Canaanites along with their style of architecture and system of farming, etc. Out of 166 elements of the language of the psalms, which in classical Hebrew are known solely or overwhelmingly from the psalms, 35 to 40 are found in closely related languages of Israel's precursors or contemporaries in the land of Canaan.

Comparison with the two Books of Chronicles shows that the psalter uses many words which were dead not only in the secular realm but also cultically by the time that Chronicles was composed in the mid fifth century B.C.

The early origin of Israel's psalms is corroborated by the important place of King David. Again to quote R. Tournay, "One cannot contest the place occupied by David in the musical annals of his people. A reputable musician already in his youth (1 Sam 16:18), he might have invented some of Israel's musical instruments (Amos 6:5; 1 Chron 23:5). . . . Lovable singer of Israel (2 Sam 23:1), he composed some beautiful touching profane elegies (2 Sam 1:17-27; 3:33). . . . The Chronicler, without doubt himself a musician and levite, considers David as the organizer of the liturgy and of sacred music in his eulogy of the poet-king (1 Chron 15-17)." Sirach's eulogy to David has already been quoted in this introduction (Sir 47:8-9).

While admitting the presence of psalms in Israel's earliest, even pre-monarchic period, nonetheless, almost all the psalms underwent a long evolution over the centuries. The problem of dating the psalms is similar to the difficulty of locating the origin of the major eucharistic prayers and other material in the *Sacramentary*. In this latter case we are dealing with the origins of Christianity as well as with a long history of major changes, up to and including the Second Vatican Council. Tournay-Schwab, therefore, who recognize the impact of King David upon the psalms, will also locate important psalms like 2 & 110 in the late postexilic period of Israel's history.

The Bible provides minimal information about the use of the psalms in the life and liturgy of ancient Israel. General facts come to our attention: dancing during a cultic celebration at the sanctuary of Shiloh (Judg 21:19-22); a vague reference to "singing men and singing women" in 2 Sam 19:35 or "noise of your songs. . .the melody of your harps" in Amos 5:23. Lev 23 lists the principal holy days. The guild or family of Asaph is accorded a principal role as leaders of song (Ezr 2:41; Neh 7:44). A medley of psalms is sung by Asaph, to which the people respond with the refrain: "Amen! Hallelujah!" (1 Chron 16:7-36).

Very few specific references occur in the psalter, attaching individual psalms to liturgical ceremonies: Ps 65 would seem to belong to a time after the rainy season; Ps 67 to the harvest season; Ps 95 accords with a liturgical procession, possibly from the spring Gihon to the top of the Jerusalem mount (see commentary). Pss 15 and 24 are associated with ceremonies at one of the gates of the sanctuary; Ps 132 with a procession to the sanctuary; Pss 20 and 26 with religious action in the temple enclosure.

In another series of passages we find that psalms or religious songs are quoted within the body of other books of the Bible: Jeremiah's confessional curse of the day of his birth is interrupted with a hymn (Jer 20:13); Amos or his canonical editor spliced into his prophecy other hymnic fragments (Amos 4:13; 5:8-9; 9:5-6). The same dependence upon ritual works seems in evidence in 1 Chron 16.

Gradually psalms were assigned to each day of the week, as noted elsewhere in this introduction.

Yet when we gather the hard data about the use of the psalms in the preexilic and postexilic liturgy, very few specific facts are available. It is possible that fewer psalms were composed directly for the temple liturgy than we often suppose to have been the case. The temple, moreover, exercised less direction in the formation of the psalter than we are inclined to think. Tournay and Schwab propose that an important role in this process was performed by religious laity. They rose to the need felt by the decline and disappearance of prophecy, by the laxity and political careerism of the priesthood and by the recurrent threat of paganism within Israel (*cf.,* Isa 56-66).

It is also a matter of continual discussion how and when the psalms were introduced into synagogue services. Massey H. Shepherd, Jr., points out some similarities and dissimilarities between early Christian and synagogal use of the psalms. Similar to early Christianity, the synagogue did not provide for the psalms to be sung by special choirs but rather by individual cantors; nor were the psalms accompanied by musical instruments, despite such precedence in the temple and the evidence of psalms like Ps 150. Musical instruments were now associated with pagan worship — as if that had not been the case in preexilic Israel! In the synagogue the psalms were recited almost in a monotone, with inflections and cadences. It is helpful to add that in isolated examples, as with the Yemenite Jews once in southern Arabia, melodic patterns were found, close to very ancient Christian chants, Byzantine, Ambrosian and Gregorian.

In the use of the psalms early Christianity introduced its own variations distinct from the synagogue. For instance, the recitation or singing of a psalm between the biblical lessons of the liturgy was unknown in the synagogue before the eighth century. Nor did the synagogue have a sequence for reciting or singing *all* 150 psalms nor again any cycle for special times of the year, except the Hallel (Pss 113-118) and the Great Hallel (Pss 135:4-21 + 136); see commentary. It was already mentioned here that a three year cycle of reading the psalms may have accompanied the temple reading of the Torah.

At the beginning of the Christian period, psalms were still being added to the psalter and the arrangement was not definitely settled. The Greek Septuagint includes a Ps 151. A scroll from the eleventh cave at Qumran, dated A.D. 30-50, is inscribed with all or part of thirty-nine canonical psalms but in a non-canonical order; these, moreover, are broken up by eight other non-canonical psalms, the Septuagint Ps 151 and other variations. Hymns indeed were popular at Qumran; the members produced a scroll of their own compositions. Unlike other major parts of the Bible, the sacred collection of psalms was not yet definitively closed; additions were still being made.

Yet, as our discussion modulates from the Jewish setting to the Christian, it is significant that the disciples of Jesus accepted what is now our canonical book of Psalms without additions or substitutions. Christianity did not write its own Book of Psalms.

The psalms were important for Jesus and his first disciples. Jesus quoted more often from the psalms than from any other Old Testament book. In the New Testament there are some ninety-three quotations from over sixty psalms. The first recorded sermon of St. Peter in Acts 2 and the first of St. Paul in Acts 13 base important aspects of their presentation upon the psalms (Pss 16, 110 & 132 in Acts 2; Pss 2, 16, 89, Isaiah and Habakkuk in Acts 13).

Relying upon the research of Balthasar Fischer, we summarize and divide the church's approach to the psalms in this way: up to A.D. 200, the psalms tended to be read as a prophetical book about Christ; between A.D. 200 & 400, the psalms were prayers addressed *to* Christ who is the Yahweh of the psalms; from A.D. 400 into the Middle Ages, due to the influence of Augustine, the psalms were the prayers *of* Christ, whose mystical body embraced all men and women of faith.

In this triple formula we glimpse the marvelous simplicity of the liturgical-contemplative life. The psalms are *about* Christ. They throw open the portals of Christ's soul and permit us to see what are Christ's reactions in times of sorrow and joy, persecution and triumph, poverty and wealth. Introduced thus into Christ's heart, our prayers *to* Christ are not sung at a distance but in the depths of the godhead. God has "raised us up with him, and made us sit with him in the heavenly places in Christ Jesus" (Eph 2:6). Immersed in the overwhelming silence of this infinite grandeur, our prayers like our thoughts are absorbed into those of Christ; they become truly the prayers *of* Christ.

The Christian use of the psalms evolved into an ever clearer pattern. In the New Testament there are general references to psalms, hymns and spiritual canticles (Col 3:16-17; Eph 5:19-20). Tertullian notes that at services the scriptures are read and psalms sung. The oldest extant liturgies speak of three biblical readings, from the Old Testament, the epistles and the gospel; this order has been restored in the Roman Catholic Church for Sundays and major feastdays. These ancient liturgies, as ours today, provide for a psalm to be sung by a cantor, with refrains by the entire congregation, after the Old Testament reading.

Once the early church was granted freedom, an impressive development took place in all that referred to public liturgy: architecture, music, hymns, prayers, etc. Some of the hymn writing was intended to counteract the songs composed by Arian heretics, which were becoming popular among non-Arians. The Roman liturgy introduced psalms also as an opening processional, at the offertory and again at communion. These and other details are available in the study of Massey H. Shepherd, Jr.

It must be confessed that the use of the Psalter, the prayer book of the synagogue, by the Christian Church created its own difficulties. The original meaning of the psalms, in their Old Testament and Jewish setting, had to be respected. In fact, the exegetical school of Antioch (mainly in the person of Diodore of Tarsus and Theodore of Monsueptia) reacted strongly to the allegorizing approach of Alexandria which saw a Christological meaning in almost every phrase. For the school of Antioch only four psalms (Pss 2, 8, 44 & 109 in the Greek Septuagint numbering) were direct prophecies of Christ. The others were taken as containing moral teaching of a general nature, or as referring to events within the history of Israel.

In the recent reform of the Divine Office or Breviary (see below) the Church has also shown a concern to blend as far as possible the historical with the Christian understanding of the Psalms. In the "General Instruction on the Liturgy of the Hours" (1970), the Church recognizes that "each psalm has a literal sense which even in our times cannot be neglected" (no. 107) and repeats the Vatican Council's call for "more intensive biblical instruction, especially with regard to the psalms" (no. 102). Each psalm, however, is also provided with a dual heading: the first indicating the nature of the psalm, the other one being a phrase from the New Testament or from the Fathers added as an invitation to pray in a Christian way (*cf.*, no. 111). The real link between the present and the past as we pray the psalms is "the Holy Spirit, who inspired the psalmists, always present with his grace to believing Christians" (no. 102).

Psalms are a conspicuous part of the Divine Office, a collection of prayers and readings, strongly influenced by early monasticism in its evolution. At first there were three "hours" for prayer, corresponding to Jewish worship: morning sacrifice, the noon peace offering (*minhah*), and the evening incense service. Night vigils, corresponding perhaps to prayers at night in the psalter, were incorporated. St. Benedict arranged for a weekly "cursus" or cycle for reciting all 150 psalms. Pope Damasus introduced this practice at Rome. In 528 Justinian made it obligatory for all clerics. Taking a clue from Ps 119:164 about singing seven times daily, St. Basil divided the divine office into seven periods of prayer throughout the day and night. The church at Rome gathered together material from various books into which the divine office was scattered and produced the "Breviarium," a Latin word meaning "brief" or "short." The Franciscans popularized the Breviarium; it became the official prayer book of parish priests. Pope Pius V regulated a yearly cycle of readings, selected from all the books of the Bible. The Breviarium was further reformed by Pope Pius X and considerably shortened at Vatican II. Since the council the psalms are read/sung on a monthly cycle, divided over five periods of prayer each day, two of which are much more important and obligatory than others.

VIII
Numbering and Versification of the Psalms

The division of the Bible into chapters and verses was a long process. During the first centuries of the Christian period, the rabbis seriously counted "verses" and words in the different books of the Bible and appended the results at the end of the book. Our present system of chapters depends principally upon Archbishop Stephen Langton (d 1228) while that of verses upon the work of Robert Estienne in 1551. Variations show up in our English Bible for the following reason that the Hebrew text and the ancient Greek combined or divided some psalms differently. For instance, Pss 9-10 in the Hebrew remained one psalm in the Greek; Pss 146-147 in the Greek are joined as a single psalm in the Hebrew. As the following schema shows, there are still other variations. The Hebrew enumeration was followed, of course, in all Hebrew Bibles, but also in translations from the Hebrew at the time of the Protestant reformation. The

Greek enumeration was reflected in the Latin Vulgate and in Roman Catholic books and liturgical documents. Since the epochal encyclical letter of Pope Pius XII, urging a return to the original languages in translation and interpretation (1943), Roman Catholic editions of the Bible have incorporated the Hebrew enumeration, sometimes with the numbering of the Greek Septuagint in parenthesis. Liturgical books remain with the liturgical tradition of the Vulgate system of numbering the psalms.

Another factor enters to confuse the situation still more. The verses within the psalms are counted differently, depending whether one includes the title as a separate verse (or verses in a couple instances; *cf.,* Pss 51; 54; 60). Because the titles were not used in the singing or recitation of the psalms liturgically, many ritual books omitted them. As mentioned earlier in this introduction, the Hebrew text, on the contrary, not only includes the titles within the system of versification but also prints them with the same type of lettering as the rest of the psalm. This Hebrew style of versification devised by Rabbi Nathan in 1448, is reflected in the Greek Septuagint, the Latin Vulgate, the English Catholic Rheims-Douay, the Jerusalem Bible (French edition), the New American Bible. The practice of *not* including the titles in the versification is seen in Protestant English-language editions of the Bible and the Jerusalem Bible (English edition).

This commentary is based upon the Revised Standard Version (RSV), a translation in the tradition of the King James Bible and from a committee of Anglican and Protestant scholars. A special edition of the RSV, called the *Common Bible*, an ecumenical edition according to its subtitle, not only includes the seven apocryphal or Deuterocanonical books, normally not found in Protestant editions of the Bible, but also places these seven books according to their order in Roman Catholic editions. This commentary, based on the RSV translation, will always refer to the psalms (and other parts of the Bible as well) according to the enumeration and versification in the RSV.

These details about the numbering and the versification of the psalms show up as follows:

Hebrew, RSV, NAB, JB	Greek, Vulgate, Rheims-Douay
Pss 1-8	1-8
9-10	9
11-113	10-112
114-115	113
116	114-115
117-146	116-145
147	146-147
148-150	148-150

As an example of versification:

	Hebrew, NAB JB (French)	RSV, JB (English)	Rheims-Douay
title	51:1-2	title	title
body of psalm	51:3-21	51:1-19	50:1-19

IX
Outline Of Psalms According To Literary Form *

HYMNS OF PRAISE

Motivation from Nature: Pss 8, 19A, 29, 33, 89:6-19, 104, 148

Motivation from History or Torah: Pss 19B, 24, 46, 47, 48, 68, 76, 78, 81:1-5b, 100, 105, 113, 114, 117, 122, 133, 134, 135, 136, 145, 146, 147, 149, 150

Yahweh-King: Pss 24, 29, 47, 93, 95, 96, 97, 98, 99, 149

Canticles of Zion: Pss 42-43, 46, 47, 48, 76, 84, 87, 122

Entrance or Processional Liturgies: Pss 15, 24, 68, 95, 100, 132

PRAYERS OF SUPPLICATION & LAMENT

For the Assembly: Pss 12, 14, 44, 53, 58, 60, 74, 79, 80,
83,   85, 89, 90, 94, 106, 123, 126, 137, 138, 144:1-11
For the Individual: Pss 3, 4, 5, 6, 7, 9-10, 13, 17, 22, 25,
  26, 27, 28, 31, 35, 38, 39, 40, 41, 42-43, 51, 52, 54, 55,
  56, 57, 59, 61, 63, 64, 69, 70, 71, 77, 86, 88, 102, 109,
  120, 130, 139, 140, 141, 142, 143
For the Sick: Pss 6, 13, 16, 28, 30, 31, 38, 39, 41, 69, 88,
  91
For Repentant Sinners: Pss 6, 25, 26, 32, 38, 51, 90, 130
Curse Psalms: Pss 10:15; 31:17-18; 40:15; 55:15; 58:6-11;
  59:10-13; 68:22-23; 69:22-28; 83:9-18; 137:9; 139:18-21;
  140:8-10

THANKSGIVING PSALMS

For the Assembly: Pss 22:22-31, 30, 34, 65, 66, 67, 75,
  92, 107, 111, 118, 124, 138
For the Individual: Pss 9-10, 18, 23, 30, 31, 32, 35, 40,
  41, 92, 103, 116, 120, 144:1-11

PRAYERS OF CONFIDENCE

  Pss 11, 16, 20, 23, 27, 57, 62, 91, 115, 121, 125, 129,
  131

WISDOM PSALMS

  Pss 1, 15, 19B, 24, 33, 34:11-21, 36, 37, 49, 73, 78,
  90:3-12, 92, 101, 111, 112, 119, 127, 128, 144:12-15,
  145
Alphabetical or Acrostic: Pss 9-10, 25, 34, 37, 111, 112,
  119, 145
Concerning the Law: Pss 1, 19B, 119

ROYAL PSALMS

Coronation or Anniversary: Pss 2 (or 1-2), 72, 89:1-37,
  101, 110, 132
Intercession: Pss 20, 21, 144:1-11

Supplication: Pss 61, 89
Marriage: Ps 45
Thanksgiving: Ps 18

PROPHETICAL PSALMS

Pss 15, 50, 81, 82, 95:7d-11

OTHER CLASSIFICATIONS

Hallel Psalms
Egyptian Hallel: Pss 113-118
Great Hallel: Pss 136 (+ 135:4-21)
Morning Hallel: Pss 146-150

Morning Prayer: Pss 3, 5, 16, 27:1-6, 57, 59, 63, 88, 92, 143

Evening Prayer: Pss 4, 8, 16, 17, 27:7-14, 38, 63, 77, 91, 141, 143

Seven Penitential Psalms: Pss 6, 32, 38, 51, 102, 130, 143

(*) Although all psalms are listed here, some are included more than once. At times a psalm overlaps categories or else defies a single, definite classification. Not only psalms but also categories evolved over the centuries; some subsections, like "Canticles of Zion," will include psalms that do not correspond to the larger heading of "Hymns of Praise." We also note the following repetitions: Ps 14 = Ps 53; Ps 40:13-17 = Ps 70; Ps 108 = Pss 57:7-11 + 60:5-12.

Method and Style of This Commentary

Each psalm is studied according to four stages of its presence in Israel and in the Christian community:

(I) According to the *origin* of the psalm in the socio-religious background of ancient Israel and the *absorption of later modifications* from the life and worship of Israel;

(II) According to the psalm's *literary form and structure*;

(III) According to *key words or phrases* and other important or difficult items within the psalm;

(IV) According to the *impact of the psalm today* in public worship, private devotion or social-moral questions.

Method Recommended for Using This Commentary

1st) Always read the text of the psalm before studying the commentary.

2nd) After reading Sections I & II of the commentary, re-read the text of the psalm in order to become more deeply appreciative of the word of God in the Bible and in the context of its origin.

3rd) After studying Section III of the commentary of each psalm, reread the psalm in the light of its key words and phrases. Also, check the biblical references cited, so as to see how the psalm and its key phrases are enriched by the larger patterns of biblical theology.

4th) After reflecting on Section IV and on the relevance of the psalm to our world today, it is crucial to see how the psalm applies to your own needs and inspirations. Then read the psalm carefully and prayerfully again.

BOOK I
(PSALMS 1-41)

Psalm 1

I

[1]Blessed is the man
  who walks not in the counsel of the wicked,
 nor stands in the way of sinners,
  nor sits in the seat of scoffers;
[2]but his delight is in the law of the Lord,
  and on his law he meditates day and night.
[3]He is like a tree
  planted by streams of water,
 that yields its fruit in its season,
  and its leaf does not wither.
 In all that he does, he prospers.

II

[4]The wicked are not so,
  but are like chaff which the wind drives away.
[5]Therefore the wicked will not stand in the judgment,
  nor sinners in the congregation of the righteous;

III

[6]for the Lord knows the way of the righteous,
  but the way of the wicked will perish.

(I) If the psalter was compiled during the postexilic age (539 B.C. onward) as the principal song book of the Jerusalem temple, this introductory psalm reminds us that neither the psalter nor the temple belonged exclusively to Israelite priests and other religious leaders. Ps 1 is rightly considered a sapiential psalm with close ties to such books as Proverbs which speak seldom of liturgical matters, not even of Israel's great historical moments, the basis of theology and worship. Sapiential literature remains close to the everyday world of human existence and seeks to live here in a godly way. Ps 1, therefore, does not ring with the glorious tones of a sanctuary hymn like Pss 8 or 29, nor echo salvation history like Pss 104, 105 and 114; yet it shows a close association with Israel's sacred institutions. It reminds us that Israel's liturgy ritualizes God's redeeming presence in secular life and is to be judged acceptable or not by its impact on justice and sincerity. Thereby liturgy and the psalms offer true worship to God.

Ps 1 was added late to the psalter. Some New Testament manuscripts and early ecclesiastical writers seem oblivious of Ps 1 and refer to Ps 2 as the first psalm (*cf.,* Codex Bezae; Origen on Acts 13:33). When one of the final editors of the Psalter added Ps 1, this person linked it carefully with Ps 2. The first psalm begins and the second ends with *Blessed* or *How happy that one*, a literary device called "inclusion." Because Ps 2 originally belonged to the coronation of a new king, Ps 1 is thereby associated with the Davidic royalty at Jerusalem. There are associations with still other parts of the Bible. Some connection exists between Ps 1 and Jer 17:5-8, and there is a remote possibility of some relation of Ps 1:3 with the poetry of an Egyptian scribe, Amen-en-Opet. Ps 1 also harmonizes with Deuteronomic literature in Joshua and the Book of Deuteronomy, literature that resonates the theology of the northern kingdom, which was closer to Moses and less centralized or less controlled than the religious situation at Jerusalem. In many subtle ways then, Ps 1 represents a medley of many biblical traditions, more secular than sacred, yet always related to the way of the Lord's direction and providence, even to finding one's deepest pleasure in the Lord's Instruction. The author was not a great poet, thinker or moralist. This psalmist was a person of experience, reflection and moderation, but most of all a person of strong conviction, totally dedicated to the Lord in the path of daily life.

The redactor integrated Ps 1 with the five books that comprise the Psalter. The opening phrase of Ps 1, *Blessed is that one*, or better translated in a less liturgical way, closer to the Hebrew *'ashre, How happy that one*, is found towards the end of the first two books: Ps 41:1 within Pss 1-41; Ps 65:4 within Pss 42-72; it also occurs in the final psalm of the third and fourth books (Pss 73-89 and Pss 90-106 — *cf.,* 89:15 and 106:3) and it appears very often in the fifth book, Pss 107-150, 8 times in Ps 119 alone. Ps 1 was clearly meant to be a coalescing force in the psalter and by its own secular contact to keep the prayer of Israel closely in touch with the total life of Israel and this life closely attached to God.

(II) The psalm is divided into vv. 1-3, the way of the just; vv. 4-5, the way of the wicked; v. 6, the concluding judgment on the two ways. In contrast with the pre-exilic age (before 587 B.C.) and its struggle between Israel and the gentile non-elect people, this psalm, perhaps by prophetic or sapiential influence, identified the crucial struggle as that within Israel between the just and the wicked.

(III) *Blessed* or *How Happy* translates the Hebrew word *'ashre* (not the more liturgical, ritualistic word *baruk* — *cf.,* Ps 104), closely connected with right living in one's daily life. The word occurs 45 times in the Hebrew Bible, of which 26 times are in the Pss and 12 occurences in the wisdom literature, especially in the oldest section of Prov (14:21; 16:20; 20:7). The *happy person* fears God (Ps 112:1; Prov 28:14), behaves righteously (Ps 119:1-2), cares for the poor (Ps 41:1; Prov 14:21) and follows the Lord's instructions (Prov 29:18). Because of association with wisdom literature, the word might even be translated: *How envious* or *to be envied* is that person....

Another key word in Ps 1 is *the way* (66 times in the psalter, 16 times in Ps 119, frequently also in wisdom literature). The word, *way* (in Hebrew, *derek*), came into popular

use with the later prophets, Jeremiah and especially Ezekiel
(107 times); Second Isaiah considers it to be the way of the
Lord (Isa 55:9) along which the exiles return to their promised land (Isa 40:3) and so retrace in spirit the first exodus
out of Egypt (43:16, 19). It becomes even clearer that this
way belongs to the Lord and can be found only by obedient
faith and humble submission to divine guidance. People are
never the master of this right way, only the Lord. Ps 1 ends
by stating that *the Lord* [and we add, the Lord alone] *knows
the way of the righteous.* We find here an unusual, even
intriguing combination of practical common sense (very
visible in the wisdom books) and the mysterious guidance of
the Lord (prominant with the prophets). Again we note the
ecumenical or inclusive attitude of Ps 1.

The law of the Lord extends beyond the Mosaic Torah or
the first five books of the Bible, even though this law is
always based on the Mosaic covenant, is mediated through
the Holy Scriptures, and ought to be the subject of continuous meditation, *day and night* or as Deut 6:7 stated, "when
you sit in your house, and when you walk by the way, and
when you lie down, and when you rise." The Hebrew word,
meditate (*hagah*), means to mumble, sigh, whisper or reflect
aloud (see Pss 9;16); it presumes a visible manifestation (Isa
3:14; 8:19; Ps 90:9; Josh 1:8), and therefore it commits a
person totally, body and mind, as the Lord's way sinks
deeply within. Therefore, one's *delight* in the law of the Lord
reveals an interior peace and satisfaction that center upon
the person of the Lord (Pss 19:8-9; 119:2, 10). This interior
satisfaction in the Lord orientates us to the proper meaning
of *the fear of the Lord* (Ps 19:9; Prov 1:7), a healthy fear, lest
we stray from the heart's greatest delight. Such wandering,
unfortunately, is easily possible when one is successful (Ps
37:7-9).

A steady momentum moves the psalm forward: *How
happy that one who walks...stands...sits...like a tree
[trans]planted by streams of water that yields its fruit in its
season...[and] rises* [a better word than *stand* to translate
qum in v. 5] *in the* [decisive] *judgment* [with] *the congregation of the righteous.* This impetus towards a final, perma-

nent state of justice — a divine gift where one has been transplanted by the Lord *by streams of water* may be at least a vague, intuitive glimpse of the eschatological judgment in favor of the righteous within the heavenly assembly, even a fleeting perception of the messianic community (*cf.,* Isa 65:8-10, 13-16; 66:10-11, 18-23; Dan 12:1-3). This sense of God's final judgment is hidden within the comparison of the wicked to *chaff* (v. 4), which occurs with fierce finality in Zeph 2:2; Isa 17:13.

(IV) Ps 1 begins with *aleph*, the first letter of the Hebrew alphabet, *'ashre*; its final word, *to'bed*, starts with the last letter of the alphabet, *taw*. The letters aleph and taw symbolize all the letters and words in between. Ps 1 thereby embraces the entire psalter, even all the Holy Scripture. Ps 1, moreover, places us in meditation *day and night* and reaches even beyond time. We are reminded of Jesus, the alpha and the omega (of the Greek alphabet, Rev 1:8; 21:6; 22:13), the joyful fulfillment of the law (Matt 5:17-19; 6:33). While we are expected to work strenuously, body and mind, the reward at the end of the way of the Lord is a grace beyond all merit on our part.

Psalm 2

I

¹Why do the nations conspire,
  and the peoples plot in vain?
²The kings of the earth set themselves,
  and the rulers take counsel together,
  against the Lord and his anointed,
    saying,
³"Let us burst their bonds asunder,
  and cast their cords from us."

II

⁴He who sits in the heavens laughs;
  the Lord has them in derision.
⁵Then he will speak to them in his wrath,
  and terrify them in his fury, saying,

[6]"I have set my king
     on Zion, my holy hill."

III

[7]I will tell of the decree of the Lord:
  He said to me, "You are my son,
     today I have begotten you.
[8]Ask of me, and I will make the nations your heritage,
     and the ends of the earth your possession.
[9]You shall break them with a rod of iron,
     and dash them in pieces like a potter's vessel."

IV

[10]Now therefore, O kings, be wise;
   be warned, O rulers of the earth.
[11]Serve the Lord with fear,
   with trembling [12]kiss his feet,
  lest he be angry, and you perish in the way;
     for his wrath is quickly kindled.

V

Blessed are all who take refuge in him.

(I) Pss 1-2 together introduce the entire psalter. They are
united by the literary device of "inclusion," the identical
formula of *How happy...'ashre...* at the beginning and at
the end of the combined psalms. Ps 2, in fact, concludes in
vv. 11-12 with sapiential instruction, the sole preoccupation
of Ps 1. While Ps 1 comes from the sapiential movement
with a more humanistic outlook, Ps 2 originated in a more
political setting, the coronation ceremony of new kings at
the Jerusalem temple and royal palace. Because royalty
protected the sapiential movement — King Solomon
became the wise person par excellence (*cf.,* 1 Kgs 4:29-34) —
the combination of sapiential Ps 1 and royal Ps 2 as a
prologue to the psalter is not surprising. Ps 2, moreover,
with its roots in the Davidic dynasty, leads more immediately to the cluster of "Psalms of David," concentrated in
the First and Second Books of the Psalter. In Book One (Pss
1-41), all except Pss 1, 2, 9-10 and 33 are called "Psalms of

David"; in Book Two (Pss 42-89), this title is found before Pss 51-65, 68-70. Two other collections in the first two Books of Psalms are associated with the Jerusalem temple (Psalms of Asaph, Pss 50, 73-83; Psalms of Korah, Pss 42-43; 44-49; 84-85; 87-88) and are appropriately introduced by the royal Ps 2. Royalty exercised supreme authority over the temple and could function on occasion as priests (1 Kings 3:4; chap. 8).

Ps 2 is related to several other texts prepared for a coronation or a royal anniversary: 2 Sam 7; Isa 9:2-7; Ps 89:19-37; Ps 110. Important features of the ceremony can be pieced together as well from the coronation of Solomon (1 Kgs 1:32-48) and of Joas (2 Kgs 11:12-20). According to R. de Vaux, the rubrics included: a) positioning of the crown prince "near the pillar" or upon a dais in the temple (2 Kgs 11:14; 23:3); b) bestowal of royal insignia, diadem or crown, and a solemn inscription affirming the "divine birth" of the king (2 Kgs 11:12); c) anointing with oil and the gift of the Spirit (1 Sam 9:16; 10:10; 2 Sam 2:4; 5:3; 1 Kgs 1:39; 2 Kgs 9:3, 6); d) acclamation by the people (1 Kgs 1:34-39; 2 Kgs 11:12, 14); e) enthronement in the palace (1 Kgs 1:46; 2 Kgs 11:19); and f) homage from high officials and foreign dignitaries (1 Kgs 1:47).

The royal psalms, like royalty itself, at first represented a radical innovation in Mosaic religion. The less centralized structure of tribal federation, inherited from the days of Moses and Joshua, was collapsing around 1050 B.C. and the people demanded of the prophet Samuel "a king to govern us like all the nations" (1 Sam 8:5). Political and military conditions forced this change upon Samuel and eventually God gave his sanction. Not even David, however, could go so far as to build a temple (2 Sam 7:4-7); Solomon swung the royal revolution full circle by constructing the temple. Israel had returned to the ways of Canaanite kings and Egyptian pharaohs whom earlier they had despised and conquered! The Davidic royalty was granted unconditional, divine promises: "Your house and your kingdom shall be made sure for ever before me; your throne shall be established for ever" (2 Sam 7:16). The king was considered inviolable (1 Sam 24:7, 11; 26:9, 11, 23). Royalty became as deeply imbedded in Israel's *religious* traditions as the Mosaic covenant; it was a *conditio sine qua non* for the prophet Isaiah (Isa 7-9). When the Babylonians destroyed the temple and exiled the king, God seemed to have betrayed Israel (Ps 89:38-51). Israel continued to recite or sing the royal psalms, now no longer in honor of the incumbant king but as a carrier of hopes for a heavenly deliverer or messianic king. God would revive the dynasty mysteriously, supernaturally.

Ps 2, then, like the other royal psalms, had a long history, from non-Israelite pressure and modeling, to religious impowerment of Jerusalem kings within Israel's sacred traditions, to a non-political, possibly a non-military revival in the distant future. In its origins Ps 2 reaches back into the early period of Israelite monarchy and political life; in its evolution it occupies a prominent place in Israelite religion, even in NT understanding of Jesus' resurrection (see below).

(II) While the structure of Ps 2 is rather simple, the interchange of speakers is debated. The following explanation is based upon the texts, cited above, for the coronation ceremony, in which a respected prophet anoints the crown prince and declares him king.

Vv. 1-3. The earthly setting for the coronation ritual. During an interregnum, vassal states tended to revolt (Isa 14:28-31) and palace intrigues ran rampant (1 Kgs 1-2). Chaos prevailed even in the cosmos; no king was present as God's representative in maintaining balance and good order in the physical universe (Pss 8:1b-2; 89:9-37). Verses 1-2 were sung by the temple choir about the kings in revolt while in v. 3 a special choral group speaks in the name of these kings: *Let us burst their bonds....*

Vv. 4-6. The heavenly setting, mirrored in the temple, for the coronation ritual. In vv. 4-5 the temple choir speaks about Yahweh's serenity and power; in v. 6 Yahweh speaks in his own name through a prophet who anoints the crown prince with oil.

Vv. 7-9. The enthronement, spoken by a prophet in the name of Yahweh: v. 7a, the solemn inscription of divine edict, referred to above; v. 7b, the words of consecration, again in Yahweh's name. As in any liturgical action, words and actions together achieve what they symbolize. They explain one another. At the central point of the liturgy, however, symbolism fades away and there is a sense of God's immediate presence (*cf.,* Ps 12:5). Ultimately, royalty does not depend upon popular choice but upon divine anointing. Verses 8-9 reflect other ritual actions like homage and tribute from foreign kings and the bestowal of the royal scepter.

Vv. 10-12a. Advice to the vassal kings and indirectly to the newly crowned King of Jerusalem, which can be linked to the instruction in Ps 1. The blessed or happy person is now seen to be the king who must *delight in the law of the Lord* and as Ps 2:12b concludes, *take refuge in him.*

(III) Verse 1 opens with a rhetorical question, very effective for getting attention. *Nations. . .peoples* may reflect the domain of David's empire, the only time that the Jerusalem capital competed on the world scene, but the phrase tends to be a stereotype for greatness (*cf.,* Pss 76:12; 102:15; 148:11; Isa 40:23). In the late postexilic age it presaged the Messiah's universal kingdom, yet only in a vague way as in Dan 7-9. The word, *plot,* is the same Hebrew word, *hagah,* as in Ps 1:2 and implies whispering, intrigue, repeated attempts.

V. 4, *He who sits in the heavens,* a dramatic contrast with the futile, feverish activity in vv. 1-3. The phrase continues a biblical image of Yahweh's enthronement in the heavens above the earth, surrounded by spirits or divine servants —Pss 8:5; 11:4; 82; 104:1-4; Exod 19:11; 1 Kgs 22:10-23. Yahweh *laughs,* not out of ridicule nor disdain but from sovereign security and total self-control, patiently allowing creatures to learn the hard way, sometimes the only way (*cf.,* Pss 37:13; 59:9).

Verses 6-8 insist upon the first person, "I," that it is "I Yahweh and no one else." *Zion* at first signified the Jebusite city conquered by David and called the "city of David" (2 Sam 5:7); later it designated the growing metropolis of Jerusalem (Isa 10:24) and still later that part of the city on the NE, occupied by the temple (Ps 132:13). The ancient Greek Septuagint translates v. 6, "I am established as his

king on his holy mountain," and corroborates the position
that the psalm is spoken mostly by the king, not by the
anointing prophet; we prefer the RSV reading, closer to the
Hebrew.

Verse 7a, *decree of the Lord*, in Hebrew *ḥoq*, refers not
only to the solemn inscription given like a royal seal to the
crown prince, but also to Yahweh's assurance to establish
good order in the universe and to subdue forces of chaos
(*cf.,* Jer 5:22; Job 28:26; Ps 148:6; Prov 8:29).

V. 7b, *He said to me*, spoken by the anointing prophet or
priest, as appointed by Yahweh to speak in the Lord's own
name the words of consecration over the crown prince.

V. 7b, *You are my son, today I have begotten you.* By this
rite of divine adoption, the king incorporated in himself all
the people of Israel, also called Yahweh's "first-born child"
(Exod 4:22; *cf.,* Hos 11:1). We are reminded of the covenant
formula: "I am your God; you are my people" (Jer 7:23;
11:4; 31:33; etc.). Yet, the source of this royal title is traced
to non-Israelite countries, like Egypt where the king was
considered divine, or Babylon where he was annually suf-
fused with a divine spirit. In Israel, however, the kings never
claimed divinity, and were not accused of this crime by the
prophets. Verse 8, *ask of me*, reflects Solomon's prayer at
Gibeon (1 Kgs 3:5).

Verses 11-12 are textually corrupt, or at least uncertain in
meaning, due to a copyist's error in the late postexilic age;
this person even used the common language of his or her
time, the Aramaic *bar* instead of the Hebrew *ben* for *son*,
already present in v. 7. The Greek Septuagint is still different and compounds the textual problem. This deterioration
can happen in a text that is in frequent use. The emendation
of A. Bertholet is generally followed. *Kiss his feet* reflects a
normal way of bestowing homage (Ps 72:9; Luke 7:38, 45).

V. 12d. *Happy are all who take refuge in him.* The psalm
in some places seems fierce and angry; yet it ends on a note
of peace and tenderness. The sequence of thought in this
psalm is close to a hymn to the Babylonian god, Marduk.
We quote it to show that biblical religion was not different
or unique in its individual words or actions but rather in its

pervading spirit and consistent morality. In an ancient Akkadian creation epic, the *Enuma elish*, we read: "O Marduk, thou art indeed our avenger. We have granted thee kingship over the universe entire. When in Assembly thou sittest, thy word shall be supreme. Thy weapons shall not fail; they shall smash thy foes! O Lord, spare the life of him who trusts thee..." (*ANET*, p. 66; Tablet IV, lines 13-17).

(IV) The New Testament discreetly overlooked some of the verses in Ps 2 (*cf.,* v. 5) and carefully adapted others, like v. 6 about Mount Zion. Jesus fulfills the psalm by becoming king, not at his birth of the Davidic line, acquired through his foster-father Joseph (Matt 1:16-17; Luke 1:32), but rather through his resurrection from the dead, enthronement at God's right hand and sending of the Spirit (Acts 4:25-26; 13:33; Heb 1:5; 5:5). This fulfillment is certainly in continuity with the Hebrew Scriptures, yet it could never be deduced ahead of time from the literal meaning of the words. The OT prepares for the mystery of Jesus but still leaves us walking the way of faith for surprises beyond our best expectation. The difficulty and revolt of kings in Ps 2 may truly represent our own impatience and intransigency, our revolts and sinfulness, when we reject God for not acting according to our plans and our interpretation of Scripture. Only when we live within the continuity of God's people and by faith *take refuge in him*, so as to allow God the liberty to fulfill his promises beyond our best hopes, will Jesus be crowned king in our lives, within the family of *a kingdom of priests and a holy nation* (Exod 19:6).

We also note the interdependence of Israelite religion and politics, or divine inspiration and non-Israelite religion. Israel's most important insights into God's will for the nation evolved through political crises. The formulation of messianic hopes came originally from Egyptian and Babylonian documents and ceremonies, a profound lesson for the missionary enterprise of the church which is tempted to impose its western customs, ceremonies and styles of leadership upon Africans, Asians and Central or South Americans.

Psalm 3
A Psalm Of David, When He Fled From Absalom His Son.

I

¹O Lord, how many are my foes!
  Many are rising against me;
²many are saying of me,
    there is no help for him in God.

Selah

II

³But thou, O Lord, art a shield about me,
  my glory, and the lifter of my head.
⁴I cry aloud to the Lord,
  and he answers me from his holy hill.

Selah

⁵I lie down and sleep;
  I wake again, for the Lord sustains me.
⁶I am not afraid of ten thousands of people
  who have set themselves against me round about.

III

⁷Arise, O Lord!
  Deliver me, O my God!
  For thou dost smite all my enemies on the cheek,
    thou dost break the teeth of the wicked.

IV

⁸Deliverance belongs to the Lord;
  thy blessing be upon thy people!

Selah

(I) According to its title, Ps 3 inaugurates the first series of *Psalms of David* (Pss 3-41) and states further that David composed this particular one *when he fled from Absalom his son*. Davidic authorship, therefore, does not necessarily situate a psalm within the sublime chambers of a sanctuary but within the agony and weakness, hopes and triumphs of our common humanity. Absalom's revolt is told in 2 Sam

15-18 and climaxes in David's tearful cries of adieu: "O my son Absalom, my son, my son Absalom! Would I had died instead of you, O Absalom, my son, my son!" (2 Sam 18:33). Ps 3 itself is so general that it can be applied to any sorrowful situation, especially when the sufferer feels abandoned and betrayed, hemmed in by hostile people. The reference to the temple, *his holy hill* (v. 4), not only tends to place this psalm in an age later than David's, who was prevented from constructing the temple (2 Sam 7:4-7), but it also gives a clear charter to bring every human problem into God's sacred presence. The title, however, *Psalm of David*, may mean that it was sung on days of national mourning, anniversaries of sorrow or defeat, in the presence of the king.

(II) Although the psalm includes an upbeat of confidence, it seems best to consider it a *psalm of lamentation* for the *morning* prayer of an *individual* worshipper. This person may represent the larger community. Despite its general application, it resonates an intimate rhythm of sorrow and cry for help. The psalm can be divided between: vv. 1-2, an appeal to Yahweh; vv. 3-6, an expression of confidence; v. 7, a second cry for help; v. 8, concluding words of confidence, perhaps sung as a refrain by the entire congregation, at least the closing phrase, *your blessing upon your people*. Several key words are repeated throughout the psalm: variations of *rabab, to be numerous* (vv. 1 [twice], 2, 6); *yeshu'ah, salvation*, spoken by the enemy in v. 2, by the psalmist in v. 7 and possibly by the entire congregation in v. 8; *qûm, to rise*, said of the enemy in v. 1 and of Yahweh in v. 7. This skillful use of contrast is enhanced by still other devices: v. 1 combines *sar, foes*, which literally means "to restrict, shut off, close in upon" with *yeshu'ah, salvation*, which in its earliest sense indicated something spacious or abundant.

Ps 3 is closely related to Ps 4 as morning and evening prayer, even to the repetition of key words or phrases:

3:1a Lord, how many are my foes (*ṣar*)	4:1b in my *distress* (*ṣar*)
3.2 *Many* are *saying* of me	4:6 there are *many* who *say*
3:3b my *glory* (*kebodi*)	4:2a my *honor* (*kebodi*)

3:4 I *cry aloud* to the Lord	4:1a *Answer* me when I *call*
and he *answers* me	4:3b The Lord hears when I
	call
3:5 I *lie down* and *sleep*	4:8a I *lie down* and *sleep*
(*shakab*)	(*shakab*)
	4:5b on your *bed* (*shakab*)

(III) Vv. 1-2. Each of the first three lines should probably begin with: *How many*...The psalmist feels personally helpless, totally alone before a converging multitude of hostile people.

Vv. 3-6. This expression of confidence begins abruptly, *But* [*on the contrary*] *You, O Lord.* While the enemy uses a general word for *God, 'elohim*, who, they say, has abandoned the psalmist, the latter invokes the sacred name of *Yahweh — Lord* and begs for the Lord to intervene from personal concern. *Shield* recalls God's special promise to Abraham (Gen 15:1) as well as the great prayer of thanksgiving, attributed to David (Ps 18:1). *my glory* is rich in theology, indicating the Lord's wondrous, redemptive presence among his people. The Lord's glory is manifest in the psalmist. St. Ireneus wrote: "Gloria Dei, vivens homo — the glory of God [is] the living human being." V. 4, *he answers me* is the pivotal point of the psalm; God's word, spoken silently in the heart, turns distress into new life (see Ps 22:21, commentary). *from his holy hill*, the place of the temple and the Lord's special presence, where the Lord not only breaks the loneliness of the psalmist by a renewed union with the entire congregation at prayer but also fulfills the prayer of Solomon: "Hearken thou to the supplication of thy servant and of thy people Israel, when they pray towards this place ...and when thou hearest, forgive" (1 Kgs 8:30). V. 5, *lie down, sleep, wake again* — indicate a morning prayer: night, a symbol of evil and powerlessness (Gen 1:2-5; Jer 13:16), has surrendered to light.

V. 7, a second cry for help and for the humiliation of the enemy (*smite*...*on the cheek — cf.,* 1 Kgs 22:14; Isa 50:6; Matt 5:39; John 18:22).

V. 8, a final cry of confidence. The Hebrew is dramatically

succinct: "With Yahweh, salvation; with your people, your blessing."

(IV) This psalm accompanies the church throughout Holy Week and tells of the Lord's endurance of persecution and betrayal, death and sleep in the earth, awakening to a new day in the resurrection (Justin; Augustine). It teaches us to deal with breach of faith by a stronger personal bond with the Lord; redemption must begin within the heart. It is also interesting to note that this psalm has been used in the ancient ritual of exorcism against evil spirits.

Psalm 4
To The Choirmaster: With Stringed Instruments. A Psalm Of David

I

¹Answer me, when I call, O God of my right!
  Thou hast given me room when I was in distress.
  Be gracious to me, and hear my prayer.

II

²O men, how long shall my honor suffer shame?
  How long will you love vain words,
    and seek after lies?   *Selah*
³But know that the Lord has set apart
    the godly for himself;
  the Lord hears when I call to him.

⁴Be angry, but sin not;
  commune with your own hearts on
    your beds, and be silent.   *Selah*

⁵Offer right sacrifices,
  and put your trust in the Lord.

⁶There are many who say, "O that we
    might see some good!
  Lift up the light of thy countenance
    upon us, O Lord!"

III

⁷Thou hast put more joy in my heart
   than they have when their grain and
   wine abound.

⁸In peace I will both lie down and sleep;
   for thou alone, O Lord, makest me
   dwell in safety.

(I) While Ps 3 is a traditional morning prayer, its counterpart, Ps 4, has been long used for evening prayer. Ps 3 is
more aggressive and militaristic (vv. 6-7), Ps 4 is more
sombre and more insistent upon trusting in the Lord (v. 5).
Ps 3 seems to sweep out more readily into the human side of
life, Ps 4 settles more persistently into liturgical ceremonies
and religious language. We meet a convergence of ritual or
at least official language, particularly in the Hebrew text of
Ps 4: *i.e.*, right or justice, vv. 1, 5 (*ṣedeq*); prayer, v. 1
(*tephilah*); glory or honor, v. 2 (*kabod*); the godly, v. 3
(*ḥesed*); sacrifice, v. 5 (*zabaḥ*); light of thy countenance, v. 6.
The author was possibly a priest or someone who handled
legal inquiries within the religious setting of the sanctuary.
Yet he was caught in a tangle of intrigue, lies, fraud and
perjury (v. 1-2), perhaps at a time of drought (v. 7) when
people are always tempted to prey on the helpless for food.
Even though the last suggestion is only conjectural, nonetheless, the psalm speaks for anyone who has been betrayed
and must stand solely by their conscience and their absolute
trust in God.

(II) For these reasons we consider Ps 4 to be like Ps 3, a
psalm for individual lament, yet united with a congregation
at worship. It does sustain a persistent note of trust in God,
but not strong enough for this to be a psalm of confidence.
V. 1, introductory call for help, possibly sung antiphonally
by the assembly; vv. 2-6, a vigorous report of the difficulties,
with vv. 3-4 addressed to the conspirators (v. 3 enumerating
their intrigue; v. 4 as advice) and vv. 5-6 addressed to the
congregation at worship (v. 5, possibly a late addition that

breaks the meter and rhythm); and finally vv. 7-8, the good results, addressed to Yahweh (v. 7) or spoken as a personal reflection (v. 8). The Hebrew text of Ps 4 has been disturbed, possibly by the interchange of many speakers in the liturgy; the rhythm also tends to be uneven.

(III) V. 1, the opening call for help. *Thou hast given me room*: resonates the semi-nomadic origin of Israel (*cf.,* Gen 26:22, where Isaac called a new place *Rehoboth,* the same Hebrew word in Ps 3:1, "for now the Lord *has made room* for us, and we shall be fruitful in the land"); the word contrasts the open prominade of the temple courtyard with the confining and worrisome intrigue of evil people. *Be gracious,* in the Hebrew implies undeserved mercy; God's goodness far exceeds our best efforts.

Vv. 2-6, the difficulties. Amazingly enough, the psalmist is still willing to trust and dialogue with the adversaries, masters of deceit as they are. The word, *godly — ḥasid,* in v. 3 implies a bond of blood or covenant, which united the devout person closely as the the Lord's very own. V. 4, *be angry,* follows the Greek Septuagint (*cf.,* Eph 4:26); the Hebrew reads, "be deeply moved" or "tremble" (NAB), here by the Lord's concern for his own people — a willingness by the psalmist to appeal to ancient memories of contemplative prayer and mystic love, imbedded within every Israelite. V. 5, *right sacrifices,* worship honoring the Lord's fidelity and generous care (*cf.,* Deut 33:19; Pss 51:18-19; 118:19-21). V. 6, *light of thy countenance,* echoing the priestly blessing in Num 6:24-26; Pss 31:16; 80:3, 7, 9).

Vv. 7-8, anticipated thanksgiving for the good results, already experienced *in my heart.* God's gift of interior peace imparts more than strength of conscience; a glow of spiritual joy spreads peace and security over the psalmist's entire life. The emphasis in the final line rests upon the person of Yahweh; the Hebrew reads in part, "Indeed, it is you, Yahweh, the only one."

(IV) A final reflection upon Ps 4, before we lie down and *sleep* (v. 8), can be drawn from Lev 26 where God speaks to his chosen people:

If you walk in my statutes and observe my commandments,...you shall eat your bread to the full, and dwell in
your land securely. And I will give peace in the land, and
you shall lie down, and none shall make you afraid....I
will make my abode among you...and walk among you,
and will be your God, and you shall be my people.

Or Ps 4's insistence upon God's justice echoes the third Song
of the Suffering Servant (Isa 50:4-9a).

Psalm 5
*To The Choirmaster: For The Flutes. A Psalm Of
David.*

I

[1]Give ear to my words, O Lord;
    give heed to my groaning.
[2]Hearken to the sound of my cry,
    my King and my God,
    for to thee do I pray.
[3]O Lord, in the morning thou dost hear my voice;
    in the morning I prepare a sacrifice for thee, and watch.

II

[4]For thou art not a God who delights in wickedness;
    evil may not sojourn with thee.

[5]The boastful may not stand before thy eyes;
    thou hatest all evildoers.
[6]Thou destroyest those who speak lies;
    the Lord abhors bloodthirsty and deceitful men.

[7]But I through the abundance of thy steadfast love
    will enter thy house,
 I will worship toward thy holy temple
    in the fear of thee.
[8]Lead me, O Lord, in thy righteousness
    because of my enemies;
    make thy way straight before me.

III

⁹For there is no truth in their mouth;
    their heart is destruction,
their throat is an open sepulchre,
    they flatter with their tongue.
¹⁰Make them bear their guilt, O God;
    let them fall by their own counsels;
because of their many transgressions
        cast them out,
    for they have rebelled against thee.

¹¹But let all who take refuge in thee rejoice,
    let them ever sing for joy;
and do thou defend them,
    that those who love thy name may exult in thee.

IV

¹²For thou dost bless the righteous, O Lord;
    thou dost cover him with favor as with a shield.

(I) This prayer of lament, deeply personal and resonating an individual's suffering under lies and deceit, reaches out for support to the people assembled for morning sacrifice in the temple. Betrayed even by leading members of the community, the psalmist has not lost faith in Israel. The language is so general and classic, that it is difficult to identify any special moment of Israel's history or any particular member of the community; Ps 5 belongs to everyone of every age.

(II) Two sets of key words run through the psalm, and if underlined in one's Bible, almost every line would have one or more words emphasized. One series threads the sense of justice/injustice through the verses; the other repeats a synonym for words or speaking. It seems that the psalmist was victimized by calumny, the innocence of his or her person violated by deceit and spite. In fact, the psalm is organized around this diptyque of opposition:

vv. 1-3, Appeal to Yahweh to heed my groaning

vv. 4-6,	vv. 9-10,
Evil and God, incompatible	Deceit of evil people

vv. 7-8,	vv. 11,
The righteous worship God	The righteous are blessed

v. 12, Conclusion: liturgical Acclamation/Blessing

The key verse occurs at the center: v. 8, *Lead me, O Lord, in thy righteousness...make thy way straight before me.* Not just God, but God at the center of community life and worship, blesses the righteous and covers them with favor (v. 12). This interaction between the God of Israel, the psalmist and the wicked shows up in the dramatic way three lines are introduced, particularly in the Hebrew text: v. 4, *But THOU*, O God; v. 7, *BUT I*, on the contrary; v. 9, *In THEIR mouth no truth.*

(III) Vv. 1-3, an introductory appeal to Yahweh. It is not that God is deaf and blind but that the psalmist must acknowledge the Lord's presence within a heart sinking beneath the polished deceit of certain community leaders and close friends. *my groaning*, the same Hebrew word, *hagah* as in Pss 1:2; 2:1, here reflects not only the mumbling and stammering sound of someone in great sorrow and tension but also the deep feelings beneath the words of this psalm. *my King and my God*: Yahweh was thought to be enthroned on the *kipporeth* or mercy-seat, the gold covering upon the ark between the outstreched wings of the cherubim (Exod 25:17-22; Is 6:1-4). From this *throne* God *judges the people* with equity (Ps 9:8). The author of the psalm, like the prophet Isaiah, each a layperson, not a priest, commune directly with Yahweh within the Holy of Holies. There is a severe tension here between the sacred and the secular, the awesome and the routine, a strain that relaxes in the person of Yahweh. *Morning*, twice in v. 3, was a normal time for prayer and temple sacrifice: Exod 29:38-40; Lev 6:12-13; 2 Kgs 3:20. In fact, the morning and evening sacrifice of the temple lies behind the ancient Christian prayer of Lauds and Vespers, the latter accompanied with incense. Morning was also a symbol of deliverance: out of Egypt (Exod 14:20-24); from the Assyrians (Isa 38:26); in the eschatological age (Isa 33:2). *prepare a sacrifice*: literally in the Hebrew, simply *prepare*, with the object being a legal case (Job 23:4; 33:5) that could lead to a final settlement and a ritual of atonement in the temple (Lev 19:20-22; Num 5:5-10). The object may also be one of the many temple sacrifices. Because the psalm is dealing continually with justice/injustice within the context of community prayer, the former explanation seems more helpful.

Vv. 4-6. Evil and God, incompatible. The references to evil reflect the Decalogue, the basic law of human behavior, essential for community security and happiness (Exod 20; Deut 5).

Vv. 7-8. The righteous worship God *towards thy holy temple*: not only was it customary to pray in the direction of the Holy of Holies (1 Kgs 8:30, 38, 42; Dan 6:10) but synagogues in Galilee, after the destruction of Jerusalem, were pointed towards Jerusalem, like Islamic mosques towards Mecca.

Vv. 9-10. Deceit of evil people. V. 9, *their heart — sepulchre* represent a meaningful play on words in the Hebrew, *qirbam — qeber*. *open sepulchre* occurs again in Jer 5:16 about foreign invaders, whose "quiver is like an open tomb [that devours] your harvest and your food... your sons and your daughters." The psalmist is close to eliminating *bloodthirsty and deceitful* Israelites (v. 6) from the true Israel, but he never takes the next step to say that just and honest foreigners might qualify. V. 10, *make them bear their guilt*, a single word in the Hebrew, from the root *'asham*, which can refer to sacrifices for sins of inadvertence (Lev 1-7). When a person, rejected for willful sins (Ps 34:21-22), makes restitution, the willful sin is then relegated to one of inadvertence. A priest must agree that the conditions were met; sacrifice is then offered (Lev 19:20-22; Num 5:5-10). The psalmist's word, then, carries a heavy theology which leads either from guilt to atonement, or from guilt to destruction/rejection. Old Testament religion may not seem adequately pious, but it keeps its feet on the ground and its God on planet earth!

Vv. 12-13. Liturgical acclamation and blessing, that echo Pss 1:1; 2:11; 4:7, center on the person of Yahweh who imparts a strong blessing and a joy which no deceitful words can tarnish.

(IV) Ps 5 enables us to weather the worst crises of betrayal within family or community, of scandal within religious circles. We begin each morning with a prayer that is real and hopeful.

Psalm 6
To The Choirmaster: With Stringed Instruments; According To The Sheminith. A Psalm Of David.

I

¹O Lord, rebuke me not in thy anger,
  nor chasten me in thy wrath.
²Be gracious to me, O Lord, for I am languishing;
  O Lord, heal me, for my bones are troubled.
³My soul also is sorely troubled.
  But thou, O Lord — how long?

II

⁴Turn, O Lord, save my life;
  deliver me for the sake of thy steadfast love.
⁵For in death there is no remembrance of thee;
  in Sheol who can give thee praise?

III

⁶I am weary with my moaning;
  every night I flood my bed with tears;
  I drench my couch with my weeping.
⁷My eye wastes away because of grief,
  it grows weak because of all my foes.

IV

⁸Depart from me, all you workers of evil;
  for the Lord has heard the sound of my weeping.
⁹The Lord has heard my supplication;
  the Lord accepts my prayer.
¹⁰All my enemies shall be ashamed and sorely troubled;
  they shall turn back, and be put to shame in a moment.

(I) A critically sick person makes a personal appeal to Yahweh, seven times invoking this intimate name for God, three times stating how *terrified* he or she is (vv. 2b, 3a, 10a) at the prospects of death (v. 5). Physically and spiritually spent, the psalmist has been pushed to the outer limits of human endurance. The same honesty with which physical weakness is admitted prevents the psalmist from any false claims of innocence. Justice is on the side of Yahweh, but so are mercy and compassion (*cf.,* Exod 34:6-7). Especially in the Hebrew text one notices a continuous tension between "I — the psalmist" and "You — Yahweh," between life and death, grace and sin. What the psalm lacks in poetic imagery and stylistic elegance, it recoups quickly in the effective use of questions and imperatives: "Rebuke me not! — how long? — turn, O Lord! — in Sheol who can give you praise? — Depart from me, you workers of evil!" This intense personal interaction gives new life to the many, stereotyped phrases in the psalm, found elsewhere, not only in other psalms, but also in Jeremiah and Job. This fact alone places Ps 6 within the repertoire of temple prayers.

(II) Grammatical details like questions and imperatives enable us to identify the strophic arrangement: vv. 1-3, *Pity, Lord*, begins with an imperative, ends with a question; vv. 4-5, *Prayer for healing*, also starts off with an imperative, concludes with a question; vv. 6-7, *Suffering*; vv. 8-10, *Prayer heard*, opens with an imperative. This dramatic interchange, along with the heavy use of familiar cultic phrases, may account for the psalm's frequent use in the liturgy both of Israel and later of the church. The title of the psalm may leave us guessing about specific details, but it also leaves a definite impression of liturgical use. During the first two centuries A.D., the psalm was recited daily in the synagogue and in the Latin church. The reference to the "eighth — *Sheminith*" led to theological speculation about circumcision among the Jews (on the eighth day after birth) and about the new creation and resurrection among Jews and Christians. "Eighth," being the day after God rested from creation, alluded to the new creation and the healing of all woes. Ps 6 is also the first of the seven penitential psalms

(Pss 6, 32, 38, 51, 102, 130 and 143), a collection probably known as such by Augustine, clearly mentioned by Cassiadorus (+ A.D. 583), once recited each Friday in Lent after morning Lauds by monastic communities and on other occasions, like the sacrament of anointing the sick.

(III) Vv. 1-3. *Pity, Lord.* The psalm presumes a connection between sin, God's anger, sickness and suffering. As such it compares with King Hezekiah's attitude in Isa 38:10-20 but differs from Job and Jeremiah who reacted against this ancient theology, that suffering always presumed (personal) sin (*cf.*, John 9:2). Granted a strong sense of corporate unity, each sin within a community was bound to affect every member of the family or tribe, innocent or not. The word order from v. 1 speaks its own message: literally, *Lord, not-in-thy-anger rebuke me.* The psalmist admits that he or she deserves rebuke but begs God not to do it *in thy anger.* v. 2, *languishing*, a rare but dramatic word, some form of which refers to drought (Jer 14), locust plague (Joel 1), devastating evil (Hos 4:3), apocalyptic collapse of the earth (Isa 24:4). *bones*, the center of physical pain (Pss 22:14; 17; 31:10), a term at times interchangeable for the person (Ps 35:10).

Vv. 4-5, *Prayer for healing. How long, O Lord?* An unfinished question of desperation, frequent in the Bible (@ 30 times) and in Babylonian prayers — perhaps dulled by overuse, yet still "audacious, direct, categorical" (Jacquet). *thy steadfast love,* an appeal to the covenant bond between Yahweh and Israel. *death—Sheol*: Israel's belief in the afterlife was far less developed than that found in Egypt; Israel's was closer to the dull, dark, listless existence, reflected in Babylonian literature (*cf.*, Pss 94:17; 143:3), with no return (Job 7:9), abode of foreigners and Israelites alike (Isa 14:15), with some, yet very inactive presence of Yahweh (Amos 9:2; Pss 88:5; 139:8). The psalmist's dread of Sheol is similar to that of King Hezekiah (Isa 38:18). In rejecting the elaborate, mythological system of the after life within Egyptian theology, Israel "threw the baby out with the bath water." Israel's official theology remained underdeveloped until a very late period when the doctrine of bodily resurrection for the just was accepted (Dan 12:1-3; 2 Macc 7:23). Popular piety always maintained some idea of contact with the dead, their continued existence, and their return to a happy life (Gen 5:24; 1 Kgs 17:17-24; 2 Kgs 2:11; 4:32-37; 13:20-21). Perhaps the question-form of v. 5 indicates a doubt about the rigid theology and a leaning towards the popular piety of life after death.

Vv. 8-10. If, as seems likely, Ps 6 was recited within temple worship, the functioning priest may have recited an "oracle of salvation" after v. 7, a cultic promise of God's intervention (*cf.,* Gen 15:1; 26:24; Isa 43:1; Joel 2:21-22; Dan 10:12). The psalmist responds with confident faith. Twice he states: *the Lord has heard,* verifying the power of prayer because of the personal concern of the Lord. The formula is so strong that it might even be translated, *the Lord fulfills* my request.

(IV) Ps 6 allows the desperately sick person to place their distress, their suffering, their doubts, their desperation honestly before the Lord. It stresses the realism of biblical prayer and the strength of biblical faith.

Psalm 7
A Shiggaion Of David, Which He Sang To The Lord Concerning Cush A Benjaminite

I
¹O Lord my God, in thee do I take refuge;
 save me from all my pursuers, and deliver me,
²lest like a lion they rend me,
 dragging me away, with none to rescue.

II
³O Lord my God, if I have done this,
 if there is wrong in my hands.
⁴if I have requited my friend with evil
 or plundered my enemy without cause,
⁵let the enemy pursue me and overtake me,
 and let him trample my life to the ground,
 and lay my soul in the dust.   *Selah*

III

⁶Arise, O Lord, in thy anger,
  lift thyself up against the fury of my enemies;
  awake, O my God; thou hast appointed a judgment.
⁷Let the assembly of the peoples be gathered about thee;
  and over it take thy seat on high.
⁸The Lord judges the peoples;
  judge me, O Lord, according to my righteousness
  and according to the integrity that is in me.
⁹O let the evil of the wicked come to an end,
  but establish thou the righteous,

IV

thou who triest the minds and hearts,
  thou righteous God.
¹⁰My shield is with God,
  who saves the upright in heart.
¹¹God is a righteous judge,
  and a God who has indignation every day.

¹²If a man does not repent, God will whet his sword;

V

he has bent and strung his bow;
¹³he has prepared his deadly weapons,
  making his arrows fiery shafts.
¹⁴Behold, the wicked man conceives evil,
  and is pregnant with mischief,
  and brings forth lies.
¹⁵He makes a pit, digging it out,
  and falls into the hole which he has made.

VI

¹⁶His mischief returns upon his own head,
  and on his own pate his violence descends.

¹⁷I will give to the Lord the thanks due
  to his righteousness,
  and I will sing praise to the name of
  the Lord, the Most High.

(I) A lament for an individual sufferer, falsely accused of a serious crime, possibly of murder, who takes refuge in the temple, both for personal safety and for adjudication of the case and a declaration of innocence. The agitated and angry state of the psalmist's mind seems to be reflected even in the rugged condition of the psalm: the Hebrew text has many difficulties and vague references, the poetic rhythm shifts from the very common 3+3 beat (vv. 1-5, 12b-17) to the sorrowful 3+2 beat typical of a lament (vv. 6-12a). Some scholars divide the psalm into two or three originally independent poems, each about the topic of evil and retribution, which were not too smoothly stitched together.

(II) The division of Louis Jacquet, based on rhythm, spirit and vocabulary, deserves attention:

Ps 7A, with a 3+3 beat and a moderate amount of self-control, shows a convincing development: vv. 1-2, appeal to Yahweh; vv. 3-5, protestation of innocence; vv. 12b-15, intrigues of the adversary; vv. 16-17, release from danger and thanksgiving to Yahweh.

Ps 7B, with a 3+2 beat and a more intense reaction, calls for an eschatological judgment and a final settlement for peace: v. 6, appeal for judgment; vv. 7-8a, the great trial; vv. 8bc-9ab, the reign of justice.

Ps 7C, with a 3+2 beat, shows a sepiential influence: vv. 9cd-10, God's presence with the just; vv. 11-12a, sanctions against evil.

For a quick summary, Ps 7A, the earliest poem, handles the problem of retribution from the immediacy of Yahweh's daily providence in the sphere of social justice; Ps 7B, from a prophetical background, demands instant, eschatological justice with social-religious sanctions; Ps 7C, graced with sapiential moderation, is also the most purely religious in its treatment of evil. Ps 7, however, reaches us in its canonical state as a single psalm, and for simplicity's sake we will study it consecutively.

(III) Vv. 1-2, Appeal to Yahweh. *I take refuge*, a phrase frequent in the psalms (*cf.,* Ps 2:11; 5:11), possibly here with the hope of sanctuary protection or asylum against adversaries (Num 35:9-28; 1 Kgs 1:49-53; 2:28-34). V. 2, *a lion*:

these existed in this country till the time of the Crusaders (*cf.,* Amos 3:12; Jer 2:20; Pss 10:9; 17:12).

Vv. 3-5, Protestation of Innocence. The repetition of *if ...if...if* follows the form of a solemn oath (*cf.,* 1 Sam 3:17; Ps 137:5-6). V. 5, three stages of punishment: *pursue, trample down, lay my life in the dust* (*i.e.,* death) with three allusions to the psalmist: *me* (literally, *my soul—nephesh,* the Hebrew word for throat, breathing and life-indicator); *my life* (*hayyim* in Hebrew = vitality, peace, joy, integrity, also a title for the "living God" in Ps 43:2); *my soul* (*kabod* in Hebrew = glory, weighty manifestation of God's redemptive presence — see commentary on Ps 3). The final word, *kabod,* is sometimes changed to read *kabed* (= *liver,* among ancient Semites the organ of strong emotions, as in Lam 2:11).

Vv. 6-9ab, Eschatological judgment. V. 6, *Arise, O Lord,* a call which is associated with the ark of the covenant and its symbolism of God's presence with the Israelites in the desert or later in war (Num 10:35; Ps 68:1; 1 Sam 4:1-4) and with God's action for the defenseless (Ps 9:18-19; Isa 51:17). V. 7, *assembly of the peoples.* Yahweh presides over a worldwide judgment (*cf.,* Ps 50:1-4; Amos 1:3—2:16; Isa 43:10-14) or with a slight change of the Hebrew, over an assembly of the powerless gods (*le'ummin* to *'elohim, cf.,* Ps 82; 1 Kgs 22:19-23).

Vv. 9cd-12a, Sapiential Reflection on good and evil. V. 9b, *triest the minds and hearts.* The word *triest* connotes an exploration of dark places (*cf.,* Jer 12:3) within the *mind* (Hebrew = *leb* or heart, the area for thinking) and *heart* (Hebrew = *kelayoth* or kidney, the area for judging and for conscience). God peers deeply within our person, into our most hidden motivation and real intentions — *cf.,* Rev 2:23. Biblical anthropology imparts different psychological functions than we do today to the organs of the human body.

Vv. 12b-15, Intrigues of the adversary. Textually, v. 12 is very difficult; the subject is left vague, simple "he." We read the "he" in v. 12b to mean the adversary whose wickedness steadily increases, as in v. 14, *the wicked person conceives evil, is pregnant with mischief, and brings forth lies.*

Vv. 16-17, Release from Danger and Thanksgiving to Yahweh. A person is destroyed by their own mischief, a fact of life with frequent testimony in the sapiential literature (Prov 26:27) and especially in Jeremiah (Jer 2:5, they *went after worthlessness and became worthless*; Jer 2:19, *your wickedness will discipline you.*)

(IV) If this psalm seems to be harsh towards the wicked, it is one example among many in the Bible that the Scriptures do not develop a theology of sin for obstinate and deceitful people but a theology of redemption and grace for humble, honest people. So long as anyone legitimizes injustice and insolence, there can be no hope; for the repentant sinner (*cf.,* Ps 6), God is waiting to forgive and to transform life (*cf.,* Exod 34:6-7). The *lex talionis* (eye for an eye — Exod 21:24) is realistic, not only according to the texts from Jeremiah, quoted above, but also according to the NT (*cf.,* Matt 7:2; 26:52; 2 Cor 5:10). The Scriptures do not remove the suffering that often follows sin, but show how these sorrows can be purifying and redemptive, within the covenant bond that includes Jesus who became "sin" for our sake (2 Cor 5:21). Social justice permeates religious justification.

Psalm 8
To The Choirmaster: According To The Gittith. A Psalm Of David.

I

¹O Lord, our Lord,
    how majestic is thy name in all the earth!

II

Thou whose glory above the heavens is chanted
² by the mouth of babes and infants,
    thou hast founded a bulwark because of thy foes,
      to still the enemy and the avenger.

³When I look at thy heavens, the work of thy fingers,
    the moon and the stars which thou hast established;
⁴what is man that thou art mindful of him,
    and the son of man that thou dost care for him?

⁵Yet thou hast made him little less than God,
  and dost crown him with glory and honor.
⁶Thou hast given him dominion over
    the works of thy hands;
  thou hast put all things under his feet,
⁷all sheep and oxen,
    and also the beasts of the field,
⁸the birds of the air, and the fish of the sea,
  whatever passes along the paths of the sea.

III

⁹O Lord, our Lord,
  how majestic is thy name in all the earth!

(I) Yahweh is praised as creator of the universe, but we must note at once that this praise returns to the Lord from men and women gifted not only with strong, spontaneous faith but also with the appreciation to transform its sound and action into ecstasies of delight. The language is highly poetic. Several key words add a touch of elegance: the exclamation *mah* (= how? or what? in vv. 1 and 4 — *How majestic!...what* is the human family?); the play on sound between name and heavens (*shem* and *shamaim* in vv. 1a, 1b, 3a, 9). There is, besides, an effective use of grammar which enables the religious assembly to interact vigorously through choral exclamations (*How majestic!* in vv. 1a and 9), questions (*What is a human being?* in v. 4), contemplative mood of wonder (*When I look at thy heavens* in v. 3), rapid enumeration (*sheep, oxen, beasts of the field, birds, fish* in vv. 7-8).

Because of the accumulation of royal terms and imagery, it is possible that the psalm was originally composed in honor of a reigning monarch at Jerusalem. Through the king God was thought to maintain the stability of the universe (see commentary on Ps 2); later when the Davidic monarchy disappeared, Yahweh became the exclusive center of praise. The psalm speaks of *Our Lord*, a title for kings in 1 Kgs 1:11, 43, 47 but directed to Yahweh only in postexilic literature like Neh 10:30 or Ps 135:5. Other regal terms occur: *majestic* (vv. 1a, 9), *glory* (in Hebrew, *hodeka*, v. 1b), *crown with glory and honor* (v. 5), *dominion* and *under his feet* (v. 6).

If this explanation is correct, then the psalm reflects political fortunes and misfortunes of the Davidic dynasty. As the royal court gathered titles and protocol from neighboring countries, psalms were composed for the monarchs. After the suppression of the dynasty by Babylonian and Persian armies, these psalms passed into Israel's understanding of God and were further integrated with other biblical traditions, like the stories of creation and the closeness of God to humanity in Gen 1:1—2:4a (the Priestly Tradition, "P") or the stories of humanity and animals in Gen 2:4b—3:24 (Yahwist Tradition, "J"). We sense in Ps 8 a strong interaction as well with the wisdom tradition behind the Book of Job (Job 7:17; 26:12) as well as with other psalms (Pss 65:12; 103:4). As we shall see, the evolution of Ps 8 continued into New Testament times.

(II) A typical hymn of praise, Ps 8 opens and closes with the community's acclamation of Yahweh in wonder and joy (vv. 1a and 9) and the motivations for praise through the body of the psalm, sung by a select choir (vv. 1b-8). The assembly probably repeated the initial refrain after each line or might even have chanted it continuously *sotto voce*. The psalm fits into an evening service, on account of the reference to one's looking at *the moon and the stars* (v. 3) with no allusion to the sun or light.

(III) Title: The phrase, *according to the Gittith*, in some way relates to the Philistine city of *Gath*, either to a musical instrument or to a melody popular in this city. David had close association with the Philistines, having lived with them while a fugitive from Saul (1 Sam 27:1-7) and employed them as personal bodyguard (2 Sam 8:18). Again we notice foreign, political influences in the composition and singing of the psalms.

V. 1a, Congregational refrain. *O Lord, our Lord*: the Hebrew employs two different words, *Yahweh 'adonenu*; the Greek Septuagint always translated Yahweh as *kurios* or Lord and so ended up with *Lord, our Lord*. *thy name*: in the Bible name signified the principal characteristic(s) of a person's work or vocation. People's names were changed when they were given a special vocation (Abraham, Gen 17:5; Peter, Matt 16:18; Paul, Acts 13:9). Strange as it may seem, the refrain implies that Yahweh has a special call or "vocation" to surround his human family with majestic wonder.

Vv. 1b-2. This first of the stanzas to be sung by the special choir has serious textual problems and consequently many different translations. The rough condition of the Hebrew text may reflect the history of the psalm and its evolution from honoring the Davidic king to centering upon Yahweh. Behind the struggle with enemies and jealous powers there lies the common feature of Semitic creation stories: the creator-God(s) had to overcome chaos and hostile forces in order to establish peace and fertility on planet earth. According to the NAB, the biblical account of creation in Genesis is introduced with just an allusion to the primeval chaos:

> In the beginning, when God created the heavens and the earth, the earth was a formless wasteland, and darkness covered the abyss, while a mighty wind swept over the waters (Gen 1:1-2).

Just as the reign of a new king began with revolts across the kingdom (*cf.,* Ps 2:1-3), likewise the renewal of creation involved divine conflicts. The Bible, therefore, is envisaging a continual re-creation (like the coronation of each new king) rather than first creation, Yahweh's endeavor to restore order against the chaos precipitated by human disobedience and pride rather than the "easy" and sublime manner of first creating the world out of nothing. For these and other reasons "creation" was linked with royalty, the Torah, and wisdom (Prov 8:22-36; Sir 24; Deut 6 and 32). Many biblical passages reflect the titanic battles against chaos at re-creation: Pss 74:12-17; 89:9-18; Isa 51:9-10. After defeating chaos and spreading a beautiful world of peace before the human family, it is natural to hear the sound of new life, that of *babes and infants* (Kraus).

Vv. 3-4. The second stanza contrasts the awesome universe with tiny human beings; even a giant is only a babe compared to the heights of the heavens and the distant home of the stars! *What is man...the son of man*: the Hebrew words (*'enosh* and *ben-'adam*) do not restrict themselves to the male sex but refer to both men and women. A more adequate translation might be: *What is the human family ...the child of earth?* The term, *son of man*, is difficult to change because of its long, established use in the Bible from Old into New Testament. One of its persistent characteristics is lowliness: son of man or *ben-'adam* alludes not only to God's first creation of male and female to the divine image (Gen 1:27) but also to the origin of *'adam* from mother earth (*'adamah*). Overwhelmed by divine visions, the prophet Ezekiel falls to the earth and is addressed as *ben-'adam*, one with the *'adamah*; Job, overcome by God's continuous, probing gaze, cries out: *What is man ('enosh)...let me along till I swallow my spittle* (Job 7:17, 19; *cf.*, 25:4-6). The persecuted saints, buried in the earth, are referred to collectively as *a son of man* [coming] *with the clouds* [to be given] *dominion and glory and kingdom* (Dan 7:13-14). *Son of man* or *child of earth*, accordingly, denotes the human family in its lowly origin and humiliated, even persecuted, condition, yet by the Lord's love transformed into someone just *little less than God.*

Vv. 5-8. Humankind's highest *glory and honor* are divine gifts, not human achievements. Moreover, human dignity ranks above that of the animals, not because of a spiritual soul nor because of life after death but because of God's special remembrance. While the opening refrain, *Yahweh, Our Lord*, resonates the more restrictive covenant theology that Israel is the Lord's special people and Yahweh is *Israel's* God, the rest of the psalm hints to God's universal regard for all men and women. The allusions to the two creation accounts of Genesis, which embrace the universe and all humankind, bolster the universal aspects of Ps 8. V. 5, *little less than God* probably read in its original form "little less than the gods," meaning the members of the divine assembly (see commentary on Pss 2:4; 82). The Greek translation continues this tradition, "for a little while less than the angels," in which the substitution of the word, "angels," removes any danger of polytheism in the word "gods," while the temporal phrase, "for a little while," focuses on the short time till the appearance of the messiah. When the Epistle to the Hebrews quotes Ps 8:5, it identifies the messiah as Jesus (Hebr 2:8). In vv. 8-9 the poet associates domestic and wild animals with humankind, with unique attention to the birds and fishes whose way through the air or water seems very mysterious and directionless yet it is always with a keen perception for the place of food, mating and hibernation —an exceptionally fine but unusual image of divine providence; it always leads us mysteriously but surely to our true "home."

(IV) The NT rereading of this psalm carefully respects its OT ancestry. When the psalm is quoted by Jesus, Matthew's Palm Sunday account integrates its main elements: the royalty of David, *Hosanna to the Son of David!* (Matt 21:9), the struggle against chaos and pride when *Jesus entered the temple of God and drove out all who sold and bought* (21:12), the new creation in healing *the blind and the lame* (21:14), all within the setting of the Mosaic covenant (Jesus was about to celebrate the Pasch) and its absorption within the world (*the chief priests and the scribes saw the wonderful things...and were indignant*) typified by the spontaneity of the children. The quotation of the psalm in 1 Cor 15:20-28 includes references to the new Adam-humanity and the new kingdom, to a conflict with the enemies, the last of which is death, and to the new creation (*cf.*, Eph 1:15-23). The NT also makes clear that Jesus suffered our struggle with evil in his own body, that was crucified and buried; as we seem to die in our goals and in our weakness, we find a new dignity and a new creation in Jesus, risen from the dead.

Psalms 9-10
To The Choirmaster: According To Muthlabben. A
Psalm Of David.

Ps 9

I

¹I will give thanks to the Lord with my whole heart;
 I will tell of all thy wonderful deeds.
²I will be glad and exult in thee,
 I will sing praise to thy name, O Most High.

³When my enemies turned back,
 they stumbled and perished before thee.
⁴For thou hast maintained my just cause;
 thou hast sat on the throne giving righteous judgment.

⁵Thou hast rebuked the nations, thou
  hast destroyed the wicked;
 thou hast blotted out their name for ever and ever.
⁶The enemy have vanished in everlasting ruins;
 their cities thou hast rooted out;
 the very memory of them has perished.

⁷But the Lord sits enthroned for ever,
 he has established his throne for judgment;
⁸and he judges the world with righteousness,
 he judges the peoples with equity.

⁹The Lord is a stronghold for the oppressed,
 a stronghold in times of trouble.
¹⁰And those who know thy name put their trust in thee,
 for thou, O Lord, hast not forsaken those who seek
  thee.

¹¹Sing praises to the Lord, who dwells in Zion!
 Tell among the peoples his deeds!
¹²For he who avenges blood is mindful of them;
 he does not forget the cry of the afflicted.

II

¹³Be gracious to me, O Lord!
  Behold what I suffer from those who hate me,
  O thou who liftest me up from the gates of death,
¹⁴that I may recount all thy praises,
    that in the gates of the daughter of Zion
    I may rejoice in thy deliverance.

¹⁵The nations have sunk in the pit which they made;
    in the net which they hid has their own foot been
      caught.
¹⁶The Lord has made himself known,
    he has executed judgment;
    the wicked are snared in the work
    of their own hands.

                    Higgaion. Selah

¹⁷The wicked shall depart to Sheol,
    all the nations that forget God.

¹⁸For the needy shall not always be forgotten,
    and the hope of the poor shall not perish for ever.

¹⁹Arise, O Lord! Let not man prevail;
    let the nations be judged before thee!
²⁰Put them in fear, O Lord!
    Let the nations know that they are but men!

                            Selah

Ps 10

III

¹Why dost thou stand afar off, O Lord?
  Why dost thou hide thyself in times of trouble?
²In arrogance the wicked hotly pursue the poor;
    let them be caught in the schemes
    which they have devised.

³For the wicked boasts of the desires of his heart,
    and the man greedy for gain curses
    and renounces the Lord.
⁴In the pride of his countenance the

wicked does not seek him;
all his thoughts are, "There is no God."

5His ways prosper at all times;
thy judgments are on high, out of his sight;
as for all his foes, he puffs at them.
6He thinks in his heart, "I shall not be moved;
throughout all generations I shall not meet adversity."

7His mouth is filled with cursing and
deceit and oppression;
under his tongue are mischief and iniquity.
8He sits in ambush in the villages;
in hiding places he murders the innocent.

His eyes stealthily watch for the hapless,
9   he lurks in secret like a lion in his covert;
he lurks that he may seize the poor,
he seizes the poor when he draws him into his net.

10The hapless is crushed, sinks down,
and falls by his might.
11He thinks in his heart, "God has forgotten,
he has hidden his face, he will never see it."

12Arise, O Lord; O God, lift up thy hand;
forget not the afflicted.
13Why does the wicked renounce God,
and say in his heart, "Thou wilt not call to account"?

IV
14Thou dost see; yea, thou dost note trouble and vexation,
that thou mayst take it into thy hands;
the hapless commits himself to thee;
thou hast been the helper of the fatherless.

15Break thou the arm of the wicked and evildoer;
seek out his wickedness till thou find none.
16The Lord is king for ever and ever;
the nations shall perish from his land.

[17]O Lord, thou wilt hear the desire of the meek;
     thou wilt strengthen their heart,
        thou wilt incline thy ear
[18]to do justice to the fatherless and the oppressed,
     so that man who is of the earth may strike terror no
     more.

(I) These two psalms manifest a complex literary form
and have suffered greatly from modifications (some scholars will even say, mutilations) within a long history of use
within temple services and instructions. Nonetheless it is
generally agreed that as they now exist in the Bible, they
constitute a single poem. In fact, the ancient Greek Septuagint, followed by the Latin Vulgate and the ancient liturgical
texts of the church, calls them simply Ps 9. Because the
Greek Septuagint was the standard Bible of early Christianity, both the Greek and Latin churches adopted its division
of the psalms, generally one behind the Hebrew text from
this point onward. Most modern Bibles follow the Hebrew
enumeration, yet the liturgical books of the post-Vatican II
Catholic church remain consistently within the ancient
Greek-Latin tradition.

Many convincing reasons are present for uniting the two
psalms: the alphabetical or acrostic arrangement which
extends throughout both psalms; the ancient Greek-Latin
tradition; the absence of any title at the beginning of Ps 10,
something rather unusual in the first book of the Psalter;
continuity of ideas and vocabulary.

(II) Scholars are divided in deciding upon the dominant
spirit or literary form. Some call it a "mixed form," similar
to Pss 36, 40, 89, 90, 139. Is it a lament (Kuntz, Dahood),
thanksgiving and confidence psalm (Beaucamp), thanksgiving alone (Podechard), or sapiential like Ps 1, because of the
alphabetical arrangement and the concern over retribution
for good and evil? These seemingly academic questions lead
to some practical insights into Israel's liturgy and its concern for the poor and persecuted members of the community. Similar to a number of ancient Egyptian texts, the
temple liturgy at Jerusalem may have begun with praise and

thanksgiving (like Ps 9) and then proceeded to petition for help and sorrow over difficulties, to end with confidence (like Ps 10). Because the entire prayer was directed to Yahweh, a personal and compassionate God (Exod 34:6-7), the psalmist responded in various personal ways: with rejoicing and singing, with doubts, anger and prayers, with praise, lament and confidence. Somewhere along the way of this long evolution, with each step equally inspired with God's presence, the alphabetical or acrostic arrangement was introduced — but never perfectly as several letters are missing or reversed. This method of beginning new lines or stanzas with succeeding letters of the alphabet has many values: for memorization; for maintaining self-control and discipline amidst a depressing or explosive situation; for sustaining an impression of calm objectivity; for inculcating the sacredness of each letter and smallest particle of God's word. Also in the postexilic age, the eschatological feature of Yahweh's final judgment against a world of injustice was emphasized within the psalms.

Another approach to the psalm is given by a study of key words or ideas: the gentile nations, 10 times; the poor, 10 times; insolent and deviously wicked people, 15 times —plus all of 10:2-9; the state of being vanquished or lost, 5 times; God's justice, 8 times; and God's enthronement in the temple, 5 times. We sense, therefore, several serious tensions within the psalm: between the Israelite nation and foreign countries; between the suffering of the poor and the success of the wicked; between Yahweh, always present in the temple and seemingly absent in times of distress; between Yahweh's warm compassion and stern justice in the cause of the poor.

The division of E. Beaucamp is helpful in directing us through this complex psalm.

Ps 9:1-12, *a psalm of thanksgiving*: an enthusiastic introduction (vv. 1-2); the body of the psalm appreciative of Yahweh's *personal* help (vv. 3-6) and *general* assistance (vv. 7-10); a lively conclusion (vv. 11-12).

Ps 9:13-20, *a lament*, beginning and ending with an oath in vv. 13-14 and 19-20; in between, an account of the wicked who eventually punish themselves and of the just who are not forgotten (vv. 15-18).

Ps 10:1-13, *a lament and cry of distress*: starting with a question, does Yahweh care? (vv. 1-2), continuing with the Lord's reaction to the wicked (vv. 3-6) and their reaction to their victims (vv. 7-11), and concluding with a demand, *Rise O Lord!* (vv. 12-13).

Ps 10:14-18, *a final song of confidence.*

(III) This long psalm may be complex and textually diffi-cult, yet the English version proceeds smoothly enough, particularly with the help of our outline. We will comment on a few important or difficult phrases.

9:1-12, *a psalm of thanksgiving.* Vv. 1-2, this opening call to thank Yahweh contains characteristic phrases for public liturgy: *give thanks, tell* or announce, *be glad, exult, sing praise.* The psalm evidently was not intended simply for private meditation but for group interaction in the sanctu-ary. *thy wonderful deeds:* the needs of the poor and the persecuted are linked with Yahweh's great redemptive acts in Israel's history, even with creating the world (Pss 71:16; 75:1; 78:4; 136:4). V. 5, *rebuke*, a Hebrew word, indicative of a strong passion and violent struggle for justice (Isa 17:13; 51:20; 54:9; Nah 1:4; Ps 106:9). V. 8, *the world, the peoples*, these words, like the entire verse, are almost verbatim out of Ps 98:9, and hint to the universal outreach of the psalm, precipitated by the struggle for justice which does not depend upon race or nationality but upon sincerity and compassion. The psalm, however, is not consistent in its approach to gentiles, and like the Old Testament generally it does not reach a clear voice for universal salvation. V. 10, *seek:* another key word in this psalm and in the Hebrew Bible. The meaning of the Hebrew word, *darash*, modulates between search, inquire, demand, avenge, create, investi-gate, interpret — therefore, to track down the topic or person diligently and to react appropriately. V. 12, *avenges blood:* because of intimate family and community bonds, blood that was spilt demanded that blood be renewed, avenged, and thereby protected (*cf.,* Num 35:9-29). Israel had no police force, only the force of personal ties of blood.

The same Hebrew word for redeemer (*go'el* = bloodbond) can also be translated, "avenger of blood."

Ps 9:13-20, *a personal lament*. V. 14, *gates of the daughter of Zion*, a feminine image of God who protects and encloses life. Cities, generally surrounded with walls, are thought of as mothers pregnant with children; therefore cities are always feminine gender in the Hebrew language. Zion, where the God of life was enthroned, became a symbol for God, who begot and enclosed life. V. 15, *their own foot [has] been caught:* see commentary on Ps 7:16-17. V. 16, *higgaion*, from the Hebrew root, *hagah* (see commentary on Ps 1:2), with the meaning to meditate, muse, whisper (Lam 3:62), groan (Ps 19:14), play the harp (Ps 92:3). Here, it is a liturgical reminder for silent meditation (with quiet musical background?). V. 19, *Arise, O Lord!*, this call for Yahweh's help in personal or community distress uses the language of the exodus and Israel's movement through the desert (Num 10:35; Ps 68:1-2).

Ps 10:1-13, *a community lament*. V. 3, the text is uncertain, but everyone agrees that the phrase, *"There is no god,"* means something like "God doesn't care, so forget about religion." Philosophical atheism does not exist in the Bible! The new translation of the Jewish Publication Society, usually quite literal, paraphrases in this instance: "The wicked, arrogant as he is, in all his scheming [thinks], 'He does not call to account; God does not care.'"

Ps 10:14-18, *a song of confidence*. The psalm ends with faith in Yahweh, compassionate towards the orphan and the oppressed and determined never to let devious or wicked people, whether in the community or in the world at large, tyrannize the defenseless folk and drive them from their homes.

(IV) We know that no quick solution is in sight for many forms of injustice in today's world. Therefore, we need a long psalm to sustain us over the long haul: over our moments of anger (*Why do you hide yourself, Lord, in times of trouble?* — 10:1) and humiliation (*the wicked boast* —10:3); through our moments of confidence (*the needy shall not always be forgotten* — 9:18) and of strength in our weakness (*do justice to the orphan* — 10:18). We need the self-control, imparted by an alphabetical psalm and community prayer. We also remember the persecuted but prayerful Jesus (John 11:41), the suffering but liberated church (Rev 19). We are reminded by Paul, introducing a quotation from this psalm, that *all of us, both Jews and Greeks, are under the power of sin* (Rom 3:14). As we recite this psalm in our state of oppression and suffering, Paul reminds us that we ourselves may belong to the oppressors!

Psalm 11
To The Choirmaster. Of David.

I

¹In the Lord I take refuge;
 how can you say to me,
 "Flee like a bird to the mountains;
²For lo, the wicked bend the bow,
  they have fitted their arrow to the string,
  to shoot in the dark at the upright in heart;
³if the foundations are destroyed,
  what can the righteous do"?

II

⁴The Lord is in his holy temple,
 the Lord's throne is in heaven;
 his eyes behold, his eyelids test, the children of men.
⁵The Lord tests the righteous and the wicked,
 and his soul hates him that loves violence.
⁶On the wicked he will rain coals of fire and brimstone;
 a scorching wind shall be the portion of their cup.
⁷For the Lord is righteous, he loves righteous deeds;
 the upright shall behold his face.

(I) Centering in the Jerusalem temple where the Lord is ever present to defend the powerless and the persecuted, this psalm mingles a didactic style of advice (about the rewards of the just) with an attitude of confidence *in the Lord*[within whose temple] *I take refuge*. Technically Ps 11 is not a hymn of praise nor a lament, for it does not address Yahweh directly in the second person; its more reflective discourse about Yahweh links it with a didactic approach, as in Ps 1, but especially with prayers of confidence (Ps 16).

Little can be said about the date except that there is no solid reason for placing it after 587 B.C. and the fall of Jerusalem. A few comparisons with Jeremiah or Job make us lean towards the end of the pre-exilic period, perhaps around 600 B.C. The psalm presumes internal problems with Judaism, particularly among those devoted to Yahweh and the temple. Some friends advise against remaining in Jerusalem or within the temple. Was the temple personnel turning against the psalmist? Or did the danger come from the abuse of power in the royal government and their blatant aggressiveness to enter the temple and violate the right of asylum (*cf.,* 1 Kgs 2:28-32, when Solomon ordered the execution of Joab who had "fled to the tent of the Lord and caught hold of the horns of the altar"). In any case the psalmist might have been an important official, at odds either with temple or royal government and hounded with intrigue and betrayal of trust, even with bad advice from well meaning friends. His confidence was rooted in the Lord alone.

(II) Many small difficulties plague the Hebrew text — like a singular subject with a plural verb in v. 7b — due either to neglect of the psalm or to its overuse particularly in popular piety. The poetic meter, moreover, is very uneven. Yet the general structure seems clear enough: vv. 1-3, false advice from friends; vv. 4-7, true confidence in Yahweh.

(III) Vv. 1-3, *False advice.* The psalm begins and ends firmly: *In the Lord I take refuge... The Lord is righteous* (vv. 1 and 7). *Refuge*, a very frequent word in the psalms: 22 out of its 37 occurrences in the entire OT are in the Book of Psalms. The word is prominent at the beginning of the psalter, as in Pss 2:11; 5:11; 7:1; 11:1; 16:1, etc., very visible at the beginning or end of a psalm. Spiritually, we begin and end with our firmest support in Yahweh. *Flee:* the Hebrew word means to flutter or to fly zigzag, therefore to be distraught or in panic as one attempts to outmaneuver a clever enemy who has the advantage. *to the mountains:* frequent enough in the Bible (Judg 6:2; 2 Sam 23:14; 1 Macc 2:28; Matt 24:16), because the mountainous area between the central ridge (2-3,000 feet above sea level) and the Jordan rift (7 to 13 hundred feet below sea level) is dangerous, precipitous and filled with many hiding places. In Gen 19:24 Lot was advised to flee to the mountains, to save himself and his family from the destruction about to hit Sodom and Gomorrah. V. 3, *foundations:* what normally would be the support of the psalmist: the institution of priesthood or royalty; the tried and true traditions and customs of Israel — these seem to have crumbled, at least according to the psalmist's well-meaning friends. To the psalmist the advice of religious leaders amounted to a betrayal of God and God's promises to the chosen people.

Vv. 4-7, *Confidence in Yahweh.* Though God dwells *in his holy temple,* nonetheless his *throne is in heaven.* Not only is the Jerusalem temple a mirror of the Lord's heavenly home, but God's power and love, his promises and righteousness, surpass the limits and wonder of anything made by hand (*cf.,* 1 Kgs 8:27-30; Isa 66:1; Acts 7:46;50). Jeremiah interacted in a similar way towards the Jerusalem temple; if the temple is destroyed, "it shall not come to mind," for there is still "the presence of the Lord in Jerusalem" (Jer 3:17). V. 3, *his eyelids test:* the verb is a favorite one of Jeremiah and Job, who suffered as "you, O Lord, tested my heart" (Jer 12:3) or as a person is tried "every moment" (Job 7:18). V. 6, *fire and brimstone* [sulphur]: another reference like v. 1 to Sodom and Gomorrah (*cf.,* Deut 29:23; Ezek 38:22). Even though Abraham argued with God for the safety of these two cities, there was a limit to God's patience, a determination that justice prevail (*cf.,* Gen 18:22-33). V. 7, *behold his face:* the Hebrew reads, "behold their own face," not Yahweh's, a theological scruple or correction, because of other statements in the Torah that "no one shall see my face and live," says the Lord (Exod 33:20); even to hear the Lord's voice may mean death (Exod 20:19; Deut 5:24-26). The psalmist, however, is confident to behold the Lord's face, referring not just to the special presence of God in the

Jerusalem temple but also to righteousness and social justice, promoted by God's word as heard in the Scriptures and properly preached in the sanctuary. We already read in v. 7, *The Lord...loves righteous deeds.*

(IV) The New Testament encourages us to find God not only in the sanctuary (Matt 5:34-35) but also in the moral decisions of the church (Matt 18:15-19). These are the foundations of conscience. At times, moreover, we like Jesus might be forced by conscience "to withdraw again to the mountains" by ourselves (John 6:15); at other times we are compelled to remain within community, even when the house seems to be collapsing (Mark 8:31-33) or to follow Jesus' example who "set his face to go to Jerusalem," though it meant his death (Luke 9:51). Sooner or later we ourselves and the entire world must face a judgment of "fire and brimstone" (Luke 17:29-30; Rev 14:10). Through these severe tests we will contemplate the presence of God, liturgically and mystically on earth (1 Cor 11:23-26; Acts 7:56), eternally and immediately in glory (1 Cor 13:12; Rev 22:4).

Psalm 12
To The Choirmaster: According To The Sheminith. A Psalm Of David.

> ¹Help, Lord; for there is no longer
>   any that is godly;
>   for the faithful have vanished from
>   among the sons of men.
> ²Every one utters lies to his neighbor;
>   with flattering lips and a double heart they speak.
>
> ³May the Lord cut off all flattering lips,
>   the tongue that makes great boasts,
> ⁴those who say, "With our tongue we will prevail,
>   our lips are with us; who is our master?"
>
> ⁵"Because the poor are despoiled, because the needy
>   groan,
>   I will now arise," says the Lord;
>   "I will place him in the safety for which he longs."

⁶The promises of the Lord are promises that are pure,
   silver refined in a furnace on the ground,
   purified seven times.

⁷Do thou, O Lord, protect us,
   guard us ever from this generation.
⁸On every side the wicked prowl,
   as vileness is exalted among the sons of men.

(I) One of the most destructive crimes against family, community and church is confronted head-on in Ps 12, the internal disease of deceit, intrigue, cleverness, power-plays and pride. These misdeeds usually seem small and "venial," in no way comparable to the "mortal" sins of the flesh or to violent crimes like slavery and stealing. Yet these offenses that seem small cut into the heart of family and church, and so they can tear apart the basic fabric of human existence. If we cannot believe a spouse, a brother or sister, a religious minister or priest, then the entire structure of family and church collapses. We think of the betrayal of Jesus by "one of the twelve, one who is dipping bread into the dish with me" (Mark 14:20). In Old Testament times we turn to the classical prophets like Hosea: "There is no faithfulness or kindness, and no knowledge of God in the land; there is swearing, lying, killing, stealing, and committing adultery" (Hos 4:1-2). Jeremiah reflects the dark side of Ps 12, when he hears God say to him:

> For even your brothers and the house of your parent,
>   even they have dealt treacherously with you; they are in
>   full cry after you;
> believe them not,
>   though they speak fair words to you (Jer 12:6).

Comparison with these pre-exilic classical prophets indicates a date of composition between 700 and 600 B.C.

(II) This ugly impression of deceit and lying within Ps 12 is reinforced by the repetition of key words for "speaking": *dabar*, twice; *'amar*, 4 times; *flattering lips*, 3 times; *tongues*, twice; besides such words as *sobs* and *groaning* — all within 8 verses. The orchestration of cries, dialogue and response shows up in a careful view of the structure of this communal lament:

v. 1a'   Call for help, sung repeatedly by the entire assembly.
vv. 1a"-2 Cause/motivation for this desperate call, sung by
           the major choir.
v. 3   Prayer, addressed to Yahweh, by small choir, no. 1.
v. 4   Spoken in the name of the wicked, by a small choir,
           no. 2.
v. 5   Oracle, pronounced in Yahweh's name, by priest
           or prophet.
v. 6   Antiphonal response to Yahweh's words, by small
           choir, no. 2.
v. 7   Prayer of Confidence, by small choir, no. 1.
v. 8   Conclusion, similar to the opening lament, by the
           major choir.

This reconstruction, of course, remains conjectural; we know little about the rubrics of temple worship, even in the days of Jesus. Yet, the interaction of speakers and the modulation of pronouns first, second or third person, within the psalm support this dramatization of Ps 12.

(III) V. 1a'. *Help, Lord!* The verb *yasha'*, to save or to help (see Ps 3), normally requires an object; only here and in Ps 118:25 is the object missing, so that the call remains unfinished, like a drowning person who does not shout, "Help me!" only the abrupt and desperate, "Help!"

Vv. 1a"-4. Here the reasons or motivation for the lament are voiced by different choral groups. *godly*, in Hebrew *hasid*, repeats the covenant word for family or tribal loyalty, binding the Israelites together as though by blood; this bond is sealed by Yahweh's presence in their midst (Exod 34:6-7). *faithful*, in Hebrew *'emunim*, from the root *'amen*, means simply, be truly and authentically who and what you are, so that everyone in community can trust and depend on you. (One of the most consistent and some would say most fanatic groups in the state of Israel today call themselves *gush 'emunim*, "assembly of the faithful."). *sons of men:* the Hebrew word includes women as well as men, *i.e., all* Israelites. The psalmist feels totally alone in faithfulness. V. 4: *our lips are with us:* the Hebrew can also be translated, "our lips are our weapons [of war]," according to a suggestion of Dahood.

V. 5, the oracle, pronounced by prophet or priest in God's own name. Whenever liturgical or sacramental ceremonies approach the heart of the action, symbols tend to melt away and there is an immediacy of God's presence and action —as we find in the institution of the eucharist in the NT. After saying what Jesus did, "*he* took bread. . .*he* gave thanks," the words of consecration are spoken immediately by Jesus in his own name: "This is *my* body. . .the new covenant in *my* blood" (Luke 22:19-20). (See commentary on Ps 2:7.) *I will place him in the safety for which he longs:* the Hebrew is much more succinct: *I place salvation; wait for it.* While the entire congregation has been chanting continuously the opening word *Help* or *Save* (from *yasha'*), God now responds almost with the identical word: *I place salvation* (from *yasha'*). While the dialogue within the larger community has been devious and treacherous, that between God and the persecuted psalmist is intimate, dependable and supportive.

V. 6, *promises*, literally in the Hebrew, *words of the Lord*, are said to be *pure*, that is, not contaminating, nor betraying, nor spreading evil, but securing a healthy bond of intimate union.

V. 8, the psalm ends where it began: *the wicked still prowl*, and the final phrase, *sons of men*, is even repeated from v. 1.

(IV) While the psalm may seem to get nowhere and to accomplish nothing, it has achieved what is sometimes the most heroic non-action possible, simply *to remain*, persevering in faithfulness and in the memory that Yahweh has heard the groaning of the needy. Jesus too struggled with lies and treachery (John 8:44-47). Jesus was able to suffer ever more intensely, convinced that the Father has heard his cry for deliverance. We read in a theological commentary on his agony in the garden:

In the days of his flesh, Jesus offered up prayers and supplications, with loud cries and tears, to him who was able to save him from death, and he was heard for his godly fear. Although he was a Son, he learned obedience through what he suffered; and being made perfect [that is, having completed the full cycle of human existence, even death] he became the source of eternal salvation to all who obey him (Heb 5:7-9).

When reduced to nothing yet waiting with faith, a person enables God to accomplish small wonders during life and the final wonder of the resurrection at the end of time.

Psalm 13
To The Choirmaster. A Psalm of David.

I

¹How long, O Lord? Wilt thou forget me for ever?
   How long wilt thou hide thy face from me?
²How long must I bear pain in my soul,
   and have sorrow in my heart all the day?
How long shall my enemy be exalted over me?

II

³Consider and answer me, O Lord my God;
   lighten my eyes, lest I sleep the sleep of death;
⁴lest my enemy say, "I have prevailed over him";
   lest my foes rejoice because I am shaken.

III

⁵But I have trusted in thy steadfast love;
   my heart shall rejoice in thy salvation.
⁶I will sing to the Lord,
   because he has dealt bountifully with me.

(I) A gem of poignant beauty, Ps 13 reflects the most profound emotions: desolation and even panic in vv. 1-2, as four times in quick succession it cries out: *How long, O Lord, how long, how long, how long;* exquisite joy and total confidence in vv. 5-6, *I have trusted . . . my heart shall rejoice*

...I will sing. This diamond of many reflections is united around the word heart, filled with sorrow in v. 2, rejoicing in v. 5. Because there is no appeal for divine judgment against the enemies who boast and exalt over their victim (vv. 2 and 4), a scholar like H. J. Kraus prefers to call the psalm a "song of prayer," rather than a lament; E. Beaucamp, on the contrary, is tempted to entitle it "a psalm of penitence," for only indirectly does the psalmist ask for any favor. Yet, on rereading the poem, we find all the elements of a lament: plaint, supplication, confidence, thanksgiving.

From the reference to death in v. 3, it is possible that the psalmist was critically ill, but certainly not, as one commentator suggested, with a "purely mental" sickness. The psalmist manifests too much integrity and self-control, carefully integrating too many contrasting emotions, to be considered mentally deranged or spiritually off center. Whatever be the cause of pain, certainly the most grievous sorrow is located in separation from Yahweh. Because death was thought to cut off any active relationship with Yahweh, the prospects of dying could plunge an Israelite into heart-rending agony (see Ps 6 commentary).

(II) The Hebrew text is well preserved, almost as if no one would dare tamper with the poem's delicate beauty. The structure is quite simple: vv. 1-2, lament; vv. 3-4, supplication; vv. 5-6, thanksgiving.

(III) Vv. 1-2, *lament.* Four times, *how long!* a phrase, found frequently enough in the OT and always with urgency or even exasperation, so that even God can be at the end of divine endurance: *i.e.,* Num 14:11-12. "How long will this people despise me? And how long will they not believe in me in spite of all the signs which I have wrought among them? I will strike them with pestilence..." The Lord, however, relented when Moses pleaded with the Lord's "steadfast love." Again, when Job's comforter remarked, "How long will you hunt for words?... Why are we counted as cattle?" Job replied, "How long will you torment me and break me in pieces with words?" (Job 18:1-2; 19:1; *cf.,* Jer 47:6; Hab 1:2; Ps 62:3). The tender sorrow of the psalmist appears in such questions put to the Lord, as: *forget me?...hide thy face from me?*...*sorrow in my heart?* Has the Lord really forgotten the psalmist who can never forget the Lord? The psalmist feels reduced to a non-person in God's eyes and faced with that most devastating moment of human existence, the silence of God.

Vv. 3-4, *supplication.* God is implored to *consider*: a Hebrew word that connotes careful, intense scrutiny: *i.e.,* Gen 15:5; 1 Kgs 18:43; Isa 63:15; Ps 91:8. *O Lord, my God*: the pronoun communicates an affectionate, tender relationship. *lighten my eyes*: we reveal our deepest emotions, our spiritual peace or agony, our worry and anxiety through the eyes. The psalmist seems to ask for very little, just a reflection from the light of God's eyes (*cf.,* Ps 19:8). The stanza ends with a strong, even violent word: *I am shaken,* reserved for the rending of mountains (Isa 54:10), the tottering of kingdoms (Ps 46:3).

Vv. 5-6, *thanksgiving.* It is difficult to account for this sudden shift: was the psalmist quickly brought back to health? It is also possible that the psalm was composed over a long period of sleepless nights, tormenting ridicule, desolate prayer, poignant memories, all of which gradually evolved into peace; even in the process of dying, a person's anger or dejection often commutes into comtemplative peace. *Steadfast love:* the basic quality of the covenant with Yahweh and with the Israelites among themselves (see Ps 12:1 commentary).

(IV) Ps 13 reminds us that the biblical process of redemption includes the sanctification and complete purification of the just. God does more than convert sinners; God purifies the elect seven times over (Ps 12:6) and leads the servant Job to ecstatic vision (Job 38-42). "Those I love, I reprove and chastise" (Rev 3:19). There can be a delicate touch of love in exquisite pain.

Psalm 14
To The Choirmaster. Of David.

I

¹The fool says in his heart, "There is no God."
  They are corrupt, they do abominable deeds,
  there is none that does good.

²The Lord looks down from heaven
    upon the children of men,
  to see if there are any that act wisely,
  that seek after God.

³They have all gone astray, they are all alike corrupt;
  there is none that does good,
  no, not one.

II

⁴Have they no knowledge, all the evildoers
  who eat up my people as they eat bread,
  and do not call upon the Lord?

⁵There they shall be in great terror,
  for God is with the generation of the righteous.
⁶You would confound the plans of the poor,
  but the Lord is his refuge.

III

⁷O that deliverance for Israel would come out of Zion!
  When the Lord restores the fortunes of his people,
  Jacob shall rejoice, Israel shall be glad.

(I) Ps 14 is almost identical with Ps 53 except that Ps 14 refers to God most of the time as *Yahweh*, while Ps 53 always addresses God as *'elohim*. This usage of divine names corresponds with the practice within the first three books of the psalter: Book One (Pss 1-41), where Ps 14 occurs, is often called the Yahwist collection, while Pss 42-83, the Elohist collection, extend through Book Two (Pss 42-72) and most of Book Three (Pss 73-89) and employ the name *'elohim*. Ps 14 is not as well preserved as Ps 53; in fact it is "hopelessly corrupt," according to W. O.

E. Osterley. Another recent commentator, E. Beaucamp, admits with a backhanded compliment: "The profound sense of this short psalm remains for the most part enigmatic"!

According to Robert A. Bennett, two important Hebrew words within Pss 14 and 53 provide a clue to the origin and evolution of the psalms: *nabal* or fool; *'esah* or counsel. Each word began their long history with closest ties to the secular realm of human existence. *nabal* was associated with the moral outcast and later with sacrilege. At first the foolish action, with serious harm upon the community was related to sexuality (Gen 34:2; Deut 22:21; Judg 19:23; 1 Sam 13:11). Later *nabal* was seen more generally as a threat to societal stability, as in Prov 30:21-23. With the prophets *nabal* indicts the entire nation of Israel for betraying their bonds with God and with one another: *i.e.,* Isa 9:15-17, ". . . the prophet who teaches lies. . . those who lead this people astray. . . everyone is godless and an evildoer, and *every mouth speaks folly*"; *cf.,* Jer 17:11; Nah 3:6. Throughout Israel's long history *nabal* or foolishness was connected with the disintegration of family, community and covenant loyalty. At first it reflected disastrous effects in secular family life and from there it is transferred to the more purely religious realm.

Another word with a prominent place in Pss 14 and 53 is *'esah*; it is positive for the most part and generally refers to counsel by which prudent decisions are made: *i.e.,* advice at the royal court by Ahithophel (2 Sam 15:12, 34; 16:20, 23). From the domestic or political realm it passed into the religious sphere of God's decisions, yet often enough these are affected by politics and social justice: *i.e.,* Isa 28:29, where the prophet demands respect for the normal processes of family and community relationship and draws examples from agricultural work; Isaiah then concludes: "This also comes from the Lord of hosts; he is wonderful *in counsel* and excellent in wisdom"; *cf.,* Isa 5:19; Pss 16:7; 32:8; 33:11. The interaction, therefore, of foolishness and good counsel in Pss 14 and 53 affirms God's lordship over the bonds of family, politics and international affairs.

(II) The foolish one, therefore, does not necessarily deny that God exists but rather doubts for all practical purposes whether God makes any difference in family life and in political decisions (*cf.,* Pss 10:4; 15:1). Pss 14 and 53, like the Hebrew words, *nabal* and *'esah*, combine a strong prophetical and sapiential thrust — all within the setting of a communal *lament*, as the poetic meter (3 + 2) would indicate. Vv. 1-3, the sapiential section, a meditation on universal corruption; vv. 4-6, the prophetical section that Yahweh will intervene on behalf of oppressed people; v. 7, the concluding prayer.

(III) vv. 1-3, *a sapiential meditation. abominable deeds,* leading to social and religious disintegration, like those of King Ahab whose dynasty was rejected (1 Kgs 21:26) or of Judah who was to be put to shame even by Sodom and Samaria (Ezek 16:52). *none that does good:* St. Paul quotes this passage in terms of general human corruption (Rom 3:10); the psalmist will later recognize the presence of God *with the generation of the righteous* (v. 5). Humankind is not totally corrupt! After v. 3 several important Greek manuscripts incorporate lines from Rom 3:10-18 where St. Paul cites a *catena* of OT passages: Pss 5:9; 10:7; 14:1; 36:1; 140:4; Isa 59:7-8; Prov 1:16; these verses were reduced again to Hebrew and were inserted into one Hebrew manuscript (Kenn 649). Many interesting questions (or conclusions?) emerge for the general interpretation of the Bible: a) if so many disparate texts are blended together, then the Bible was explained more as an integral book of faith within Israel and the church, than as a historical document in its various political and social settings; b) Paul quotes the OT to understand better the Christian faith, not to prove it correct, and later church tradition will read the OT from a Christian perspective of faith in Jesus; c) no single verse or section of the Bible contains the entire truth but must be balanced by religious positions elsewhere in the Scripture.

Vv. 4-6, *Prophetical defense of the oppressed.* If there is *no knowledge,* then there is no deep, inner sense of what is happening nor a responsibility towards Yahweh and the nation. *eat my people:* not only is there a leaven of good

Israelites (again not everyone is corrupt) but these good people are being devoured as though by ravenous animals: *cf.,* Isa 9:18-20, "Wickedness burns like a fire...they snatch on the right, but are still hungry, and they devour on the left and are not satisfied." Vv. 4-5 have several illusive references to religious assemblies in the temple and make us suspect a priesthood that is greedy, self-serving and oppressive, certainly out of touch with moral issues and social needs (*cf.,* Mic 3 which echoes phrases with Ps 14).

V. 7, *a conclusion,* like most psalms, on a positive note! *Zion,* particularly the temple, is the home of life and goodness. *restore the fortunes of his people:* can equally read, *secure the return of his captive people,* a translation that would locate Ps 14 during the Babylonian exile (?) when pagan foreigners and those Israelites who apostatized and passed over into their ranks are to be identified with the fools within the psalm.

(IV) A series of NT passages enables us to return in a meditative spirit to this psalm: Luke 18:8, "When the Son of man comes, will he find faith on earth?"; John 15:19, "If you were of the world, the world would love its own; but because you are not of the world, but I chose you out of the world, therefore the world hates you"; Rom 8:22-23, "the whole creation has been groaning in travail together until now... as we wait for adoption as children, the redemption of our bodies"; 2 Cor 5:21, "For our sake God made him to be sin who knew no sin, so that in him we might become the righteousness of God."

Psalm 15
A Psalm Of David

I

¹O Lord, who shall sojourn in thy tent?
   Who shall dwell on thy holy hill?

II

²He who walks blamelessly, and does what is right,
   and speaks truth from his heart;

³who does not slander with his tongue,
   and does no evil to his friend,
   nor takes up a reproach against his neighbor;

⁴in whose eyes a reprobate is despised,
   but who honors those who fear the Lord;
   who swears to his own hurt and does not change;
⁵who does not put out his money at interest,
   and does not take a bribe against the innocent.

III
He who does these things shall never be moved.

(I) Strong prophetical and sapiential strands thread through Ps 15 and influence its requirements for entering the temple precincts or more precisely for participating in temple services. The psalm opens with a question about the proper dispositions to *sojourn in thy tent* (v. 1); the next ten lines list the expectations. In several places the Bible speaks of lay people, coming to the priest with inquiries: *i.e.,* Hag 2:11, "Ask the priests this question...." In Zech 7:1-4, when the people inquire of the priests and the temple prophets about fasting, the prophet Zechariah responded with language echoing Ps 15: "Render true judgments, show kindness and mercy, each to the brother and sister, do not oppress the widow, the fatherless, the sojourner, or the poor; and let none of you devise evil against brother or sister in your heart." The same prophet showed notable interest in the temple and the high priest. The prophets, therefore, may at times seem anti-temple and anti-liturgy. At the same time, they did not back down on the need to integrate moral expectations with ritual requirements (*cf.,* Isa 33:14-16; Mic 6:6-8).

Ps 15 may have constituted the text for an "entrance liturgy," similar to the penitential rite at the beginning of the Christian Eucharist. It could have served as well for instruction in the schools or in temple preaching. The psalm was intended for an examination of conscience, particularly for sins of the tongue or for the abuse of wealth. Other crimes like murder, adultery or apostasy are not included, though conspicuously present in the Decalogue; nor does the psalm reckon with liturgical matters like sacrifice or prescriptions for clean and unclean. The prophetical and sapiential impact on Ps 15 is quite evident.

(II) The structure is obvious enough: v. 1, the question, spoken by the lay person; vv. 2-5ab, the answer as given by priest or instructor; v. 5c, a final promise for the just person. The answer in vv. 2-5ab is rather carefully arranged with two sets of five requirements (vv. 2-3 and 4-5ab), each with two positive and three negative points.

(III) V. 1, *the question.* While the questioner is seeking security and uprightness, the words not only reflect the ancient semi-nomadic existence of Israel but also the transitory nature of human life. *sojourn* means a resident alien, like Abraham in the land of Canaan (Gen 15:13) or like the way of Israel in the land of Egypt (Exod 23:9). *dwell* is the old Hebrew word for living in a tent, a type of shelter that was easily dismantled as the family moved onward; this word was later reserved for God's dwelling place. God too can move onward, as happened at the time of the exile (Ezek 10:18-19, 22-25); God can appear to prophets in a foreign land (Ezek 1:1; Isa 40:1-11). Immorality, therefore, would not only keep a worshipper out of the temple but would also force God to take leave of the sinful people.

Vv. 2-5ab. The answers are first rather general (v. 2) and then become more specific (vv. 3-5ab). This is not a complete catalog of sins; the priest or prophet could add or adapt. Repeated over and over again in the temple liturgy, it became somewhat stereotyped and needed revitalization by personal examination of conscience and of seeking forgiveness anew. V. 2, *truth from the heart,* not simply clever words on the lips (*cf.,* Isa 29:13, "this people...honor me with their lips while their hearts are far from me"). V. 3, *nor takes up a reproach:* almost verbatim in Sir 5:14; it includes defamation of character. V. 4, *in whose eyes a reprobate is despised,* the Hebrew here is difficult and has many different translations. It speaks of people, despised and reprobated by others; even if they harbor doubts about their own integrity, yet they are determined to remain true to their conscience. *swears to his own hurt:* textually another *crux interpretum* (a cross for interpreters)! Dahood translates it: "He swore to do no harm and did not waver." V. 5, *money at interest:* interest rates in the ancient Orient turned between 33½% and 50% and were condemned in the Bible for seeking to gain from fellow Israelites in their weakness and need (Exod 22:25; Deut 23:19). Money or currency did not come into use until the Persian period (after 539 B.C.); the massive, international banking system of the modern world, with stock markets and purchasing on credit, was unknown. When the church reversed this clear biblical prohibition against loaning money at interest, a dramatic adaptation of the inspired scripture to the social fabric of post-biblical times took place.

(IV) Louis Jacquet calls our attention to a rabbinical homily of the third century. Rabbi Simlai declared that in Ps 15 David reduced the 613 commandments of Moses to 11 (reading two commandments in v. 2a), then Isaiah further refined them to 6 (Isa 33:15, very similar to Ps 15), Micah to 3 (Mic 6:8); Isaiah again was able to bring the number down to 2 (Isa 56:1); finally Amos and Habakkuk to a single commandment: 'seek the Lord and live' (Amos 5:4) and 'the just shall live by faith' (Hab 2:4). While Jesus insisted upon the ten commandments (Mark 10:17-19), he also synthesized these in the more perfect call to give to the poor (Mark 10:21). On another occasion Jesus summarized the entire moral law in the love of God and the love of neighbor as oneself (Luke 10:27). Sometimes we need the specific directions of the decalogue or the 613 commandments of Moses. At other times inspiration is our basic need. Sometimes we must be told in detail how to avoid serious sin. There are other moments when we spontaneously strive to be perfect. Ps 15 is adaptable.

Psalm 16
A Miktam Of David.

I

¹Preserve me, O God, for in thee I take refuge.
²I say to the Lord, "Thou art my Lord;
  I have no good apart from thee."

³As for the saints in the land, they are the noble,
  in whom is all my delight.

⁴Those who choose another god multiply their sorrows;
  their libations of blood I will not pour out
  or take their names upon my lips.

II

⁵The Lord is my chosen portion and my cup;
  thou holdest my lot.
⁶The lines have fallen for me in pleasant places;
  yea, I have a goodly heritage.

⁷I bless the Lord who gives me counsel;
  in the night also my heart instructs me.
⁸I keep the Lord always before me;
  because he is at my right hand, I shall not be moved.

III

⁹Therefore my heart is glad, and my soul rejoices;
  my body also dwells secure.
¹⁰For thou dost not give me up to Sheol,
  or let thy godly one see the Pit.

¹¹Thou dost show me the path of life;
  in thy presence there is fullness of Joy,
  in thy right hand are pleasures for evermore.

(I) The author of Ps 16 belongs to that group of God's creatures, endowed with gracious temperament, sincere heart and intuitive perception; these cannot but suffer more than the rest of us. The suffering, however, does not spread gloom, for it springs from an exquisite peace and leads in the final words of Ps 16 to the *fullness of joy, at thy right hand pleasures evermore.* Since we are known by the company we keep, it helps to point out the biblical companionship of this psalmist: vv. 5-6 converge with Jeremiah 10:16 and 51:19; v. 10 with Jer 2:2. We note a special association of Ps 16 with Isa 57:1-19 which also deals with idolatry, persecution and the entry of devout Israelites into peace. Other references in Ps 16:10-11 lead us into the sapiential movement, especially Prov 5, which contrasts *sheol* to the *path of life for all time.* As we might expect of someone, close in kinship with Jeremiah and Third Isaiah (Is 56-66), there are also other references to a northern, Deuteronomic theology about the Lord, who is *my chosen portion and my cup* (Deut 10:9).

The psalmist, accordingly, gravitates towards books of prayer and suffering like Jeremiah, of compassion and divine choice like Deuteronomy, of hope and mystic response like Third Isaiah, of moderation and family virtue like Proverbs. Perhaps it is better to leave the psalmist in this companionship that spanned several hundred years and blended prophetical, sapiential and liturgical traditions, rather than attempt any precise date. If the question of date must be raised, most of the facts seem to favor the early postexilic age between 500 and 450 B.C. as the time of final redaction.

It is generally agreed that the poet is a levite: the phrases in v. 5 echo those about levitical priests:

> At that time the Lord set apart the tribe of Levi to carry the ark of the covenant of the Lord, to stand before the Lord to minister to him and to bless in his name, to this day. Therefore, Levi has no portion or inheritance with his brothers; the Lord is his inheritance...(Deut 10:8-9).

Yet, if the psalmist was a levite, he did not stand on dignity and privilege distinctly superior to the rest of the people. The levites, in fact, symbolized all Israel in their dedication to the Lord (Pss 73:26; 119:57; Num 3:40-51). The phrase, *godly ones, hasid* in Hebrew, is never used of the levites but of all the covenant people (*cf.,* Ps 12:1). As we shall see, the levite-poet was probably suffering from a serious illness (*cf.,* vv. 7-10).

(II) Even though a strong note of lament or sorrow is heard, Ps 16 belongs to the prayers of confidence; the tone is set by the opening phrase, *I take refuge in you.* The rhythm picks up momentum, from 2 + 2 at the beginning till 3 + 3 + 3 at the conclusion (v. 11). The language too becomes ever more intense: from *'el,* a very common word for God in v. 1a, to the emphatic and more personal *'adonai 'attah, Thou art my Lord* in 2a. Each word in the final verse echoes a key word from earlier lines in the psalm. All in all, a carefully structured poem. The psalm develops in the following way: vv. 1-4, Call for help and reasons; vv. 5-8, Expression of confidence; vv. 9-11, the reward of confidence.

(III) Vv. 1-4, *Call for help and reasons.* These verses reflect, it seems, a conflict among the levites, some of whom had introduced idolatrous or superstitious worship. The Hebrew in vv. 3-4 has been disturbed perhaps by theological attempts to correct the statements of the dissident levites. The psalmist issues a strong endorsement of personal faith: *in thee I take refuge,* even though others say *all my delight* is derived from other gods, here called *the saints.* These other levites *multiply their sorrows* with the implication of fertility rites and sexual excess (*cf.,* Isa 57:7-8). If religious leaders lose their fervor by catering to careerism and sensuality, their downfall and loss of faith take on devastating proportions (*cf.,* Isa 14:12-19).

Vv. 5-8, *Expression of confidence.* The levites possessed no landed property, a situation precipitated several centuries earlier by their violent act against the Shechemites (Gen 34:25-31) and their punishment for this by the patriarch Jacob (Gen 49:5-7). Details are blurred by centuries of time, but the history of the Levites revived with Moses, himself of the same tribe, who entrusted them with priestly functions (Exod 2:1-10; Deut 33:8-11). Their propertyless and precarious position continued — only it was now transformed into a religious symbol, applicable to every Israelite: each person was God's specially chosen one and each was completely dependent upon the Lord. It is amazing indeed that in a culture where landed property was essential for full membership (*cf.,* Lev 25), the levitical priests possessed no property. This counter-culture symbol reminded everyone, in the words of God, that "the land is mine; you are strangers and sojourners with me" (Lev 25:23). Levites continually challenged the Israelites to consider their property as leased to them from the Lord in order that all the people might share in the produce and security. V. 7b is a rich mine of religious insight: *night*, plural in the Hebrew and referring either to night vigils of prayer or to long nights of sickness and loneliness, or to both; *my heart*, literally "my kidneys" (*cf.,* Ps 7:9, commentary; the seat of conscience and judgment), disquieted and nervous through the sleepless nights; *discipline*, the Hebrew word, *yasar*, means to strengthen and purify by hardship and punishment: *cf.,* Isa 53:5, the servant "was wounded for our transgressions. . . upon him was the *chastisement* [from *yasar*] that made us whole and with his stripes we are healed." Because Yahweh was venerated as the God of life (*cf.,* Pss 42:2; 84:2), it was a severe trial of faith for a levite, a leader of worship, to be sick.

Vv. 9-11, *The reward of confidence.* The physical sense of pain and joy continues, from kidneys in v. 7, to heart, soul and body in v. 9 (see Ps 7:5, 9). In v. 10 *sheol* and *pit* both refer to death and the grave; the psalmist evidently had been suffering from a mortal illness but is now cured. V. 11 resonates the entire psalm, at times repeating key Hebrew words, in a joyful, confident spirit:

show me (Lord counsels me, v. 7a)	*in thy presence* (before me, v. 8a)
life (kidneys, heart, soul, body, vv. 7-9)	*pleasures* (in pleasant places, v. 6a)
	thy right hand (same in v. 8b)
joy (my heart is glad, v.7)	*evermore* (always, v. 8a; also 9b)

(IV) The Hebrew text was finalized at a time when the *official* religion of Israel had no clearly formulated position on conscious survival after death in God's presence (Ps 6:5). Yet neighboring nations and because of them many Israelites in their personal devotions anticipated some kind of happy life after death. The levite, as a proponent of the official position, could not do much more than hint vaguely of immortal life. If Yahweh is faithful with a young, seriously sick person (who often enough died), then there *must* be life with God after death, at least for these. By the time that Ps 16 was translated into Greek, after 200 B.C., Israel began to officially accept immortality — even though the temple priests, later called the Sadducees, never did (Acts 23:6-8). Ps 16:8 reads in the Greek, "I *see* the Lord before me always [throughout eternity]; *pit* in v. 10b becomes "corruption," a reference to the corpse that will be freed of corruption and raised from the dead. A similar re-reading of Ps 16 to express the "new" belief in bodily resurrection and personal immortality is not only found in the Dead Sea Scrolls and in the midrash or rabbinical expositions of the psalms but clearly in the New Testament (Acts 2:24-28). In quoting Ps 16 as a "proof text" of the resurrection, Luke was not relying upon the original sense of the psalm but upon its later absorption of popular belief in the resuscitation of the body in eternal happiness for the just. Finally, in the spirit of Ps 16, we should not rest with doctrine but with the *person* of the Lord: *in thee I take refuge* (v. 1), or as it was expressed in one of the great "I AM" passages of John's gospel: "I am the resurrection and the life" (John 11:25).

Psalm 17
A Prayer Of David.

I

¹Hear a just cause, O Lord; attend to my cry!
Give ear to my prayer from lips free of deceit!

²From thee let my vindication come!
　　Let thy eyes see the right!

II

³If thou triest my heart, if thou visitest me by night,
　　if thou testest me, thou will find no wickedness in me;
　　my mouth does not transgress.
⁴With regard to the works of men, by the word of thy lips
　　I have avoided the ways of the violent.
⁵My steps have held fast to thy paths,
　　my feet have not slipped.

III

⁶I call upon thee, for thou wilt answer me, O God;
　　incline thy ear to me, hear my words.
⁷Wondrously show thy steadfast love,
　　O savior of those who seek refuge
　　from their adversaries at thy right hand.

⁸Keep me as the apple of the eye;
　　hide me in the shadow of thy wings,
⁹from the wicked who despoil me,
　　my deadly enemies who surround me.

IV

¹⁰They close their hearts to pity;
　　with their mouths they speak arrogantly.
¹¹They track me down; now they surround me;
　　they set their eyes to cast me to the ground.
¹²They are like a lion eager to tear,
　　as a young lion lurking in ambush.

V

¹³Arise, O Lord! confront them, overthrow them!
　　Deliver my life from the wicked by thy sword,
¹⁴from men by thy hand, O Lord,
　　from men whose portion in life is of the world.
　May their belly be filled with what thou hast stored
　　up for them;
　　may their children have more than enough;
　　may they leave something over to their babes.

VI

¹⁵As for me, I shall behold thy face in righteousness;
   when I awake, I shall be satisfied with beholding thy
   form.

(I) Pss 16 and 17 may come from the same author, not just because of their neighborly position in the psalter but on account of literary and conceptual parallels. Identical Hebrew words occur, like the rare negative *bal* (16:2, 4; 17:3, 5), the right hand of the Lord (16:8; 17:7), the divine name *'el*, somewhat unusual in the Yahwist section of the psalter (16:1; 17:6 — see Ps 14); the request, *preserve me* (16:1; 17:8). Similar religious ideas or actions also show up: *i.e.,* secret prayer at night (16:7; 17:3); feet which do not stumble on the way of the Lord (16:8; 17:5); desire to behold the face of the Lord (16:8, 11; 17:15); the contrast between the just and the wicked (16:2-6; 17:14-15). As L. Jacquet and J. Leeven also mention, the agony or *cri de coeur* is not pushed to the background as in Ps 16 but is heard from center stage in Ps 17. The piercing, even bitter cry from the heart is roused by outrage and betrayal within the religious community, possibly within the ranks of the levitical priesthood (see Ps 16). Ps 17, a lament for an individual, stirs from a spiritual night of the soul and most likely as well from long night vigils in desperate prayer (vv. 3 and 15). The psalmist feels caught within intrigue and false accusation, losing what a person in such a position values most, good reputation and the quiet contemplation, essential for religious ministry.

(II) Serious difficulties disrupt the Hebrew text and as E. Beaucamp remarked, the ancient versions prove only an embarrassment for they seldom clarify the difficulty! We encountered similar textual problems with Ps 16. The general meaning, however, is clear enough and the structure easy to follow:

vv. 1-2, Initial appeal for help vv. 10-12, Serious danger
   3-5, Declaration of   13-14, Punishment upon
      innocence   adversary
   6-9, Supplication   15, Confident hope

This psalm may have been available for temple worship: for a night vigil; for an examination of conscience (*cf.,* Ps 15); and for a final verdict given in the temple in favor of a falsely accused person (*cf.,* Deut 17:8-13).

(III) Vv. 1-2, *Appeal for help.* Although Ps 17 is concerned almost entirely with the just cause and innocence of the psalmist, Yahweh is the ultimate source of goodness and strength. The persecuted person is courageous enough to place his or her entire life openly before *the eyes* of the Lord which always *see the right* and pierce to the heart.

Vv. 3-5. *Declaration of Innocence.* The Hebrew text is unsettled here. With a different system of vocalization and just a slight change of consonants, vv. 4-5a can read: "I have acted, O Lord, according to the word of thy lips; I have kept to the paths of the righteous; my steps have held fast to thy paths."

Vv. 6-9, *New Supplication.* V. 6 is strong and abrupt: *It is none other than I who call upon thee; it is thou, indeed, who wilt answer me, O God.* This blunt interjecting is not due to irreverence nor pride but to desperation. The psalmist appeals to the covenant bond in the phrase, *steadfast love* (in Hebrew, from *ḥesed,* see Ps 12) and to the Lord's gentle love, expressed in such endearing phrases as *apple of the eye* (Deut 32:10, "The Lord encircles and cared for the chosen one and kept that one as the apple of the eye"; *cf.,* Prov 7:2) and *shadow of thy wings,* a metaphor of the mother bird (*cf.,* Isa 49:2, in the second Song of the Suffering Servant; Hos 14:7; Lam 4:20) or else a reference to the wings of the cherubim encircling the ark of the covenant and Yahweh's presence with Israel (Exod 25:20-22).

Vv. 10-12, *Serious danger.* The psalmist does not have the luxury to discuss the theology of sin when surrounded with the act of sin. V. 10, *close their hearts:* again the Hebrew text needs slight modification, but the reference is clear enough to gross, obese indifference, like Israel in Deut 32:15 who "waxed fat, grew thick, became sleek and forsook God"; or Isa 6:10, "make the heart of this people fat."

Vv. 13-14, *Punishment upon the adversary.* The vindictive or curse element in the psalms is discussed with Ps 69. V.

14 is the most textually corrupt in the entire psalm. Again with slight modification of the Hebrew (*i.e.,* changing *mimetim*, RSV, "from men," of the Hebrew text to *temimim*, "perfect") the entire verse refers to good people who are contrasted with the wicked. Based on a suggestion of J. Leveen the first part of v. 14 would then read: "They that are perfect [in thy ways], Lord, will praise thee; as for the [wicked people] perfect [in the ways] of the world, their portion is in this life [only]." At least a hint of reward in the future life is presumed by this interpretive translation.

V. 15, *Confident hope.* The expectation to *behold thy face* may refer to full participation in the temple, the home of Yahweh (*cf.,* Ps 42:1-5). We have noted already how biblical ceremonies tended to lead into the immediate presence of the Lord (Ps 2:7; 12:5). Beaucamp remarks: what biblical theology cautiously denies (Exod 33:20, where Yahweh declares even to Moses, "You cannot see my face; for no one shall see me and still live"), liturgy affirms, at least in this instance of Ps 17. *when I awake:* some like Dahood read this phrase as an awakening "at the resurrection" (*cf.,* Isa 26:19; Dan 12:2); certainly the Greek Septuagint read it at least in terms of life after death by adding: "in the vision of your glory." This interpretation represents an advance beyond the position of the psalmist (see the discussion with Ps 16), yet quite normal, considering the flashing insights of faith in the Lord's justice while enduring extreme pain. It is the word *justice* in the first and last verse that actually hold the psalm together.

(IV) We need Ps 17 as well as our own mysterious, innocent suffering, not only to peer beyond the horizons of this earth into eternity but also to enter the heart of Jesus, falsely accused (John 8:46), innocently "made sin for our sake though he knew no sin" (2 Cor 5:21) and executed as "a curse for us" (Gal 3:13). As we recite Ps 17, we pray also for the times we ourselves have misjudged and abused innocent people. We pray for all victims of injustice, but especially those (like the author of this psalm) within the community of God's chosen people, then and now.

Psalm 18

To The Choirmaster. A Psalm Of David The Servant Of The Lord, Who Addressed The Words Of This Song To The Lord On The Day When The Lord Delivered Him From The Hand Of All His Enemies, And From The Hand Of Saul. He Said:

I

¹I love thee, O Lord, my strength.
²The Lord is my rock, and my fortress, and my deliverer,
   my God, my rock, in whom I take refuge,
   my shield, and the horn of my salvation, my stronghold.
³I call upon the Lord, who is worthy to be praised,
   and I am saved from my enemies.

⁴The cords of death encompassed me,
   the torrents of perdition assailed me;
⁵The cords of Sheol entangled me,
   the snares of death confronted me.

⁶In my distress I called upon the Lord;
   to my God I cried for help.
From his temple he heard my voice,
   and my cry to him reached his ears.

II

⁷Then the earth reeled and rocked;
   the foundations also of the mountains trembled
   and quaked, because he was angry.
⁸Smoke went up from his nostrils,
   and devouring fire from his mouth;
   glowing coals flamed forth from him.
⁹He bowed the heavens, and came down;
   thick darkness was under his feet.
¹⁰He rode on a cherub, and flew;
   he came swiftly upon the wings of the wind.
¹¹He made darkness his covering around him,
   his canopy thick clouds dark with water.
¹²Out of the brightness before him
   there broke through his clouds
   hailstones and coals of fire.

¹³The Lord also thundered in the heavens,
and the Most High uttered his voice,
hailstones and coals of fire.
¹⁴And he sent out his arrows, and scattered them;
he flashed forth lightnings, and routed them.
¹⁵Then the channels of the sea were seen,
and the foundations of the world were laid bare,
at thy rebuke, O Lord,
at the blast of the breath of thy nostrils.

¹⁶He reached from on high, he took me,
he drew me out of many waters.
¹⁷He delivered me from my strong enemy,
and from those who hated me;
for they were too mighty for me.
¹⁸They came upon me in the day of my calamity;
but the Lord was my stay.
¹⁹He brought me forth into a broad place;
he delivered me, because he delighted in me.

III

²⁰The Lord rewarded me according to my righteousness;
according to the cleanness of my hands he
recompensed me.
²¹For I have kept the ways of the Lord,
and have not wickedly departed from my God.
²²For all his ordinances were before me,
and his statutes I did not put away from me.
²³I was blameless before him,
and I kept myself from guilt.
²⁴Therefore the Lord has recompensed me according to
my righteousness,
according to the cleanness of my hands in his sight.

²⁵With the loyal thou dost show thyself loyal;
with the blameless man thou dost show thyself
blameless;
²⁶with the pure thou dost show thyself pure;
and with the crooked thou dost show thyself perverse.
²⁷For thou dost deliver a humble people;

but the haughty eyes thou dost bring down.
28 Yea, thou dost light my lamp;
the Lord my God lightens my darkness.
29 Yea, by thee I can crush a troop;
and by my God I can leap over a wall.
30 This God — his way is perfect;
the promise of the Lord proves true;
he is a shield for all those who take refuge in him.

31 For who is God, but the Lord?
And who is a rock, except our God?—
32 the God who girded me with strength,
and made my way safe.
33 He made my feet like hinds' feet,
and set me secure on the heights.
34 He trains my hands for war,
so that my arms can bend a bow of bronze.
35 Thou hast given me the shield of thy salvation,
and thy right hand supported me,
and thy help made me great.
36 Thou didst give a wide place for my steps under me,
and my feet did not slip.
37 I pursued my enemies and overtook them;
and did not turn back till they were consumed.
38 I thrust them through, so that they were not able to rise;
they feel under my feet.
39 For thou didst gird me with strength for the battle;
thou didst make my assailants sink under me.
40 Thou didst make my enemies turn their backs to me,
and those who hated me I destroyed.
41 They cried for help, but there was none to save,
they cried to the Lord, but he did not answer them.
42 I beat them fine as dust before the wind;
I cast them out like the mire of the streets.

43 Thou didst deliver me from strife with the peoples;
thou didst make me the head of the nations;
people whom I had not known served me.
44 As soon as they heard of me they obeyed me;
foreigners came cringing to me.

⁴⁵Foreigners lost heart,
    and came trembling out of their fastnesses.

IV

⁴⁶The Lord lives; and blessed be my rock,
    and exalted be the God of my salvation,
⁴⁷the God who gave me vengeance
    and subdued peoples under me;
⁴⁸who delivered me from my enemies;
    yea, thou didst exalt me above my adversaries;
    thou didst deliver me from men of violence.

⁴⁹For this I will extol thee, O Lord,
    among the nations,
    and sing praises to thy name.

⁵⁰Great triumphs he gives to his king,
    and shows steadfast love to his anointed,
    to David and his descendants for ever.

(I) This "Ode of Victory" (L. Desnoyers) or "Solemn *Te Deum*" (R. Tournay) not only represents a centerpiece of temple liturgy for celebrating royal festivals, but it also has a good chance of being one of the most authentic compositions of King David. It is repeated in a collection of ancient Davidic traditions at the end of the two Books of Samuel (2 Sam 21-24). In fact, the poem in 2 Sam 22 retains more of the ancient flavor, for it does not seem to have "suffered" as much from continual use in the liturgy and from modification induced by choirmasters and other temple personnel. Though Ps 18 was written as an individual's Song of Thanksgiving, it quickly became the property of the congregation at prayer and worship. Despite these modifications we might indeed be holding our hand on the pulse of Israel's most ancient psalmody while reciting Ps 18. Such at least is the conclusion of Cross and Freedman from a comparison of this psalm with other pieces of ancient poetry like the Songs and Blessings of Moses (Exod 15; Deut 32-33) or the canticle of Habakkuk (Hab 3).

As just indicated, Ps 18 underwent a slow process of change and at key moments was more thoroughly revised. One of these times may have been the reform of King Hezekiah. Ps 18 is linked with his reign (716-687 B.C.) not only by literary consanguinity with the traditions of Deuteronomy, brought south to Jerusalem during Hezekiah's rule after the collapse of the northern kingdom of Israel, but also by the seemingly miraculous defeat of the Assyrians outside the walls of Jerusalem (*cf.,* 2 Kgs 18-20; Isa 36-39). The Assyrian collapse looked like a photo-fulfillment of Ps 18. We are even tempted to see a play on the name Hezekiah in the phrase *Yahweh, my strength* in v. 1, which reads in Hebrew *Hizeki-ya[hweh]*.

(II) If the structure of Ps 18 at first seems to be abrupt or uneven, we need to hear and visualize its celebration within the temple. Not only are ancient recollections of David's victories preserved, but the language and strophic arrangement of the psalm reach out to a large assembly at worship. We offer this modified form of an outline by L. Jacquet:

Exordium: vv. 1-6, *Deliverance from Mortal Danger*

(I) *Allegorical Presentation of Deliverance - Theophany,* vv. 7-19

vv. 7-12, Yahweh leaves heaven amid a violent storm

vv. 13-15, Upheavals on earth

vv. 16-19, Salvation

(II) Historical Presentation of Deliverance - *Victory,* vv. 20-45

vv. 20-30, Righteousness rewarded

vv. 31-45, Warfare and Victory

Epilogue: vv. 46-49, *Thanksgiving*
+ Addition about Davidic Dynasty, v. 50

(III) The psalm's long title is addressed to the choirmaster. In liturgically celebrating the glorious achievements of King David, Israel must never forget David the poor man, fleeing for his life amid the mountains of Judah (*cf.,* Ps 11:1) nor can Israel overlook poor refugees of any age. This glorious temple *Te Deum* is rooted in social justice and secular needs!

Vv. 1-6, *Exordium*. The opening phrase, *I love thee*, or according to a better translation, *I have pity on you,* is spoken to Israel by Yahweh — or in the liturgy, by the presiding liturgical officer. This verb, *raham*, never has God as its object in the Hebrew Bible and always connotes warmth, compassion and very literally the womb of a pregnant mother. This military psalm opens with a feminine image for God! A series of divine titles comes next, very similar, in fact, to ritual texts in Babylon and Egypt. *my rock:* the word certainly symbolizes majesty and permanence, and at Jerusalem it may refer as well to that rocky height upon which stood a sanctuary in David's time and later the Solomonic temple. The natural environment of the temple provided an insight into the God who was present there. *horn of my salvation:* "horn" is a frequent image in the Bible, derived originally from the fierce strength in the horns of animals (Ps 22:21, "save me...from the horns of the wild oxen"). It was applied to the uplifted corners of the altar of sacrifice, where Israel contacted the majesty of Yahweh (Exod 27:1-2, "the altar of acacia [with] horns for it on its four corners [which] you shall overlay with bronze"), adapted to God's kindly but effective presence with the people (Ps 89:17, "by thy favor our horn is exalted"). Only in this psalm is it a *title* for Yahweh. Vv. 4-5, a litany of death-images. (For *Sheol*, see Pss 6 and 16). V. 6, *from his temple:* not only did the Jerusalem sanctuary reflect God's heavenly abode, but its magnificent liturgy also mirrored God's celestial wonder.

Vv. 7-12, *Yahweh leaves heaven amid a violent storm.* Throughout the Bible, even into the New Testament (*cf.,* Col 1:15-20, where a creation hymn ends with "the blood of his cross"), creation is pictured as a violent encounter between chaos and order, between goodness and evil, between God and the powers of darkness (see earlier comments on Pss 2 and 8). Because the king was thought to embody God's determination to bring peace and fertility into the family and land of Israel, this creation-battle against disorder and violence was prominent in the coronation of kings and in all royal festivals. Creation, therefore, was considered an ongoing process that periodically flared up with greater intensity, not only at royal deaths and coronations but also at times of general disobedience or national reform. This attitude towards creation is enunciated, for instance, within the flood story of Genesis (chaps. 6-9). Sin, which reverses the good order of creation, is never easily subdued and cast out; God, moreover, is in the thick of the battle. Otherwise we would perish from superhuman powers. Even if God acts through human instruments like a king, still the overall scenario remains supra-natural and cannot be adequately communicated simply by retelling the surface details of history. When Ps 18 and other parts of the Bible declare that *the earth reeled, . . . mountains trembled* [and] *smoke went up from his [God's] nostrils [and] thick darkness was under his feet*, we find ourselves in the midst of a type of literature, technically called mythological. The word myth, therefore, does not of itself deny historical reality but attempts primarily to communicate an awesome, even terrifying sense of the momentous battle of goodness and evil, of God and demons, being waged within the events of history. The imagery of Ps 18 is found elsewhere in the Bible: *bowed the mountains* in Ps 99:1 and in the theophany at Mount Sinai (Exod 19; see also Ps 68); *rode on a cherub*, repeated in Pss 68:4, 33; 104:3, with some relation to the cherub above the ark of the covenant where Yahweh was preeminently present among the people (*cf.,* Exod 25:10-22).

Vv. 13-15, *Upheavals on earth.* V. 15, *at thy rebuke*, always a very strong word, evoking anger or violence (see commentary on Ps 9:5).

Vv. 16-19, *Salvation.* The statement about *many waters* (v. 16) can also be rendered "mighty water," in Hebrew *mayim rabbim*, the name of one of the sea monsters in Ugaritic literature (*cf.,* Isa 51:9-10). The psalmist may be thinking again of the watery depths of Sheol (see vv. 4-5 in this psalm).

We now enter the second major section of Ps 18, *the historical presentation of deliverance and victory*, vv. 20-45. Just as another royal psalm (Ps 89) moved from a section of cosmic struggle in mythological language (vv. 5-18) to a section redolent of history and the Davidic dynasty (vv. 19-37), a similar transition occurs here. The first sub-section states the rewards of living uprightly (vv. 20-30). The emphasis is upon *righteousness.* The colossal and fearful deeds of Yahweh, just recounted in vv. 7-19, do not dispense the individual Israelite, not even the king, from obeying the will of Yahweh. God demands this cooperation and rewards it accordingly, as we observe in the entrance liturgies of Pss 15 and 24. In vv. 20-30 the psalm resonates phrases and ideas of the Book of Deuteronomy. Vv. 25-26 may seem stilted and rigid, yet God does not tolerate that he or his covenant with Israel be mocked. V. 26b, *show thyself perverse,* is a Hebrew word, used in Gen 30:8 of *wrestling, i.e.,* contending for a goal, the birth of a child. Lying behind the statement of the psalm is the larger biblical position: an evil person is punished by the evil they perpetrate (*cf.,* Ps 7). V. 27, *deliver a humble people:* the king must identify himself with the cause of the poor and defenseless. V. 29 refers to military ventures and the scaling of enemy walls.

The second sub-section, vv. 31-45, acknowledges victory which Yahweh achieved in warfare for his people. V. 35, *thy help made me great:* may be translated more adequately as a reference to the gracious condescension of Yahweh in electing Israel among all the nations of the earth (*cf.,* Deut 7:6-8, an exquisite passage of divine love, set within a context of total warfare).

Vv. 46-49, *Epilogue.* David's victories seemed to fulfill God's promises, even of blessing other nations through Israel (*cf.,* Gen 12:1-3), and so a Hymn of Thanksgiving was appropriate. Looking back from our position, many centuries later, we know that universal salvation was to come in another way, through a kingdom centered in the crucified, risen Jesus and the sending of the Spirit (Acts 2:29-36). Paul, therefore, will quote v. 49 in Rom 15:9, "that the Gentiles might glorify God for his mercy." The military victories and world empire of King David imparted an ideal of world unity within biblical tradition that would not be satisfied till Jesus' disciples were sent to the world (*cf.,* Matt

28:16-20). V. 50 was added, to sharpen the focus upon the Davidic dynasty and the covenant bond of Yahweh's *steadfast love*.

(IV) This psalm reminds us that each of our personal battles, even within the secrecy of our conscience, as well as every world struggle for justice belong to an eternal, cosmic war for the establishment of God's kingdom in our midst. *Righteousness* is a key word at the center of this psalm (v. 20). Jesus wrestled with evil even to the point of shedding his blood on the cross, fighting such fierce enemies as death, demons, world and sin (Rom 7:24-25; 1 Cor 15:20-28). In the Epistle to the Ephesians we are advised that "we are not contending against flesh and blood, but against the principalities, against the powers, against the world rulers of this darkness, against the spiritual hosts of wickedness in the heavenly places" (Eph 6:12). The mythological language of Ps 18 extends our vision to the *real* world and its mammoth dimensions. Ps 18 also enables us to sing our small *Te Deum* after minor victories and will be on hand when we join a heavenly choir at the end of life's battle. Ps 18 is ready to celebrate victory over poverty, even in limited places on this earth, victory over sickness and malnutrition in slums or over-crowded places, victory over eviction and homelessness among world refugees — in fact wherever God's gracious goodness triumphs in the cause of justice. The title of this psalm provides important orientation.

Psalm 19
To The Choirmaster: A Psalm Of David.

I

¹The heavens are telling the glory of God;
   and the firmament proclaims his handiwork.
²Day to day pours forth speech,
   and night to night declares knowledge.
³There is no speech, nor are there words;
   their voice is not heard;
⁴yet their voice goes out through all the earth,
   and their words to the end of the world.

In them he has set a tent for the sun,
5which comes forth like a bridegroom leaving his
   chamber,
   and like a strong man runs its course with joy.
6Its rising is from the end of the heavens,
   and its circuit to the end of them;
   and there is nothing hid from its heat.

II

7The law of the Lord is perfect,
   reviving the soul;
   the testimony of the Lord is sure,
   making wise the simple;
8the precepts of the Lord are right,
   rejoicing the heart;
   the commandment of the Lord is pure,
   enlightening the eyes;
9the fear of the Lord is clean,
   enduring for ever;
   the ordinances of the Lord are true,
   and righteous altogether.
10More to be desired are they than gold,
   even much fine gold;
   sweeter also than honey
   and drippings of the honeycomb.

III

11Moreover by them is thy servant warned;
   in keeping them there is great reward.
12But who can discern his errors?
   Clear thou me from hidden faults.
13Keep back thy servant also from presumptuous sins;
   let them not have dominion over me!
   Then I shall be blameless,
   and innocent of great transgression.

IV

14Let the words of my mouth and the meditation of
   my heart
   be acceptable in thy sight,
   O Lord, my rock and my redeemer.

(I) An extraordinary unity integrates this psalm which might have splintered into a pantheistic hymn, some legalistic spirituality and finally an irrational concern over inadvertent faults. The psalmist, whose spirit reached outward with optimistic wonder, did more than unite disparate poetic elements. A new meaning was given to each section of the psalm by means of two key words or themes: speech and light. The resounding word and the luminous light of the universe became a personal message of life and joy and climaxed in that unique word, almost exclusively Israelite and certainly basic to Israelite culture and religion — *go'el*, which recognized a bond of blood between all Israelites and spiritually between them and Yahweh. The final word of the psalm is *go'ali, my redeemer* (*cf.*, Lev 25:23-55 and Num 35:16-34 for the principal duties of the kinsperson — see Ps 16:5-6).

Ps 19 ends in the most intimate sphere of blood-relationship. The Israelites are not only one closely knit family but they are also Yahweh's one and only chosen people among all the nations of the earth (*cf.*, Exod 19:4-5; Deut 7:6-8). It is indeed extraordinary then that such a psalm should resemble Egyptian and Babylonian hymns to the sun and even quote from one of them (v. 4bc-6). We are surprised that the revelation from Yahweh in vv. 7-14 should be placed in a cosmic setting where God is addressed under the very general word, found among many Semitic people, *'el*. The psalmist, therefore, was no narrow devotee or rigid cultist; he was no religious fanatic who despised world culture. Just as the universe brought a sense of mystery to the revelation of the law on Mount Sinai, the Torah was not so much something new as a clarification of the mystery which surrounded all peoples.

The dating of this psalm is also a mystery! We could almost believe that it came from David in his earliest youth, "hardy and naive, rough and ardent" (Jacquet), yet the psalm reflects the sophisticated and cosmopolitan court of a Solomon as well as the advanced stage of the sapiential movement during the postexilic age. We propose an initial composition of vv. 1-6 during the early royal period, @ 950

B.C., which was integrally developed after the reform of Ezra in the postexilic age, @ 400 B.C. with vv. 7-14.

(II) This magnificent hymn then praises: the *universal God* whose mysterious word and brilliant light rebound and echo across heaven and earth (vv. 1-6); *Yahweh*, whose *unique* revelation to Israel enlivens and brightens every aspect of the chosen people's existence (vv. 7-10). Quite naturally, given the Semitic habit of attributing the law to the sun-god, the hymn modulates into a prayer that the word and the light of Yahweh direct and cleanse the Lord's servant (vv. 11-13) and so re-consecrate the bond of life (v. 14).

(III) Vv. 1-6, *A hymn of praise* to the universal God, *'el*, is provided with a liturgical *setting* in v. 1 and then teems with liturgical *action* in vv. 2-6. God's cosmic home above the heavens and Israel's temple at Jerusalem reflect one another.

V. 1, the liturgical setting of the universe is carefully arranged even in literary style; the Hebrew word-order follows the pattern of chiasm (from the Greek letter chi or "X" with one stroke down, a-b-c, and another stroke up, c-b-a. With a slight adaptation for English style the chiasm proceeds accordingly:

a	the heavens	by the firmament.	a
b	are telling	is being proclaimed	b
c	the glory of God	his handiwork	c

Each of the two verbs are participles, so that the action is continuously happening. The center words of *glory* and *handiwork* not only stress God's personal endeavor (literally, work of his hands) but also the *weighty* wonder of God's presence (the literal meaning of *glory*).

V. 2 begins the liturgical action. It employs unusual words for communicating speech and knowledge: *pours forth* connotes the bubbling sound of water as it gushes from a spring;

declares implies from its Aramaic background the whispering sound of the evening wind (*cf.,* John 3:8, "The wind blows where it wills, and you hear the sound of it, but you do not know whence it comes or whither it goes").

Vv. 3-6. It is not clear whether the negatives in v. 3 add up to a positive meaning; we think not! Do we really know what we hear during the gurgling sounds of day and the whispering breath of night? There are a thousand and one messages here. V. 4, *their voice goes out:* despite the blurred understanding and confused vocalization no one can deny the fact of a message for everyone who is open to mystery and wonder. In Rom 10:5-18 Paul quotes v. 4 to climax a catena of biblical texts on preaching. V. 5c-6, an abstract from a long pagan hymn to the sun god. There are strong sexual images of bridal tent (*cf.,* Ezek 23 where the names of the two young women are a play upon the Hebrew word for tent, *'ohel*), life-giving warmth and love, final embrace in the darkness of the night. The psalmist, perhaps like King David, was half-Israelite and half-Canaanite and called upon each background in the service of Yahweh.

Vv. 7-10, *A didactic or sapiential praise for the Torah*, Yahweh's gift of light and direction. The first three verses are like a litany, extolling the Law. Torah or law should be understood as the totality of Israel's directives and traditions as Yahweh's chosen people. As noted previously, the divine name now modulates to Israel's particular name for God, namely *Yahweh*. Beaucamp is right; we should avoid legalistic terms here and speak of exigencies, directives, will, statements, words, any form that maintains a personal relationship that *rejoices the heart* and is *sweeter than honey*. V. 7, *the simple*: best understood from the ancient Greek translation which reappears in Matt 11:25, where Jesus prays: "I thank thee, Father, Lord of heaven and earth, that thou hast hidden these things from the wise and understanding and revealed them to the *babes* [the simple ones]." V. 8, *pure*, in the sense of clean, splendid, translucent, beautiful. V. 9, *clean*, a Hebrew word that rules out anything that is contagious and secretly harmful to others.

Vv. 11-14, *Prayer and Lament.* The more intense the light, always the deeper the shadow. The purity and certain naivete of the psalmist's heart make it exceptionally sensitive to sin, even to the inadvertent fault. This third section is carefully related to vv. 1-6 and 7-10 by the image of light, or now by the dark shadow cast by light, as pointed out by Michael Fishbane. V. 12, *errors*, the Hebrew word is the same as that in Leviticus for "sins of inadvertence" or "sins [committed] unwittingly" — Lev 4:1ff, for the priest; 4:13ff, for the whole congregation; 4:22ff, for the princes; etc. Willful sins had to be corrected first, by admitting the fault publicly; second, by remedying any harm done to another; third, by bringing an offering to the priest for a sin now reduced to one of "inadvertence," so that the priest can judge if proper restitution has been made and could then publicly readmit the culprit to the community by "sacrifice." (*cf.*, Num 5:5-10).

V. 14. The psalm concludes with a re-consecration to *Yahweh, my rock* (see Ps 18:2) *and my redeemer.*

(IV) Psalm 19 engenders an optimistic spirituality and a strong ecumenical attitude. (1) It inculcates an esteem for the entire world. Our universe is translucent with God's glory! (2) The mystery of the universe should not only be interpreted and applied to daily life by law and tradition, but its mystery should never be lost or snuffed out in the process. It asks us to preserve the *mystery* of faith in all our preaching and explanation of the faith. (3) The liturgy of the universe and that of the sanctuary should echo one another, so that one helps to appreciate the other. (4) Sin is not always the result of bad will but the shadow cast by ideals and goodness within a person's delicate conscience.

Psalm 20
To The Choirmaster. A Psalm Of David.

I

¹The Lord answer you in the day of trouble!
The name of the God of Jacob protect you!

²May he send you help from the sanctuary,
  and give you support from Zion!
³May he remember all your offerings,
  and regard with favor your burnt sacrifices!   *Selah*

⁴May he grant you your heart's desire,
  and fulfil all your plans!
⁵May we shout for joy over your victory,
  and in the name of our God set up our banners!
May the Lord fulfil all your petitions!

II
⁶Now I know that the Lord will help his anointed;
  he will answer him from his holy heaven
  with mighty victories by his right hand.
⁷Some boast of chariots, and some of horses;
  but we boast of the name of the Lord our God.
⁸They will collapse and fall;
  but we shall rise and stand upright.

III
⁹Give victory to the king, O Lord;
  answer us when we call.

(I) We need to interpret this psalm as much imaginatively as theologically or historically. Israel's theology of kingship (see Ps 2) for several centuries sustained the people's faith not only in Yahweh's powerful presence in the person of the king, but also (much more implicitly) in Yahweh's intention of universal salvation. This theology identified Israel's wars as the wars of Yahweh, whether fought now under Davidic kings, or previously under Moses and the judges. We already called attention to the battle cry which rose from the ranks of Israel when the ark led the people forward, whether to a new stage in the desert (Num 10:35), into battle (1 Sam 4:5) or in liturgical procession (Ps 68:1) — see Ps 18. The remembrance of these mighty acts of Yahweh along with faith in Yahweh's promises of eternal protection to the king (2 Sam 7:16) assured the congregation, gathered at the temple in prayer, that Yahweh will give victory to the king, who was about to march into battle.

This psalm, perhaps one of the most ancient, belonged to the temple ritual for kings, particularly in time of war. It is impossible to date the psalm any more precisely than a long development during the pre-exilic period. If v. 7 implies that Israel did not yet possess chariots, then we find ourselves in the reign of David, certainly before Solomon organized an army with "soldiers, officials, commanders, captains, chariot commanders and horsemen" (1 Kgs 9:22). Yet v. 2 presumes the enthronement of the ark of the covenant in the Jerusalem temple, already constructed by Solomon, and v. 7 can be interpreted as a later prophetic challenge to excessive trust in military forces.

(II) Ps 20, as we stated, must be interpreted imaginatively. To picture the ceremony, we draw upon several biblical texts which speak of ritual acts before battle, in 1 Sam 7:7-11, where Samuel "offered a whole burnt offering... and cried to the Lord"; or after battle, in 1 Sam 13:9-12. A still more elaborate account is given in 2 Chron 20. From these ceremonies we can reconstruct the liturgical setting for Ps 20:

(A) *Prayer of Intercession* for the King, vv. 1-5,

v. 1	Prayer of Entire Assembly	When the king arrives at the sanctuary
vv. 2-3	Prayer sung by the choir for divine assistance	as holocausts and other sacrifices were offered by the priests
vv. 4-5b	Also sung by the choir, asking for victory	as tribal banners and trophies were carried in procession
v. 5c	Prayer of Entire Assembly, addressed to the king	as king steps to the center

(B) *Prayer of Thanksgiving*, anticipating victory for the king, vv. 6-8.

—	—	An oracle is given by priest or prophet
v. 6	Promise of help	Spoken by priest
vv. 7-8	Assurance of victory	Spoken by priest (or prophet?) in the presence of king and soldiers

(C) *Conclusion*, v. 9.

v. 9	Sung by the entire assembly	Perhaps repeated many times throughout the ceremony

(III) Within the *Prayer of intercession* (vv. 1-5), an appeal to the *name* of God revives the faith that God's presence in the sanctuary is not for quiet adoration alone but for actively and personally assisting his people, as we read in another psalm for warfare, "through *thy name* we tread down our assailants" (Ps 44:5). *God of Jacob*, a title for God, frequently used by the prophet Isaiah (Isa 2:5, 6; 8:17; etc.) occurs again in Ps 46:7, 11, where it confesses total reliance upon Yahweh to overcome one's enemies. Jacob is the patriarch who faced the most dangerous opposition and was promised God's continuous protection through the angels that descend and ascend — *cf.,* dream of Jacob at Bethel (Gen 28:10-17). The *burnt offerings* (v. 3) would be holocausts, totally consumed by the sacrificial fire atop the main altar and symbolizing total consecration and absolute union with God. The reference to *banners* in v. 5 may allude to the "standards" or insignia proper to each tribe (Num 1:52) and to the custom of preserving important trophies in the temple, like the bronze serpent (Num 21:8-9; 2 Kgs 18:4) and the sword of Goliath (1 Sam 21:9-10). These would feature in temple ceremonies at appropriate times.

The *Prayer of Thanksgiving* (vv. 6-9) would have been preceded by an oracle of salvation, similar to that in Ps 12:5, in which a priest promised victory. V. 7 may be a prophetic statement within the cult that the chariots and horses of the enemy and even of Israel (*cf.,* Ps 44:6) are useless without trusting in the Lord. This statement may resonate either the later prophetic call for peace and non-violence (Isa 2:2-4;

30:15-17) or the earlier prophetic summons to the "holy war" (*cf.,* the battle cry of the prophetess Deborah, Judg 4:14, "Up! For this is the day in which the Lord has given Sisera into your hand. Does not the Lord go out before you?") V. 9, this final exclamation of victory inspired the British shout of honor and loyalty, "God save the King/Queen!"

(IV) The long history of Ps 20, *from temple liturgy* for the king in time of war, *all the way to prophetic reliance* on instruments of peace with Isaiah, *into the apocalyptic movement* with firm faith that through God alone will a new world emerge out of its present, chaotic condition (Dan 7-9), all these ancient applications of Ps 20 enable us to turn to it in contrasting situations. At times it summons us to rally all of our human energy to the cause of justice, and at other times it asks us to wait with patience till God achieves, perhaps miraculously, what seems humanly impossible. The liturgical or community context of the psalm expects us to seek advice and help from others, and to give ourselves ample time for prayer and reflection, before deciding that it is "a time to rend" or "a time to sew," "a time for war" or "a time for peace" (Eccles 3:7-8).

Psalm 21
To The Choirmaster. A Psalm Of David.

I

¹In thy strength the king rejoices, O Lord;
   and in thy help how greatly he exults!
²Thou hast given him his heart's desire,
   and hast not withheld the request of his lips.   *Selah*
³For thou dost meet him with goodly blessings;
   thou dost set a crown of fine gold upon his head.
⁴He asked life of thee; thou gavest it to him,
   length of days for ever and ever.
⁵His glory is great through thy help;
   splendor and majesty thou dost bestow upon him.
⁶Yea, thou dost make him most blessed for ever;
   thou dost make him glad with the joy of thy presence.

⁷For the king trusts in the Lord;
  and through the steadfast love of the Most High
  he shall not be moved.

II

⁸Your hand will find out all your enemies;
  your right hand will find out those who hate you.
⁹You will make them as a blazing oven when you appear.
  The Lord will swallow them up in his wrath;
  and fire will consume them.
¹⁰You will destroy their offspring from the earth,
  and their children from among the sons of men.
¹¹If they plan evil against you,
  if they devise mischief, they will not succeed.
¹²For you will put them to flight;
  you will aim at their faces with your bows.

III

¹³Be exalted, O Lord, in thy strength!
  We will sing and praise thy power.

(I) Like Ps 20, this one too centers around the king and was appropriate for any royal festival or anniversary; many of the details seem to reflect a temple ceremony before marching into battle.

(II) Ps 21 is energetic, even fiercely so as in vv. 9, 10 and 12; yet in other ways it seems elusive and indirect. E. Beaucamp remarked: although the king is the principal personage, yet he is also a mute person about whom one speaks to Yahweh in vv. 2-6, or to whom one speaks about Yahweh in vv. 8-12. These two main sections would have been sung by the main temple choir. Vv. 1, 7 and 13 were intended as antiphonal responses for the entire assembly, either in praise of Yahweh (vv. 1 and 13) or in praise of the king (v. 7). These three separate verses are linked together by the repetition of words and a meter different from the main stanzas.

(III) While interceding for the king before Yahweh (vv. 2-6), the psalmist asks that God grant him *length of days for*

ever and ever. This phrase does not necessarily mean eternal
life after death (see Ps 6:5). It is an honorary title, at times
even for pagan kings (Neh 2:3; Dan 2:4); here it is to be
understood of the royal family's perpetual right to the
throne (2 Sam 7:16, 29). The words about Yahweh to the
king (vv. 8-12) are dominated by the language and spirit of
the "Holy War" (see Ps 20:6-9, or the lengthier discussion in
the commentary in this series on the Book of Deuteronomy,
chaps. 7 and 20). In this type of warfare and literary style
Yahweh is the Warrior-God to whom every object and
person are dedicated, so that nothing of the enemy's property or lives can remain in secular use anymore. Vv. 9-10
refer to an enemy city, besieged for a long time and now in
flames, whose inhabitants ("offsprings") are being
destroyed.

(IV) For the theology of the curse psalms, see Ps 69. Ps 21
challenges us to the total dedication of our lives to the Lord,
to absolute obedience to God's will, and to a strong confidence in God's fidelity. As the Old Testament moved away
from military might and through the prophets developed an
ever firmer trust in the Lord and distrust in warfare, the
struggle against evil became all the more comprehensive and
overpowering. Opposition to evil becomes particularly
intense in the apocalyptic literature. There will never be an
easy way to die and to be reborn totally in Christ Jesus. A
key word within the psalm is *strength* (in vv. 1 and 13) and to
that word we ought to relate another in v. 7, *the steadfast
love of the Most High.* Occurring at the center as a choral
refrain, *steadfast love* (in Hebrew *ḥesed*, see Ps 12) explains
the source of all strength, which is found in the covenant
bond between Yahweh and his chosen people, a bond as
fierce as love, as loyal as blood, rooted in God.

Psalm 22
To The Choirmaster: According To The Hind Of The
Dawn. A Psalm Of David.

I

¹My God, my God, why hast thou forsaken me?
   Why art thou so far from helping me, from the words
      of my groaning?
²O my God, I cry by day, but thou dost not answer;
   and by night, but find no rest.

³Yet thou art holy,
   enthroned on the praises of Israel.
⁴In thee our fathers trusted;
   they trusted, and thou didst deliver them.
⁵To thee they cried, and were saved;
   in thee they trusted, and were not disappointed.

⁶But I am a worm, and no man;
   scorned by men, and despised by the people.
⁷All who see me mock at me,
   they make mouths at me, they wag their heads;
⁸"He committed his cause to the Lord;
      let him deliver him,
   let him rescue him, for he delights in him!"

⁹Yet thou art he who took me from the womb;
   thou didst keep me safe upon my mother's breasts.
¹⁰Upon thee was I cast from my birth,
   and since my mother bore me thou hast been my God.
¹¹Be not far from me,
   for trouble is near
   and there is none to help.

¹²Many bulls encompass me,
   strong bulls of Bashan surround me;
¹³they open wide their mouths at me,
   like a ravening and roaring lion.

¹⁴I am poured out like water,
   and all my bones are out of joint;

my heart is like wax,
   it is melted within my breast;
15my strength is dried up like a potsherd,
   and my tongue cleaves to my jaws;
   thou dost lay me in the dust of death.

16Yea, dogs are round about me;
   a company of evildoers encircle me;
   they have pierced my hands and feet—
17I can count all my bones—
   they stare and gloat over me;
18they divide my garments among them,
   and for my raiment they cast lots.

19But thou, O Lord, be not far off!
   O thou my help, hasten to my aid!
20Deliver my soul from the sword,
   my life from the power of the dog!
21Save me from the mouth of the lion,
   my afflicted soul from the horns of the wild oxen!

II

22I will tell of thy name to my brethren;
   in the midst of the congregation I will praise thee:
23You who fear the Lord, praise him!
   all you sons of Jacob, glorify him,
   and stand in awe of him, all you sons of Israel!
24For he has not despised or abhorred
   the affliction of the afflicted;
   and he has not hid his face from him,
   but has heard, when he cried to him.

25From thee comes my praise in the great congregation;
   my vows I will pay before those who fear him.
26The afflicted shall eat and be satisfied;
   those who seek him shall praise the Lord!
   May your hearts live for ever!

III

27All the ends of the earth shall remember
   and turn to the Lord;

and all the families of the nations
shall worship before him.
²⁸For dominion belongs to the Lord,
and he rules over the nations.

²⁹Yea, to him shall all the proud of the earth bow down;
before him shall bow all who go down to the dust,
and he who cannot keep himself alive.
³⁰Posterity shall serve him;
men shall tell of the Lord to the coming generation,
³¹and proclaim his deliverance to a people yet unborn,
that he has wrought it.

(I) This psalm, even if it had not been quoted as often as 13 times in the New Testament, 9 times alone in the Passion Story, and had not been consecrated by the blood of Jesus (Matt 27:46; Mark 15:34), would still remain one of the most priceless gems of the psalter. Despite total abandonment, the psalmist lives within a domain of peace. The sufferer makes no allusion to sin, neither is there any appeal to personal innocence nor any defense against unjust charges. No anger lashes out against the enemy; in fact, they are never directly mentioned and are never the subject of formal curses as in most laments. Unlike the Book of Job, there are no "philosophic" disquisitions on the nature of suffering. The words are clean of any dourness or bitterness. We meet a simple abandonment into the hands of God, and in this surrender to God there is peace. The psalmist asks so little of God: only that God *hear* this cry of abandonment (v. 2). Once God induces a mystic presence so that the psalmist can whisper, "you have heard me" (v. 21 according to the Hebrew), the psalm modulates into a Song of Thanksgiving. This transition from lamentation to thanksgiving will not seem abrupt if we recall that the psalm was written over a long period of sickness and imprisonment. The earlier days, perhaps weeks and months, could never be forgotten, nor their pathetic lament in vv. 1-21 be erased, even after the psalmist felt the mystic touch of God's loving awareness and reached out of this abyss of loneliness to the community of the "great congregation" of "the afflicted" (vv. 25-26). These neglected people are invited to join with the psalmist in vv. 22-26. Years later, another member of the "great congregation" of "the afflicted" extended this prayer to still other disabled people: the gentiles (vv. 27-28), the diseased and possibly the dead (v. 29) and the unborn (v. 31).

Though severely alone in a dark prison cell, the psalmist nonetheless found companionship — or better, sheer survival — by repeating over and over the laments particularly of the prophet Jeremiah but also the Servant Songs of Second Isaiah, and then by absorbing and recasting them into new form. Not only a bond of spirituality with Jeremiah and Second Isaiah but also a close identity of words are seen as we compare, particularly in the Hebrew text, such passages as: *scorned by men* in Ps 22:6b with Jer 49:15; *all who see me mock at me* in Ps 22:7a with Jer 20:7b; *they wag their heads* in Ps 22:7b with Lam 2:15 and Jer 18:16; *thou. . . who took me from the womb* in Ps 22:9-10 with frequent references in Jer 1:5; 15:10; 20:14, 17-18 and echoing again in the Servant Songs (Isa 49:1). It is not possible to prove that the psalmist quoted from Jeremiah but there certainly seems to have been sustaining kinship of spirit not only with Jeremiah and his disciples but also with an expanding group of the "afflicted," like Second Isaiah during the exile, as well as with Job and other late "Davidic Psalms" (Pss 69, 71, 139) after the exile.

Though Ps 22 comes from an individual sufferer, it quickly became the property of the "great congregation" of the "afflicted" in Israel, each influencing the other and by sharing their spirit contributing to the inspiration of the Bible. With the help of Albert Gelin, we project these stages of development:

1st) composition of vv. 1-26, in the early postexilic age or perhaps during the exile itself, therefore between 587 and 500 B.C., by someone physically sick, imprisoned, ridiculed yet innocent;

2nd) because of its sheer beauty and its effectiveness in expressing the thoughts of a suffering person before God, it "forced" its way into temple liturgy and became the "property" of all God's afflicted ones;

3rd) within this community the psalm evolved with a sense of God's concern for foreigners and a belief of conscious survival after death; vv. 27-31 were added;

4th) from the ranks of this suffering, innocent, hopeful community came the Messiah Jesus who turned to this psalm to sustain hope and silent prayer while dying on the cross;

5th) the early disciples of Jesus reach out to this psalm to preach the saving message of Jesus' death and resurrection and to compose the gospels. What Jesus had individualized for himself, again becomes the property of the "great congregation" of the "afflicted."

(II) Ps 22 modulates so gently that we hardly notice the transitions. Even dramatic changes seem to be absorbed within the intimate I-Thou relation between the psalmist and God. We call attention to the opening phrase in many lines: *My God...Why art thou...O my God...Yet thou ...in thee...to thee...But I am a worm...all who see me ...Yet thou...upon thee...but thou, O Lord.* A careful reading detects these subsections within the individual lament of vv. 1-21:

vv. 1-2	Invocation and call for help
vv. 3-5	Motive of faith
vv. 6-8	Lament
vv. 9-10	Prayer of confidence
v. 11	Prayer for help
vv. 12-18	Lament
vv. 19-21	Prayer for help

(III) This psalm speaks for itself. With the assistance of the outline just given, we comment on individual phrases. Vv. 1-21 form the long, individual lament. V. 1, *my God ...why hast thou abandoned me?* these opening words seem to contradict themselves, for how can anyone say *My God* to a God who has abandoned his servant. Yet we never feel abandoned by strangers, only by those close to us. V. 1, *far from helping me:* the Hebrew word *far* or *distant* is repeated again in vv. 11 and 19 and sustains the sense of abandonment. The Hebrew reads *my salvation* instead of *helping me,* thereby distancing God even more poignantly from the psalmist. V. 2, *does not answer:* this verb is repeated in the transitional v. 21, *you hear me* (Hebrew text). It is the silence of God that torments the psalmist more than ridicule, false charges, sickness or imprisonment.

Vv. 3-5, here we see that the strength of the psalmist's devotion to tradition turns into a major problem. Because he or she has taken God so seriously, God's absence seems a denial of faith. V. 3a rises like staccato shouts of praise: "But thou! The holy One! The Praises of Israel!" Vv. 6-8 show a tragic reversal. The ancestors *were not disappointed* (literally, shamed) *But I am...scorned...and shamed.* Is there any hope for someone shorn of their humanity? The inhuman and mad ridicule in vv. 6-8 contrasts bitterly with the tender, helpless humanity of the babe in vv. 9-10.

Vv. 12-18 offer a terrifying assembly of images for persecution: *strong bulls, roaring lion, poured out like water, bones out of joint, heart like melting wax, throat dried up like a potsherd, tongue cleaving to my jaws, dogs round about me.* Therefore the line in v. 16c, *they have pierced my hands and my feet,* ought also to be interpreted metaphorically. In fact, the verb *pierced* is obtained only by textual clarification, repeatedly discussed by scholars. Literally it reads: "Like a lion my hands and my feet." The Jewish version translates literally and adds what seems implied, "Like lions [they maul] my hands and my feet." This line, moreover, is never cited in the New Testament, despite its frequent use of Ps 22. If applied to Jesus, this phrase would have been fulfilled whether or not Jesus had been nailed hands and feet to the cross. It would have been sufficient to belong to the "congregation" of the "afflicted." The long lament ends with the prayer, vv. 19-21, whose final word in the Hebrew is, *you have heard me, 'anithani;* with a slight change to *'aniyathi,* it can be translated, *my afflicted soul,* as in the RSV, following the ancient Greek Septuagint and Syriac. We retain the Hebrew text, first on literary grounds that vv. 19-21 form an "inclusion," repeating three words from vv. 1-2 (far off, deliver/save, and hear). Also on religious grounds, the Hebrew text enables us to see the transition to a Song of Thanksgiving, not necessarily in liberation from prison or from sickness, but in the interior realization of faith, God has heard!

The first Song of Thanksgiving (vv. 22-26) may have been preceded by an "oracle of salvation" (see Ps 12:5), once the psalm became a part of the temple liturgy. We begin to see how Ps 22 combines the elements of good liturgy: the reading of Scripture with the meditative response of Ps 22:1-21; hymns or songs of encouragement; a peace sacrifice in which a part of the animal (as in the case of the paschal lamb) is returned to the offerers for their sacred meal and shared with friends (*cf.,* Exod 12; Deut 26). In this ritual both the original psalmist and Yahweh live in the assembly at prayer. The psalm enables the past and the present to merge into one act of worship and so to proclaim now the presence of Yahweh who continues to live within the words of Scripture and the actions of the liturgy (*cf.,* 1 Cor 11:26).

The second Song of Thanksgiving (vv. 27-31) manifests the continued life of the psalmist, whose lament became a prayer of thanksgiving in the "great congregation" of the "afflicted." Other "afflicted" outlaws are now summoned to participate in the liturgy: foreigners, the sick and diseased, and even the unborn. V. 29 is troubled textually; with a slight emendation or by simply translating the Hebrew with the help of the ancient Ugaritic language, it might read, "Yea, to him all those who sleep in the earth bow down." The psalm ends with a strong affirmation of faith. The phrase, *that he has wrought it,* is stated succinctly in the Hebrew, *Indeed, he takes action.*

(IV) Christian tradition has always considered Ps 22 to be messianic. We propose that Jesus did not so much fulfill words in a book as he identified himself with the agony and faith of generations of persecuted, afflicted people. Ps 22 is not so much a detailed prediction about Jesus as it is a psalm whose fulfillment in Jesus reached even beyond the agony and innocence, the power and influence of the psalmist. The psalm leads us into the suffering heart of Jesus, but Jesus enables us to plummet to depths of spirituality, otherwise hidden to us in Ps 22. Ps 22 insists upon the utter humanity of Jesus, "obedient even unto death" (Phil 2:8), while Jesus through his death and resurrection leads us through the darkness of the psalm into the glory of the divine assembly, reflected in each Christian celebration of the Eucharist which proclaims the death of the Lord until he comes (1 Cor 11:26).

Psalm 23
A Psalm Of David.

I

¹The Lord is my shepherd, I shall not want;
² he makes me lie down in green pastures.
 He leads me beside still waters;
³ he restores my soul.

II

He leads me in paths of righteousness
 for his name's sake.

⁴Even though I walk through the valley
 of the shadow of death,
 I fear no evil;
 for thou art with me;
 thy rod and thy staff
 they comfort me.

III

⁵Thou preparest a table before me
 in the presence of my enemies;
 thou anointest my head with oil,
 my cup overflows.
⁶Surely goodness and mercy shall follow me
 all the days of my life;
 and I shall dwell in the house of the Lord
 for ever.

(I) This most popular of the psalms draws upon the quiet yet at times dangerous life of a semi-nomadic shepherd to express strength, tenderness and confidence in God. Grateful for green pasture and restful waters, the psalmist is led to an abundant table where the cup overflows. No one is lost in the crowd, for the Lord is *my* shepherd, yet each one merges into the assembly at temple worship. The psalm combines quiet personal journeys with the mighty exoduses of the nation, out of Egypt through the Sinai desert, and later out of Babylonian exile across the Arabian desert.

(II) Depending on how we translate the last line: either *I shall dwell* as in RSV, or *I shall return* as in the Hebrew, the psalm reflects two, very different moments: either the excitement upon entering the promised land to *dwell* there with grateful heart (in this case, a psalm of thanksgiving), or it shows the determination to *return* again to the temple (in this case, a psalm of confidence). The blend of such diverse moments of personal and national life, of private devotion and public liturgy, continues in the structural modulation of the psalm: vv. 1-3a develop the image of *shepherd and flock;* vv. 3bc-4 gradually abandon the metaphors to speak more directly of *Yahweh as guide* "in the valley of darkness"; vv. 5-6 are free of all figures of speech and locate us in the Jerusalem temple at the conclusion of a thanksgiving festival similar to the one in Ps 22:22-26.

(III) The opening lines (vv. 1-3a) draw upon the most popular image in the Bible, that of shepherd (Gen 49:24; Ezek 34:11-16) and probably allude as well to a most persistent theological motif, Israel's exodus through the desert either under Moses (Ps 77:16-20; Hos 11) or at the end of the exile (Jer 23:3-4; Isa 40:11), closely connected with temple liturgy (Ps 95). Almost all of these passages exude God's tender care for Israel, a spirit further personalized by Ps 23, which addresses the Lord as *MY Shepherd.*

Vv. 3bc-4 speak more directly, less figuratively. *paths of righteousness:* God's promises and holy will are fulfilled in the care and protection, shown the psalmist, and so there is a self-revelation of God (*cf.,* Ps 106:8 and Isa 40:5, "he saved them *for his name's sake* that he might make known his mighty power" and so "the glory of the Lord shall be revealed"). *Rod* was a shepherd's instrument to protect the sheep and the *staff* to support himself; as such *they* are a source of *comfort* for *me*. The last words remind us of Second Isaiah's opening message in chap. 40, "Comfort, comfort my people."

Vv. 5-6 locate us in the temple towards the conclusion of a thanksgiving sacrifice, in which part of the offering was returned for a family banquet (see Ps 22:22-26; also Ps 116:17-19, "I will offer to thee the sacrifice of thanksgiving ...in the courts of the house of the Lord"). At the end of the ceremony, the psalmist declares confidently, according to the Hebrew *shabti*, "I will return." When the psalm was adapted to the return from exile or more generally to pilgrimages to the temple, the Hebrew was changed ever so slightly to *shibti*, "I will dwell" forever in the house, that is, in the promised land with every right to take part in temple services.

(IV) Synagogal and Christian tradition called upon this psalm to accompany the faithful disciple into the house of God. In the early church it was sung at the Easter vigil service as the newly baptized rose from the baptismal font, were anointed with oil, clothed with fresh white garments and led to the table of the Eucharist for the first time. Jesus was influenced by this psalm, as well as by other shepherd images in the Bible, to speak of himself as the "Good Shepherd" who "calls his own sheep by name and leads them out" (John 10:3, 11). This psalm is frequently used for funerals, to accompany the body of the deceased person whom the Good Shepherd calls home beyond "the shadow of death" that they may "dwell in the house of the Lord forever."

Psalm 24
A Psalm Of David.

> [1]The earth is the Lord's and the fulness thereof,
>   the world and those who dwell therein;
> [2]for he has founded it upon the seas,
>   and established it upon the rivers.

³Who shall ascend the hill of the Lord?
  And who shall stand in his holy place?
⁴He who has clean hands and a pure heart,
    who does not lift up his soul to what is false,
    and does not swear deceitfully.
⁵He will receive blessing from the Lord,
    and vindication from the God of his salvation.
⁶Such is the generation of those who seek him,
    who seek the face of the God of Jacob.   *Selah*

⁷Lift up your heads, O gates!
    and be lifted up, O ancient doors!
    that the King of glory may come in.
⁸Who is the King of glory?
  The Lord, strong and mighty,
    the Lord, mighty in battle!
⁹Lift up your heads, O gates!
    and be lifted up, O ancient doors!
    that the King of glory may come in.
¹⁰Who is this King of glory?
  The Lord of hosts
    he is the King of glory!   *Selah*

(I) Composed for a solemn liturgical procession, escort-
ing the ark of the covenant through the holy city of Jerusalem and back again into the Holy of Holies of the temple,
this psalm resonates with very ancient as well as with late
pre-exilic motifs. We find here some archaic phrases, a
mixed meter and a repetitive parallelism, all of which locate
the psalm with Israel's earliest poetry, like Exod 15, Judg 5
or Hab 3. At the same time we hear echoes of many biblical
passages which describe the attitude for approaching the
temple, like Isa 2:35; 33:13-16; Jer 31:12 and Pss 16 & 132.
Some of these passages gravitate towards the religious
reform of King Josiah, 621-609 B.C., *i.e.,*

Come, let us go up to the mountain of the Lord,...
    that he may teach us his ways (Isa 2:3).

> They shall come and sing aloud on the height of Zion,
> and they shall be radiant over the goodness of the Lord
> (Jer 31:12).

Like most liturgical pieces, this psalm evolved over the years, holding onto ancient phrases yet absorbing new ones, adapting itself to vigorous interaction between the assembly, temple choirs and personnel, reaching out to provide words for congregational praise (vv. 1-2, 7-10) and religious instruction (vv. 3-6). It is difficult to be more precise (were 2 or 3 original psalms combined?) or to identify the feastday on which it was sung. Later Jewish tradition added to the title, "for the first day after the sabbath," when God began to create the world.

(II) The following schema from L. Jacquet may be helpful in appreciating the structure and celebration of the psalm. It shows how it *might* have been utilized and *certainly* puts us into a mood congenial with the psalm:

In procession — the psalm celebrates

the grandeur of Yahweh	choir I	vv. 1-2
the demands of Yahweh	choir II	vv. 3-4
the favors of Yahweh	altogether	vv. 5-6

Before entering the temple, Yahweh is acclaimed as King

temple choirs	v. 7	v. 9
solo voice	v. 8a	v. 10a
cortege of levites	v. 8bc	v. 10bc

(III) Vv. 1-2 open the psalm, celebrating Yahweh's creative power over the universe (Pss 2 and 8). The earth is pictured, according to an ancient cosmogony, as suspended over subterranean waters by means of sturdy pillars which like mountains reached into the depths (Gen 7:11; Exod 20:4; Ps 136:6). *Seas* and *ocean currents* (better than rivers) reflect a very ancient Canaanite or Ugaritic mythology, in which the god Baal defeated the hostile and raging gods of the sea and was then joyfully received by the divine assembly of lesser gods (Pss 2; 8; 32). Yahweh is the conqueror of all hostile forces, imaged by sea and currents, and sustains Israel in peace. In the ancient Near East the temple reflected the strength and peace of the celestial home of the gods; the Jerusalem temple, therefore, became the center of Yahweh's governance of the universe, the source of fresh water for irrigating the world (Ezek 47; Ps 46:4), the navel from which life flowed (Ezek 5:5; 38:12).

Vv. 3-4 are often called a Torah-liturgy, with typical instructions for true worshippers. The phrases, *clean hands* (only here in the OT), *pure heart* and *not swearing deceitfully* stress a spirit of familial sincerity, and absolute loyalty to Yahweh alone. We are reminded of Jesus' words: "Blessed are the pure in heart, for they shall see God"(Matt 5:8). People such as these are on pilgrimage to the Lord's presence throughout each moment of their daily life and so are totally qualified to enter the holy place.

Vv. 5-6 generously bestow the Lord's favors from the temple, the source of life, the center of God's goodness. *vindication*, the same word for justice or righteousness, stresses Yahweh's fidelity in living up to his part of the covenant and blessing his faithful people (Pss 132:9, 15-16; Jer 31:23). *those who seek him:* a rich word, about 165 times in the Old Testament and frequent in the psalms, with connotations to search for, inquire about, turn to and repent, cry out to in sorrow, discover and worship.

Vv. 7-10 welcome the Lord in triumph. This military language is derived from early traditions about Yahweh the Warrior who defeats Israel's enemies and brings the people safely out of Egypt, through the desert; into the promised land (Num 10:35-36; Judg 5:4-5; Ps 68:7-8). These and other passages connect the people now in procession at Jerusalem with Israel's earliest pilgrimage from Egypt to the promised land; they unite the God of glory at Jerusalem with the covenant God of Sinai. The ancient doors of the sanctuary open onto Israel's glorious antiquity and even onto the heavenly home of Yahweh.

(IV) Not only does Ps 24 find an extraordinary fulfillment in the words of Jesus in the beatitude about the pure of heart who see God (Matt 5:8), but its intuition of a universal God who creates the world and declares that it is good is reflected in Paul's citation of it in 1 Cor 10:26, stating that all food is clean and therefore can be eaten with a good conscience —yet Paul at once advises restraint if the neighbor should be scandalized. We enter God's presence as a community, not as rugged individuals. We can reread Ps 24 in the context of the final judgment: "Come, O blessed of my father" (Matt 25:34), and of Jesus' entry after his death into the Holy of Holies (Heb 10:19-23).

Psalm 25
A Psalm Of David.

I

¹To thee, O Lord, I lift up my soul.
  ²O my God, in thee I trust,
  let me not be put to shame;
  let not my enemies exult over me.
³Yea, let none that wait for thee be put to shame;
  let them be ashamed who are wantonly treacherous.

⁴Make me to know thy ways, O Lord;
  teach me thy paths.
⁵Lead me in thy truth, and teach me,
  for thou art the God of my salvation;
  for thee I wait all the day long.

⁶Be mindful of thy mercy, O Lord,
  and of thy steadfast love,
  for they have been from of old.
⁷Remember not the sins of my youth,
  or my transgressions;
  according to thy steadfast love remember me,
  for thy goodness' sake, O Lord!

II

⁸Good and upright is the Lord;
  therefore he instructs sinners in the way.
⁹He leads the humble in what is right,
  and teaches the humble his way.

¹⁰All the paths of the Lord are steadfast
  love and faithfulness,
  for those who keep his covenant and his testimonies.

¹¹For thy name's sake, O Lord,
  pardon my guilt, for it is great.
¹²Who is the man that fears the Lord?
  Him will he instruct in the way that he should choose.
¹³He himself shall abide in prosperity,
  and his children shall possess the land.
¹⁴The friendship of the Lord is for those who fear him,
  and he makes known to them his covenant.
¹⁵My eyes are ever toward the Lord,
  for he will pluck my feet out of the net.

III

¹⁶Turn thou to me, and be gracious to me;
  for I am lonely and afflicted.
¹⁷Relieve the troubles of my heart,
  and bring me out of my distresses.
¹⁸Consider my affliction and my trouble,
  and forgive all my sins.

¹⁹Consider how many are my foes,
  and with what violent hatred they hate me.
²⁰Oh guard my life, and deliver me;
  let me not be put to shame, for I
    take refuge in thee.
²¹May integrity and uprightness preserve me,
  for I wait for thee.

²²Redeem Israel, O God,
  out of all his troubles.

(I) As quietly read from any English translation, Ps 25 flows smoothly enough: vv. 1-7 pray to Yahweh in the 2nd person (v. 1, an opening refrain, is typical, *To thee, O Lord, I lift up my soul*); vv. 8-15 speak about Yahweh in the 3rd person (v. 8 is again typical and sets the spirit, *Good and upright is the Lord*); vv. 16-21 return to a second person address in prayer, now more poignantly (v. 16 is an effective transitional verse even in its opening word: *Turn thou to me ...for I am lonely and afflicted*). The psalm concludes with a choral refrain, *Redeem Israel, O God* (v. 22).

On second reading, particularly in the Hebrew, we begin to see the intricacy of this exquisite lament for the individual penitent person. First, this psalm is an alphabetical or acrostic poem, even more perfect than Pss 9-10, running from *aleph* to the final letter *taw* with only slight irregularity. One of these irregularities is the addition of an extra verse beyond the 22 letters of the Hebrew alphabet; this final line begins with *pe*. As a result, the psalm opens with *aleph*, the middle verse starts with *lamedh*, and the final verse with *pe*. These three letters, when joined together, produce the Hebrew word, "to learn" or "to teach." Rather than wrap the psalm into an artificial straight jacket, the alphabetical style impresses us with the delicate faith of the psalmist: in the peaceful privilege of speaking with Yahweh, each letter and syllable became sacred. In fact, each letter of the alphabet is a gift from the Lord and can transform even one's penitential prayer into a return gift of praise (L. Jacquet). The alphabetical style, moreover, manifests a healthy control over hyper-emotionalism. The personal trust between the psalmist and Yahweh shows up also in the repetition of the divine name *Yahweh* 10 times and a reference to the Lord's *way* also 10 times. Through such words as *teach* (3 times), *make known* (3 times) and *shame* (4 times), we perceive the psalmist's sincerity, openness and nobility of character.

It is impossible to date the psalm. Its alphabetical style, its vocabulary and its concern with shame and internal foes would lead us to the postexilic age around 450 B.C. when the sapiential movement flourished and internal problems plagued the Jerusalem temple. Yet its spirit is very close to Jeremiah's (627-587 B.C.) and could lead to the late preexilic age.

(II) Ps 25 can be classified with the sapiential psalms as well as with laments for the individual, especially one who is sorrowing over personal loneliness and persecution. Following the division of lines in RSV, we arrive at these directions for reading Ps 25:

Prayer to Yahweh in 2nd person, vv. 1-7	v. 1	Introduction
	vv. 2-3	to be saved from enemies and not shamed
	vv. 4-5	following the path of the Lord
	vv. 6-7	Yahweh's covenant love
Announcement of Yahweh's Goodness in the 3rd person, vv. 8-15	vv. 8-10	Covenant love, the right way
	vv. 11-15	Pardon through the covenant; peace
Prayer of Anguish in the 2nd person, vv. 16-21	vv. 16-18	Relieve the troubles of the heart
	vv. 19-21	Saved from enemies and not shamed
Choral Refrain, v. 22		

At the center of the psalm, four sections center on covenant love and the way of the Lord; these are surrounded by references to the enemy and shame (vv. 2-3 and 19-21); at the beginning and end, the normal introduction by the individual (v. 1) and the choral refrain for the entire liturgical congregation (v. 22). This penitential prayer then rests upon the bonds of covenant and Yahweh's promise of steadfast love, fidelity and compassion.

(III) Our meditation upon this psalm can be furthered by parallel reading in the Bible. We mention a few possibilities:

v. 1, *I lift up my soul,* see Lam 3:41.

v. 2, *in thee I trust*, see Ps 22:4-5.

v. 3, *wait for thee*, see Isa 40:31.

v. 7, *sins of my youth,* see Job 13:23-28; Jer 2:2-3; 31:19.

v. 10, *steadfast love and faithfulness*, see Exod 34:6-9; Jer 32:18.

v. 16, *lonely and afflicted,* see

v. 4, *ways...paths*, see Pss   Jer 12:6; 15:10, 17.
1; 119:1-8.

(IV) The covenant which is inherited through the community leads the psalmist to an intense personal piety, which the community makes its own, to a humble spirit which never suppresses human dignity, to a lonely person who still senses the friendship of the Lord, to contrite sorrow that leads to a new awareness of the Lord's fidelity and goodness.

Psalm 26
A Psalm Of David.

I

¹Vindicate me, O Lord,
    for I have walked in my integrity;
    and I have trusted in the Lord without wavering.
²Prove me, O Lord, and try me;
    test my heart and my mind.

³For thy steadfast love is before my eyes,
    and I walk in faithfulness to thee.

II

⁴I do not sit with false men,
    nor do I consort with dissemblers;
⁵I hate the company of evildoers,
    and I will not sit with the wicked.

⁶I wash my hands in innocence,
    and go about thy altar, O Lord,
⁷singing aloud a song of thanksgiving,
    and telling all thy wondrous deeds.

III

⁸O Lord, I love the habitation of thy house,
    and the place where thy glory dwells.
⁹Sweep me not away with sinners,
    nor my life with bloodthirsty men,

¹⁰men in whose hands are evil devices,
   and whose right hands are full of bribes.

¹¹But as for me, I walk in my integrity;
   redeem me, and be gracious to me.
¹²My foot stands on level ground;
   in the great congregation I will bless the Lord.

(I) This psalm, a lament for someone unjustly accused of a serious crime, can be linked with Pss 7 and 17. As a protestation of innocence, it can be considered part of a penitential rite before entering the temple or at least before proceeding with the other ceremonies in the temple, similar to Pss 15 and 24. Some scholars see its origin in the right of asylum in the temple till an accused person can be declared innocent (Num 35:9-15; 1 Kgs 1:50-53); others, in the ritual of "ordeal," a public way of establishing the innocence or guilt of a person under suspicion (Num 5:11-31); still others, in the requirement that the priest publicly declare that debts, contagious diseases, or infractions of another's rights have been remedied (Num 5:1-10; 8:5-22). Later the psalm may have been adapted for the general use of pilgrims at the sanctuary and their desire for a ritual act of purification before admission to worship.

(II) Though written for an individual, Ps 26 has come to us within the congregational collection of prayers. Several phrases may have been sung collectively, as they seem to overload the poetic structure of the Hebrew poem: v. 1a, *vindicate me, O Lord,* or better, "Acknowledge my righteousness, O Lord"; v. 8, *I love the place...where thy glory dwells*; and v. 12, *My foot stands on level ground* (better, "in justice"); *in the great assembly I will bless the Lord.* The three stanzas were sung by an individual: vv. 1b-3, an appeal to Yahweh from one's interior sincerity; vv. 4-7, an appeal, through temple ritual, for a public declaration of one's innocence; vv. 8-11, a final appeal to Yahweh to be delivered from a sinner's death and kept close to the Lord.

(III) We note several biblical parallels. V. 2, *test my heart and my mind*: the words are heard again within the first confession of the prophet Jeremiah (Jer 12:1-5). V. 3, *steadfast love:* an appeal to the covenant (see Pss 12:1; 25:10). Vv. 6-7 may contain various ritual acts: washing hands (Exod 30:17-21; Deut 21:6-9); walking in procession (Pss 42:4; 118:27); thanksgiving sacrifice (Ps 66:13-15); possibly some type of solemn oath (Deut 21:6-7).

(IV) This prayer and temple ritual endorses and reinforces the prophetical demand of sincerity and moral integrity before God accepts sanctuary ritual (1 Sam 15:22-23; Jer 7; Mic 6:6-8), a position strongly endorsed by Jesus (Matt 9:12-13; 12:6-7, "I tell you, something greater than the temple is here. And if you had known what this means, 'I desire mercy, and not sacrifice,' you would not have condemned the guiltless"). The protestation of innocence in Ps 26 is best recited by Jesus, our "high priest holy, blameless, unstained, separated from sinners" and by ourselves only in his company (Heb 7:26).

Psalm 27
A Psalm Of David.

I

¹The Lord is my light and my salvation;
  whom shall I fear?
The Lord is the stronghold of my life;
  of whom shall I be afraid?

²When evildoers assail me,
  uttering slanders against me,
my adversaries and foes,
  they shall stumble and fall.

³Though a host encamp against me,
  my heart shall not fear;
though war arise against me,
  yet I will be confident.

⁴One thing have I asked of the Lord,
  that will I seek after;
that I may dwell in the house of the Lord
  all the days of my life,

to behold the beauty of the Lord
  and to inquire in his temple.

⁵For he will hide me in his shelter
  in the day of trouble;
he will conceal me under the cover of his tent,
  he will set me high upon a rock.

⁶And now my head shall be lifted up
  above my enemies round about me;
and I will offer in his tent
  sacrifices with shouts of joy;
I will sing and make melody to the Lord.

II

⁷Hear, O Lord, when I cry aloud,
  be gracious to me and answer me!
⁸Thou hast said, "Seek ye my face."
  My heart says to thee,
  "Thy face, Lord, do I seek."
⁹ Hide not thy face from me.

Turn not thy servant away in anger,
  thou who hast been my help.
Cast me not off, forsake me not,
  O God of my salvation!
¹⁰For my father and my mother have forsaken me,
  but the Lord will take me up.

¹¹Teach me thy way, O Lord;
  and lead me on a level path
  because of my enemies.
¹²Give me not up to the will of my adversaries;
  for false witnesses have risen against me,
  and they breathe out violence.

¹³I believe that I shall see the goodness of the Lord
  in the land of the living!
¹⁴Wait for the Lord;
  be strong, and let your heart take courage;
  yea, wait for the Lord!

(I) This poem puts us in contact with a spirit of strong confidence (vv. 1-6) and the depths of desolation and subconscious hope (vv. 7-14). The dominant meter throughout is that of a dirge or lament (3 + 2); the integrating attitude is heroic courage and unconquerable hope. This blend of confidence and lament in a single psalm is credible. From a literary viewpoint, many great poems simmer a long time through contrary tensions of disturbance and peace before they reach, sometimes suddenly, their final integral expression; from the liturgical side we have noticed already that congregational use tends to retain the archaic and also to adapt to new circumstances. The confidence in vv. 1-6 prepared for faith heroic enough to sustain abandonment even from one's own family in vv. 7-14. This faith was formed and nourished by God, continuously present, more faithful, more life-giving than *my father and my mother* [*who*] *have forsaken me* (v. 10).

(II) The *first stanza* of confidence (vv. 1-6) envelops the fearful sight of "a host encamp[ed] against me" (vv. 2-3) with the vision of the Lord *my light* (v. 1) in whose house the psalmist prays *to behold the beauty of the Lord...and make melody* (vv. 4-6). Likewise the *second stanza* of individual lament (vv. 7-14) surrounds the outcast (v. 10) first with an invitation to *seek my face* (v. 8) and with the assurance *that I shall see the goodness of the Lord in the land of the living* (v. 13). V. 14, an oracle of salvation, is a liturgical conclusion, spoken by the priest (see Ps 12:5).

(III) The language is uniquely powerful and creative. V. 1 *The Lord is my light*, only here in the OT, although similar expressions occur in Ps 43:3, *send forth thy light*; or Isa 60, where Jerusalem reflects "the light of the Lord." V. 2, *uttering slanders against me*, reads literally "eating my flesh," with the idea of living off my weakness (*cf.,* Ps 14:4). V. 4, *the beauty of the Lord* betokens loveliness and delight and reminds us of Ps 16:11, "at thy right hand *pleasures* [same Hebrew word as *beauty*] for evermore." V. 10, *abandoned by my father and my mother* recalls the agony of Jeremiah (12:6) and the haunting words of Second Isaiah, "Can a woman forget her suckling child,...yet I will not forget you" (Isa 49:15). V. 12, *give me not up*... reads in the Hebrew, "do not deliver me into the throat of my adversary" (Dahood).

(IV) Faith such as this could not have been generated by personal will power or by any private spiritual resources but solely from the Lord, present in the sanctuary. Every human support has been removed, as with St. Paul, "the life I now live in the flesh I live by faith in the Son of God, who loved me and gave himself for me" (Gal 2:20). The agony of the psalmist, endured by Jesus, shows us how *to behold the beauty of the Lord* (v. 4) in the crucified One. Finally, as Maillot-Lelièvre point out, Ps 27 provides a fitting morning prayer of confidence to the *Lord, my light* (vv. 1-6) and a sustaining evening prayer of lament and indominable hope, as we *wait for the Lord* (vv. 7-14).

Psalm 28
A Psalm Of David.

I

¹To thee, O Lord, I call;
   my rock, be not deaf to me,
   lest, if thou be silent to me,
   I become like those who go down to the Pit.
²Hear the voice of my supplication,
   as I cry to thee for help,
   as I lift up my hands
   toward thy most holy sanctuary.

³Take me not off with the wicked,
   with those who are workers of evil,
   who speak peace with their neighbors,
   while mischief is in their hearts.
⁴Requite them according to their work,
   and according to the evil of their deeds;
   requite them according to the work of their hands;
   render them their due reward.
⁵Because they do not regard the works of the Lord,

or the works of his hands,
he will break them down and build them up no more.

II

6Blessed be the Lord!
for he has heard the voice of my supplications.
7The Lord is my strength and my shield;
in him my heart trusts;
so I am helped, and my heart exults,
and with my song I give thanks to him.

III

8The Lord is the strength of his people,
he is the saving refuge of his anointed.
9O save thy people, and bless thy heritage;
be thou their shepherd, and carry them for ever.

(I) We are privileged to join the prayer of a desperately
sick person, fearful *to become* like those who go down to the
Pit (v. 1b). The lonely hours are darkened by the silence of
God (*be not deaf to me*, v. 1a) and hounded by the deceitful
words of false friends *who speak peace . . . while mischief is
in their hearts* (v. 3b). This interpretation is reinforced by
the ancient Greek Septuagint which sharpens the meaning
of v. 7b. Instead of a general word of gratitude and confidence, *I am helped*, it reads, "my flesh has revived."

(II) This individual lament follows the normal pattern:
first, the sorrow is placed honestly, even desperately before
the Lord (vv. 1-5); then a prayer of thanksgiving is provided
(vv. 6-7). It is likely that in the liturgical ceremony at the
temple, the thanksgiving was preceded by an oracle of salvation (see Ps 12:5). The same ritual added vv. 8-9, the first of
these verses possibly to accompany a sacrifice of thanksgiving for the king or *anointed one;* the other verse, a choral
refrain for all the people, composed in the postexilic days
when God was their shepherd (Isa 40:11). This final verse
manifests a tendency towards "democratization," extending
to all the people what once was a special relation between
the king and God.

(III) For the reference to the Pit or Sheol in v. 1, see Pss 6:5; 16:10. To understand the curse of the enemy in vv. 3-5, see the discussion about sin-suffering-purification with Ps 7 and the longer exposition with Ps 69.

(IV) The silence of God before a sick person brings to mind the gospel episodes in Luke 7:7, "But say the word and let my servant be healed," and in Luke 5:12, "Lord, if you will, you can make me clean." We are also reminded of the suffering servant of Isaiah who "will not cry or lift up his voice" (Isa 42:2). We think of the silence of Jesus during his Passion; before the Sanhedrin and before Pilate Jesus "was silent and made no answer" (Mark 14:61; 15:5). When Jesus cried aloud from the cross, he drew upon Ps 22, "My God, my God, why hast thou forsaken me?" which continues in the next verse, "O God, I cry by day, but thou does not answer; and by night, but find no rest," (Mark 15:34; Ps 22:1-2). God's silence is fearsome!

Psalm 29
A Psalm Of David.

I

¹Ascribe to the Lord, O heavenly beings,
   ascribe to the Lord glory and strength.
²Ascribe to the Lord the glory of his name;
   worship the Lord in holy array.

II

³The voice of the Lord is upon the waters;
   the God of glory thunders,
   the Lord, upon many waters.
⁴The voice of the Lord is powerful,
   the voice of the Lord is full of majesty.

III

⁵The voice of the Lord breaks the cedars,
   the Lord breaks the cedars of Lebanon.
⁶He makes Lebanon to skip like a calf,
   and Sirion like a young wild ox.
⁷The voice of the Lord flashes forth flames of fire.

IV

⁸The voice of the Lord shakes the wilderness,
the Lord shakes the wilderness of Kadesh.

⁹The voice of the Lord makes the oaks to whirl,
and strips the forest bare;

V

and in his temple all cry, "Glory!"

¹⁰The Lord sits enthroned over the flood;
the Lord sits enthroned as king for ever.
¹¹May the Lord give strength to his people!
May the Lord bless his people with peace!

(I) This cosmic hymn of majestic power and exquisite
beauty breaks loose with lightning that cuts through darkness, splinters oak trees and illumines the heavens, with
thunder roaring across the desert and echoing from canyon
walls, with flood waters collapsing upon earth and driving
boulders along in the fury of their tumultuous might. Borrowed from the Canaanites — or at least written in imitation
of their hymns to Hadad or Baal, god of thunder and
conqueror of the mighty waters — Ps 29 was "historicized"
to acclaim Yahweh, supreme among the awesome forces of
heaven and earth, challenging all opposition and transforming world history by the revelation at Sinai (or Kadesh),
supporting Israel against the hostile power of oceans and
deserts and enthroned forever as King in the Jerusalem
temple.

Ps 29 resonates with the majestic setting of winter storms
and the highly literary form of those most cultured people,
the Canaanites. It also began to accompany and then absorb
the liturgy and history of Israel as it celebrated the theophany of God on Mount Sinai and the final eschatological
appearance of God at the end of time. Many words and
phrases, plus grammatical features, associate Ps 29 with
such an ancient hymn as Exod 15 and with such late hymns
as Pss 93 and 96-99. Ps 29 is one of the most mythological of
hymns in the Bible, surrounding Yahweh with tutelary gods,

the *heavenly beings* in v. 1, called in Hebrew with the same name given to divine attendants of Baal's court in Canaanite mythology. The phrase is corrected by a later theological scruple in Ps 96:7 to "families of the nations"! Thunder is called the *kol Yahweh,* the *voice of the Lord*, similar to Ugaritic mythology which acclaims the *kol Baal.* Yet, Yahweh emerges supreme, for in the second part of vv. 3, 5, 7 the psalm speaks with majestic simplicity of *Yahweh.* The sacred name, in fact, is repeated 18 times! The psalm still insists that Yahweh's majesty can never be adequately communicated by words, only roared out in thunder; eventually Yahweh will submerge the earth in the violently transforming, eschatological age. Ps 29 then has a persevering quality, from the earliest pre-Davidic age to the late postexilic age of eschatological interests.

(II) The opening two verses introduce the hymn and call upon the heavenly court and its counterpart the Jerusalem temple to glorify the Lord. Three stanzas continue the praise and motivate the liturgical assembly to ring out with the *voice of the Lord* (vv. 3-4, 5-7, 8-9ab). The conclusion begins with v. 9c, *in his temple all cry, "Glory!"* where *the Lord[is] enthroned as king,* and repeats another key word from v. 1, *strength* which *Yahweh gives* to *his people* with the blessing of peace.

The Septuagint assigned the psalm to be sung (better, to be orchestrated) on the last day of Tabernacles, a feast that happily celebrated the final harvest (of grapes and olives) and also prayed for rain to break the spell of the dry season (*cf.,* Zech 14:16-18). The Talmud (tract "Sopherim") linked Ps 29 with Pentecost or the Feast of Weeks, the wheat harvest which also commemorated in the later postexilic liturgy the theophany of Yahweh on Mount Sinai and the bestowal of the law to Moses amid thunder, lightning and earthquakes (Exod 19; Ps 68). Christian liturgy has assigned the psalm to the feast of Pentecost; it has influenced the composition of Acts 2.

(III) The invitatory (vv. 1-2) is enhanced with exquisite features of ancient Semitic poetry: *i.e.,* repetition and development of words and sounds, a characteristic exhibited in many lines of the psalm: *i.e.,*

a - b - c	ascribe	to Yahweh	O heavenly beings
↓ ↓ ↓	↓	↓	
a - b - d	ascribe	to Yahweh	glory and strength
↓ ↓ ↓	↓	↓	
a - b - d+e	ascribe	to Yahweh	the glory of his name

V. 1, *heavenly beings:* in Urgaritic/Canaanite mythology, the lesser gods who form the court of the principal deity. We have already discussed this religious pattern with Pss 2 and 8; see also Ps 82. Religiously, it symbolized the majestic greatness of Yahweh; liturgically, it was reflected in the levites who surrounded Yahweh's throne in the Jerusalem temple or earlier sanctuaries; pastorally, it not only showed that Israel's religion was at home in the Canaanite setting, but in fact incorporated and transformed the best of it. It also communicated to the worshipers Yahweh's supreme control over all the elements of the universe: the mighty waves of the sea and the winter storms that threatened their land; forces of fertility and growth, once confided to Baal. V 2, *worship the Lord in holy array:* better to read, "in his wondrous manifestation [in storms or liturgy]" or "in his holy sanctuary." Not only is this new translation closer to the Ugaritic background but it also forms a parallel unit with the first line of the conclusion, *in his temple all cry "Glory!"*

Vv. 3-4, the main features of the psalm appear in this stanza. The opening phrase, *the voice of the Lord,* ought to stand alone, like the sound of thunder that stops all activity and attracts immediate attention: *The thunderous sound of the Lord! it is upon the waters...it is powerful...it is full of majesty...it breaks the cedars,* etc. We have seen that the semites viewed creation as a struggle of order against chaos, of a peaceful land against raging waters (see Ps 8; also Ps 89:9-13; Isa 51:9-10). Generally, the people were thinking of the continuing act of creation which centered in the sanctuary and in royalty, God's means of maintaining good order and the proper sequence of the seasons of the year (see also Ps 2, about royalty). The Bible seldom speaks of "first" creation for its own sake.

Vv. 5-7, the second stanza of motivation for praise, locates the action in Lebanon, where the storm crashes against the mountains that stretch over a hundred miles north to south, in two separate ranges, some peaks rising over 10,000 feet; Sirion (= Hermon, visible from the Lake of Galilee) is 9323 feet. Cedars were highly prized and used profusely in Solomon's building programs (1 Kgs 5:6-10; 6:15; 7:1-3, 11-12); they were also symbols of pride (Isa 10:33-34; Zech 11:2). V. 7 breaks the Hebrew rhythm and overall structure!

Vv. 8-9a: the storm now sweeps into the Arabian desert east of the anti-Lebanese mountain range and here spends itself, yet not without *shaking the wilderness* (literally, making it writhe like a woman in childbirth). Does this symbolize that new life comes from the creative struggle? The original form of v. 8b was not *the wilderness of Kadesh* but as the phrase actually appears in Ugaritic literature, "the holy [or awesome] wilderness," *kadesh* is the common Hebrew/semitic word for "holy." To all these people, the desert was an awesome, fearsome place. The Bible describes the desert as "the great and terrible wilderness, with its fiery serpents and scorpions and thirsty ground" (Deut 8:15). Here bandits take refuge, even David in 2 Sam 22:1; 23:15. Here too devils and hostile forces gather (Isa 13:20; 30:6). Into the desert of Egypt the demon flees in the Book of Tobit (8:3) and here too Jesus is tempted by the devil (Matt 4:1-11; Luke 4:1-13). By re-reading the word as a proper place-name, the awesome wilderness becomes Kadesh [Barnea], where the Israelites encamped during the Mosaic period, south of the promised land in the Negeb. An entirely new geographical-theological interpretation is now given to the psalm. The storm is portrayed pushing in from the Mediterranean Sea, driving against the Lebanese and Anti-Lebanese mountains and when it reaches the eastern desert cutting directly south and then making a turn again towards the west and the Mediterranean. Thus it completes its circuit around the promised land. Kadesh enabled Israel to join the Mosaic traditions from Kadesh with Canaanite mythology.

Vv. 9c-11. The conclusion portrays Yahweh, majestically enthroned above the flood (the Hebrew word is used elsewhere only of Noah's flood in Gen 6-9 and Sir 44:17), and his presence merges with the Jerusalem temple. The temple was always thought to be a mirror of the heavenly. The words, *glory* and *strength* of v. 1 are repeated in the finale. The final blessing is one of *peace*, tranquility, new creation. This peace may seem very fragile, as the storm continues to encircle the country, yet because of faith in Yahweh that peace is as secure as God's throne.

One way of summarizing this extraordinary psalm lies in its many movements: culturally and religiously from a background of Canaanite/Ugaritic mythology to an Israelite setting of worship of the one supreme God, Yahweh; again religiously and politically from Yahweh's enthronement as supreme among the gods (from a comparison with Exod 15:11; 1 Kgs 22:19-23), to a later supporting presence in the Jerusalem temple for the sake of the Davidic dynasty, to a still later, postexilic celebration of the one God enthroned at the temple (Pss 96-99); spacially from Yahweh's theophany in the heavenly sphere in the first part of the psalm to the Jerusalem temple in vv. 9c-10; thematically, from glory and strength in v. 1 to glory, strength and peace in vv. 9-11; metaphorically from the raging storm in the first part to the peaceful environment in the latter part; time-wise from quick flashes of lightning and passing rolls of thunder to the perpetual enthronement as "king for ever" in v. 10; geographically from the northern mountains of Lebanon to the southern wilderness at Kadesh.

(IV) Ps 29 brings us face to face with important liturgical principles. God did not reveal, nor Israel create its liturgical forms. The earliest hymns came from Canaanite inspiration; even its symbols for appreciating Yahweh were Canaanite creations. The Sinaitic covenant and Mosaic intuition of Yahweh provided the spirit or soul; Canaan contributed the material substance or body. Yet even this material element enabled Israel to have religious insights into the mystery of Yahweh as creating and sustaining the universe which was lacking from Mosaic times. Ps 29 also shows the way to blend cultural masterpieces with religious celebration, even if the culture retains mythological elements. To have suppressed mythology would have deprived Israel of important insights into the mystery of Yahweh. Mythology maintained the element of mystery without which religion is always in danger of being over-formalized and over-rationalized and so becoming superstitious (where human or physical aspects of religion are worshiped as divine). Provided the deity is correctly identified (as Yahweh or Jesus), then the superstition of worshiping false gods is avoided. The seven-fold repetition of *kol Yahweh* —*the voice of the Lord* (sometimes the psalm is called the psalm of the seven thunders — Franz Delitzsch) attunes us to the *power of the divine word* in biblical religion, its force in shaking the world to its foundations and in creating a new heaven and a new earth.

Psalm 30
A Psalm Of David. A Song At The Dedication Of The Temple

I
¹I will extol thee, O Lord, for thou hast drawn me up,
   and hast not let my foes rejoice over me.
²O Lord my God, I cried to thee for help,
   and thou hast healed me.
³O Lord, thou hast brought up my soul from Sheol,
   restored me to life from among those gone down to the
      Pit.

II
⁴Sing praises to the Lord, O you his saints,
   and give thanks to his holy name.
⁵For his anger is but for a moment,
   and his favor is for a lifetime.
 Weeping may tarry for the night,
   but joy comes with the morning.

III

⁶As for me, I said in my prosperity,
"I shall never be moved."
⁷By thy favor, O Lord,
thou hadst established me as a strong mountain;
thou didst hide thy face,
I was dismayed.

⁸To thee, O Lord, I cried;
and to the Lord I made supplication:
⁹"What profit is there in my death,
if I go down to the Pit?
Will the dust praise thee?
Will it tell of thy faithfulness?
¹⁰Hear, O Lord, and be gracious to me!
O Lord, be thou my helper!"

IV

¹¹Thou hast turned for me my mourning into dancing;
thou hast loosed my sackcloth
and girded me with gladness,
¹²that my soul may praise thee and not be silent.
O Lord my God, I will give thanks to thee for ever.

(I) We begin a small series of thanksgiving psalms (Pss 30-34), this first one in gratitude for a sudden, perhaps miraculous cure of a very sick person. Both v. 3 and v. 9 explicitly refer to death and the grave. The possibility of dying prematurely seems more harrowing than usual, perhaps because the psalmist was young or belonged to the temple personnel who served closely the God of Life (see Ps 16). Besides the double references to death and Sheol, there seem to be more than the usual number of references to temple services. This closeness to the temple may explain why a phrase was added to the title in the Hebrew text in between the words *A Psalm* and *of David*, thus breaking the normal pattern. At the rededication of the temple, either after the return from exile (Ezr 3:7-13) or more likely at the time of the Maccabees (1 Macc 4:52-59), these words were inserted: *A Song at the dedication of the Temple.* The

Hebrew word for dedication, *hanukkah*, makes us think of the event in Maccabees which was the origin of the feast of Hanukkah.

(II) There are problems! The rhythm is very uneven and v. 7 is almost unintelligible in the Hebrew. These disturbances may be due to frequent use in the ritual and lead us to understand better the evolution and structure of Ps 30.

Vv. 1-3, a call to praise and to thank Yahweh. After the initial call, *I will extol thee*, we meet three times the divine name *Yahweh,* in each instance introducing a motive for the individual psalmist to thank God.

Vv. 4-5 invite the entire congregation to join in a public expression of gratitude.

Vv. 6-10, an abrupt change of mood as the psalmist recounts dreadful sickness and prays for help. In this section, vv. 6-7 seem like a separate exposition, added later (?) to relate the psalm to a serious national trial like the desecration of the temple and its eventual rededication, in 1 Macc 4:36-59; 2 Macc 6:1-5; 10:1-8. Vv. 8-10 form a close unit, beginning with *to thee, O Lord, I cried* (v. 8a) and ending with *Hear, O Lord* (v. 10a).

The psalm ends with vv. 11-12 as the psalmist celebrates a return to health in the midst of temple dancing and praise.

(III) Vv. 1-3, praising and thanking God for a cure from serious sickness. From v. 2, *thou has healed me*, we see that the Bible never disentangled sickness or health from God, nor for that matter from sin and virtue. It always viewed this topic from a wide focus lens and saw the individual within the complex of community, whether it be ancestors, living people or those yet to be born. In this sense we interpret Exod 34:7, "punishing children...to the third and fourth generation for their parents' wickedness." Deut 32:39 summarized it: "As God, I kill and I make alive; I wound and I heal." The Bible does not over-simplify the mystery to state that all suffering is due to sin; neither does the Bible form an adequate theological explanation of how the parts relate to one another. Healing is not the exclusive domain of medical or social workers, nor of religious ministers. For *sheol, pit*, see Pss 6:5; 16:10; 28:1.

Vv. 4-5 invite the congregation to imitate the gratitude of the psalmist so that each person can experience the same wondrous process of healing. Liturgy does far more than recall or commemorate; it actualizes an entire episode. One important key to the mystery of sickness/suffering is provided in v. 5, *weeping may tarry for the night:* sorrow is only a short stage along the way to life's fullest joys (*cf.,* Isa 54:7, "[only] for a brief moment I forsook you," or Isa 26:20 in the Septuagint, quoted by Heb 10:37, "yet a little while, and the coming one shall come and shall not tarry"). Part of God's purpose in the *weeping* of the psalmist was to give us the consolation of Ps 30!

Vv. 6-10 place the sorrow honestly before God, a section that usually comes not after but before the expression of gratitude. The words, *I shall never be moved* (v. 6), reflect the typical problem of "religious" people who claim special privileges with God; they especially must learn that God's gifts reach beyond what they deserve. If this interpretation is correct, v. 6 is more a cleansing of the heart than a statement for our instruction and edification; the inspired word of Scripture provides us with the process *towards* sanctity, not always its best or final form! V. 9 is bothered, as are many parts of the OT, with Sheol's useless, dreary existence. How does it benefit God or anyone. *Cf.,* Isa 38:18-19; or Exod 32:11-14 when Moses argued against God and appealed to his honor before Egyptian ridicule if Israel, despite its sins, would have been destroyed.

(IV) We need this psalm in order to discover prayer and God's presence in the midst of our questions and complaints — also in order to discover ourselves in the midst of the liturgical assembly. The former provides us with an honest representation of our true self, always the base of genuine spirituality; the latter, with the assistance of family and neighbors. That the psalm became a standard part of synagogal services shows that everyone, even Israel officially as God's chosen people, needed this expression of helplessness and questioning in the passage from personal sickness and national collapse to renewed health and the rededication of the temple.

Psalm 31
To The Choirmaster. A Psalm Of David.

I

¹In thee, O Lord, do I seek refuge;
   let me never be put to shame;
   in thy righteousness deliver me!
²Incline thy ear to me,
   rescue me speedily!
 Be thou a rock of refuge for me,
   a strong fortress to save me!

³Yea, thou art my rock and my fortress;
   for thy name's sake lead me and guide me,
⁴take me out of the net which is hidden for me,
   for thou art my refuge.
⁵Into thy hand I commit my spirit;
   thou hast redeemed me, O Lord, faithful God.

⁶Thou hatest those who pay regard to vain idols;
   but I trust in the Lord.
⁷I will rejoice and be glad for thy steadfast love,
   because thou hast seen my affliction,
   thou hast taken heed of my adversities,
⁸and hast not delivered me into the hand of the enemy;
   thou hast set my feet in a broad place.

II

⁹Be gracious to me, O Lord, for I am in distress;
   my eye is wasted from grief,
   my soul and my body also.
¹⁰For my life is spent with sorrow,
   and my years with sighing;
 my strength fails because of my misery,
   and my bones waste away.

¹¹I am the scorn of all my adversaries,
   a horror to my neighbors,
   an object of dread to my acquaintances;

those who see me in the street flee from me.
12I have passed out of mind like one who is dead;
  I have become like a broken vessel.
13Yea, I hear the whispering of many—
  terror on every side!—
 as they scheme together against me,
  as they plot to take my life.

14But I trust in thee, O Lord,
  I say, "Thou art my God."
15My times are in thy hand;
  deliver me from the hand of my
    enemies and persecutors!
16Let thy face shine on thy servant;
  save me in thy steadfast love!
17Let me not be put to shame, O Lord,
  for I call on thee;
 let the wicked be put to shame,
  let them go dumbfounded to Sheol.
18Let the lying lips be dumb,
  which speak insolently against the righteous
  in pride and contempt.

III

19O how abundant is thy goodness,
  which thou hast laid up for those who fear thee,
 and wrought for those who take refuge in thee,
  in the sight of the sons of men!
20In the covert of thy presence thou hidest them
  from the plots of men;
 thou holdest them safe under thy shelter
  from the strife of tongues.

21Blessed be the Lord,
  for he has wondrously shown his steadfast love to me
  when I was beset as in a beseiged city.
22I had said in my alarm,
  "I am driven far from thy sight."
 But thou didst hear my supplications,
  when I cried to thee for help.

IV

²³Love the Lord, all you his saints!
   The Lord preserves the faithful,
      but abundantly requites him who acts haughtily.
²⁴Be strong, and let your heart take courage,
      all you who wait for the Lord!

(I) Literary critics have found this psalm one of the most troubling in the psalter, yet the disturbed and suffering heart of Jesus on the cross (Luke 23:46) and of Stephen prostrate beneath a barrage of stones (Acts 7:59) discovered peace in its words: *into thy hand I commend my spirit* (v. 5). This same versicle has been a part of the evening prayer of the church for centuries, as men and women sought God's blessing and peace at day's end. Girolamo Savonarola was writing from this psalm "at day's end," when they came to drag him off to burning at the stake.

Everyone admits that the psalmist was no creative genius but has drawn freely from other biblical passages, especially from Jeremiah and other psalms, or better shall we say that the author has drunk deeply from the wellsprings of pro-phetical tradition and liturgical prayer. We offer a few examples for comparison:

vv. 1-3a	identical with Ps 71:1-3	v. 10	and Jer 20:18
v. 7b	and Ps 10:14	v. 12	and Jer 22:8; 43:38
v. 9a	and Pss 35; 38; 39; 71	v. 13	and Jer 20:10
v. 10a	and Ps 38:10	v. 17	and Jer 17:18

Better still, shall we consider the author a mystic, contem-plating and absorbing the word of God and making the divine words a carrier of human experiences which no other words could express? Yet the psalmist did not quote, except in citing Ps 71:1-3 in the first three verses of this poem. Otherwise biblical phrases receive a new life and one per-ceives a new depth of insight into God's presence with the devout Israelite at prayer. The psalmist must have plum-meted into the depths of a loathsome disease like leprosy, so that neighbors and acquaintances reacted with revulsion (v.

11); they not only attempted to avoid the afflicted person but even plotted to get that one out of the way (vv. 13, 20).

(II) Without being overly confident we suggest reading the poem as a single psalm according to L. Jacquet's division:

vv. 1-8   Prayer of   vv. 19-22 Prayer of
            Confidence;   Thanksgiving;
vv. 9-18 Prayer of   vv. 23-24 Liturgical Addition:
            Supplication;   didactic praise.

The momentum towards vv. 19-22 would say that the psalm is principally one of thanksgiving.

(III) In the opening section (vv. 1-8), the psalmist rests his or her confidence on the *justice* or *righteousness* of Yahweh, understood in the sense that the Lord will be just in fulfilling his own promises of forgiveness and protection. For the same reason the psalmist appeals to God *for thy name's sake* (v. 3), as though God reveals his person (a synonym for name) and the secrets of his hopes and love through compassion (see Ps 23:3). These divine virtues of compassion and fidelity, conspicuous in God's revelation to Moses on Mount Sinai (Exod 34:6-7), also explain who is the Lord appearing to Moses in the burning bush, an episode to which the psalmist seems to refer in v. 7. The Lord said to Moses from the burning bush: "I have seen the affliction of my people who are in Egypt, and have heard their cry because of the taskmasters; I know their sufferings, and I have come down to deliver them" (Exod 3:7).

Vv. 9-18, *Lament.* Here the rhythm changes to that of the dirge (3 + 2) and a concatenation of penitential phrases occurs similar to Pss 6; 13; 38; 41; 88. The section opens with the classic supplication, *be gracious to me,* in Hebrew *ḥanneni,* found in Pss 4:1; 6:2; 41:4, 10; 51:1; etc. Agony seems everywhere: *my eye is wasted, my soul and body* (literally, my belly), *my years* (the haunting of memory), *my bones waste away*; it closes in on the psalmist from *adversaries,* closer still from *neighbors,* still closer with *acquaintances,* so that like Jeremiah the psalmist seems to hear *terror on every side* (Jer 6:25; 20:3-4, 10; 46:5; 49:29). This person, agonizing in bones and flesh, in memory and loneliness, ought to be allowed at least to groan, and yet even this sound is whispered back with ridicule.

Vv. 19-22. The psalm modulates in meter (again 3 + 3) and into a touching scene of the Lord's *abundant goodness* (v. 19). Too hideous and contagious for anyone else, still too anxious to refer directly to himself, the psalmist says to the Lord in v. 20: *you hide them* [people like me] *beneath the secrecy of your face* (or with a slight variation of the Hebrew word for *face*) *beneath the secrecy of your wings*. Vv. 19-20 may refer to the psalmist's readmission to the temple and a ritual of purification and thanksgiving (see Ps 26).

Vv. 23-24, a didactic type of praise, opening with a phrase unusual for the OT in its directness: *love the Lord* (*cf.,* Ps 18:1; 26:8; Deut 6:5).

(IV) Ps 31 provides a healthy norm for all biblical interpretation (see also Ps 14:3). In citing other texts or traditions, the psalmist does not feel obliged to remain within the ancient historical setting or established meaning. Inspired passages are re-inspired within the needs and anxieties, the hopes and endurance of a new setting, and as such they are shared with the entire community. Israel at prayer remains the basic norm for Israel at study with its Bible. We also see how private piety is fed by the more official traditions of Israel, and these latter in turn are enriched by the contemplative insights of the saints. Our reflections too can turn in the direction of morality: people who would have been excluded from the community and particularly from its religious leadership because of their physical condition are the very ones to penetrate most deeply into the sacred tradition and to have the most divine right of all to participate in temple ritual. Mystically, we are privileged to witness the immanent presence of God with a person who feels *like one who is dead...like a broken vessel* [who can] *hear* [only] *the whispering of many — terror on every side*. God is most present when God seems most absent, the terrifying way of the mystics.

In a discourse on Ps 31 St. Augustine wrote: "If the psalm prays, pray; if it grieves, grieve; if it is happy, rejoice; if it hopes, hope; and if it fears, be afraid. For everything that is written here is a mirror in which we see ourselves" (quoted by Claude Peifer in *The Bible Today*, April 1974).

Psalm 32
A Psalm Of David. A Maskil.

I

¹Blessed is he whose transgression is forgiven,
    whose sin is covered.
²Blessed is the man to whom the Lord
    imputes no iniquity,
    and in whose spirit there is no deceit.

II

³When I declared not my sin, my body wasted away
    through my groaning all day long.
⁴For day and night thy hand was heavy upon me;
    my strength was dried up as by the heat of summer.
                                                    Selah

⁵I acknowledged my sin to thee,
    and I did not hide my iniquity;
  I said, "I will confess my transgressions to the Lord";
    then thou didst forgive the guilt of my sin.   *Selah*

III

⁶Therefore let every one who is godly
    offer prayer to thee;
  at a time of distress, in the rush of great waters,
    they shall not reach him.
⁷Thou art a hiding place for me,
    thou preservest me from trouble;
    thou dost encompass me with deliverance.   *Selah*

IV

⁸I will instruct you and teach you
    the way you should go;

I will counsel you with my eye upon you.
⁹Be not like a horse or a mule, without understanding,
which must be curbed with bit and bridle,
else it will not keep with you.

¹⁰Many are the pangs of the wicked;
but steadfast love surrounds him who trusts in the Lord.

V
¹¹Be glad in the Lord, and rejoice, O righteous,
and shout for joy, all you upright in heart!

(I) While tears and sorrow permeate Ps 6, the first of the seven Penitential Psalms, here in the second we sense the relief once the sinner no longer covers up the offense but *confess[es] my transgressions to the Lord* (v. 5b). As A. Maillot-A. Lelièvre point out, the principal sin here is not so much disobedience but dissimulation. The key word is cover or uncover. As long as the psalmist refused to uncover the offense, *my body wasted away through my groaning all day long;* but if God uncovers the sin, then it is forgiven and the psalmist acquires a *spirit [where] there is no deceit* (v. 2b), an *upright[ness] in heart* (v. 11b), a sense of the Lord's *steadfast covenant love [that] surrounds him*, in other words, a total, interior transformation. Even though the psalmist may seem to take the initiative in admitting guilt, still the Lord was already at work, as the psalmist concedes in the prayer: *For day and night thy hand was heavy upon me* (v. 4a). By God's hidden pressure upon the conscience, the psalmist's *body wasted away* and there was *groaning all day long* (v. 3). The psalm makes it clear then that the sinful person does not decide when and how and why to return to the Lord; God takes the first, real though hidden initiative. What begins secretly, however, ends up as a public confession within a liturgical ceremony of thanksgiving.

(II) The Hebrew text is quite poor, and as E. Beaucamp says, encumbered with "glosses" or additions which are sometimes illegible (vv. 4 and 9) or useless (v. 2b and 5)! The meter is disturbed. Explanations of structure and basic form tend to be contradictory or confusing from one author to another. While a strong didactic feature is evident in vv. 1-2 and 6-10, still the overarching intent seems to be thanksgiving to God. In subdividing the psalm, it is wise to keep one eye on the text and the other eye on temple ceremony:

vv. 1-2,   a blessing spoken by the priest upon the forgiven person;

vv. 3-5,   autobiographical, the pain of concealing one's faults and the peace from confessing one's sins;

vv. 6-7,   homiletic advice, drawn by the priest from the sinner's experience, or an antiphonal response sung by the temple choir;

vv. 8-10, oracle (see Ps 12:5), spoken by the priest in the name of God, again with the accent upon instruction;

v. 11,   concluding song of praise and thanksgiving, sung by the entire congregation.

(III) The initial blessing (vv. 1-2) like Ps 51 is rich in the vocabulary for sin and forgiveness. The first word, *transgression* or *pesha'*, implies rebellion against one's legitimate superior or one's own conscience; the second, *sin* or *ḥaṭa'ah*, means to wander from God's ways like an arrow that misses the target; the third, *iniquity* or *'awon*, indicates crookedness, similar to a tree out of shape from strong winds or the collapse of earth. Therefore, something unnatural or perverted, something against normal growth and response, is implied in each word. Vv. 1-2 are quoted by St. Paul in Rom 4:6-8, to finalize his own conviction that human works by themselves are useless to obtain pardon; God must work interiorly to correct and transform what has become basically unnatural or perverted.

Vv. 3-5 follow the steps of conversion: at first, extreme weakness, physically and emotionally (vv. 3-4); then, a decision to *confess my transgression* [publicly] *to the Lord* (v. 5c); after that, the acknowledgement itself (v. 5ab); and finally, pardon (v. 5d). In delineating these steps, L. Jacquet also draws our attention to the sequence of events in the parable of the Prodigal Son (Luke 15:11-32) where the youth's resolve to return home was anticipated and surely influenced by the parent who was already waiting for him from a distance, saw the boy first, and then "ran and embraced him and kissed him."

(IV) This psalm is needed by everyone of us when we succumb to the illusion of being without sin (John 8:7). It urges us to stop covering up and to come clean; it is God's instrument in this initial stirring of grace. The interaction of the individual with God, both in a private way and then within the temple liturgy, shows the double dimensions of sin and forgiveness. In some Byzantine rites, the priest recites this psalm three times as a way of personal purification before conferring the sacrament of baptism. The Ashkenazi Jews of Eastern European origin recite the psalm as night prayer on the second day of the week (Monday).

Psalm 33

I

¹Rejoice in the Lord, O you righteous!
  Praise befits the upright.
²Praise the Lord with the lyre,
  make melody to him with the harp of ten strings!
³Sing to him a new song,
  play skillfully on the strings, with loud shouts.

II

⁴For the word of the Lord is upright;
  and all his work is done in faithfulness.
⁵He loves righteousness and justice;
  the earth is full of the steadfast love of the Lord.

⁶By the word of the Lord the heavens were made,
  and all their host by the breath of his mouth.
⁷He gathered the waters of the sea as in a bottle;
  he put the deeps in storehouses.

⁸Let all the earth fear the Lord,
  let all the inhabitants of the world stand in awe of him!
⁹For he spoke, and it came to be;
  he commanded, and it stood forth.

¹⁰The Lord brings the counsel of the nations to nought;
  he frustrates the plans of the peoples.
¹¹The counsel of the Lord stands for ever,
  the thoughts of his heart to all generations.
¹²Blessed is the nation whose God is the Lord,
  the people whom he has chosen as his heritage!

¹³The Lord looks down from heaven,
  he sees all the sons of men;
¹⁴from where he sits enthroned he looks forth
  on all the inhabitants of the earth,
¹⁵he who fashions the hearts of them all,
  and observes all their deeds.

¹⁶A king is not saved by his great army;
  a warrior is not delivered by his great strength.
¹⁷The war horse is a vain hope for victory,
  and by its great might it cannot save.

¹⁸Behold, the eye of the Lord is on those who fear him,
  on those who hope in his steadfast love,
¹⁹that he may deliver their soul from death,
  and keep them alive in famine.

II

²⁰Our soul waits for the Lord;
  he is our help and shield.
²¹Yea, our heart is glad in him,
  because we trust in his holy name.
²²Let thy steadfast love, O Lord, be upon us,
  even as we hope in thee.

(I) A glorious symphony of praise rings out to Yahweh, Creator and Ruler of the universe. Temple musicians echo the melody of heaven and earth, of dry land and ocean waters. The good order of cosmic creation continues in the history of nations and especially among the Lord's chosen people, Israel. Creation by the word of God resonates within this psalm not only with the word proclaimed and sung within the temple liturgy but also with the word of divine wisdom in the sapiential literature (Prov 8:22-31; Sir

24). The psalm, therefore, is sometimes dated in the postexilic age, the flourishing period of the sapiential literature, but there are also good reasons to place its origin very early.

Ps 33 has no title, something very unusual in Book One of the psalter (Pss 1-41); it seems to have been attracted to its present location by the final verse of Ps 32. The fact that it is not attributed to David may mean that it originated within non-Israelite circles, perhaps with the early inhabitants of Jerusalem called the Jebusites. Stylistic features link it with ancient Semitic poetry: *i.e.,*

> *binary or two-word combinations,* 18 altogether: *i.e., righteous. . .upright* in v. 1; *upright. . .faithful* in v. 4; *forever. . .to all generations* in v. 11;
>
> *stereotype phrases,* 12 altogether: *e.g., rejoice in the Lord, O you righteous,* also in Ps 97:12; *make melody to him with the harp,* also in the Hebrew text of Pss 98:5; 147:7;
>
> *word-chains: e.g.,* earth, heavens and host of heavens in vv. 5-7.

Therefore, even if Ps 33 appears as expansive as the universe and world history, it remains a highly structured poem. As mentioned already in connection with Ps 29, some of Israel's finest poetry and liturgical forms were received from foreigners. Israel clearly identified the God who was being celebrated in these psalms, as Yahweh (*cf.,* v. 12), but through these "pagan" compositions, as in the case of Ps 33, Israel received new insights into the creative power of the word, a religious idea certainly not indigenous to Israel, but prominent in the religious literature of Egypt and Babylon.

(II) Ps 33 can be considered a hymn of praise, possibly with a strong sapiential influence. The division and liturgical orchestration may have followed this pattern which we suggest if only to appreciate the close interaction within the psalm.

vv. 1-3   *Call to praise*
       v. 1 sung by the entire assembly
       vv. 2-3 by choir no. 1
vv. 4-19 *Motivation for praise*
       vv. 4-9, from the cosmos
          vv. 4-5, sung by choir no. 2
          vv. 6-9, by choir no. 1
       vv. 10-19, from human history
          vv. 10-12, about the nations; sung by choir no. 2
          vv. 13-19, about individuals, sung by choir no. 1
vv. 20-22 *Conclusion*
       vv. 20-21, by choirs no. 1 and 2
       v. 22, by the entire congregation.

(III) Vv. 1-3, the opening call to praise, introduce a phrase rich in theological and liturgical meaning: *a new song.* Elsewhere it occurs only in exilic and postexilic hymns: Isa 42:10; Ps 40:3; 46:1; 98:1; 144:9; 149:1. The idea reverberates among the New Testament hymns of the Book of Revelation 5:9; 14:3. Seeking *what* is precisely *new*, we find that it may be: literary, a new role is given to ancient hymns; or pastoral, a new deliverance by God; or ritual, a spontaneous shout or song of the people; or best of all, theological, in that God's redemptive acts are actualized in their full effect within a new generation of Israelites (see the discussion of Ps 22:22-31).

Vv. 4-9, God's justice across the universe. Not only the repeated acclamation of God's justice but the use of many covenant terms, alerts us that the world bears a quality of dependability, good purpose and irresistible momentum to be and do what God wants. Not without a touch of humor, as Maillot-Lelièvre remark, v. 6b attributes the origin of the heavenly host, worshiped as supreme deities by Egyptians and Babylonians, to the simple breathing of Yahweh! V. 9, *he spoke and it came to be*, is one of the clearest statements of the power of God's word and leads to an important insight into biblical liturgy. Words alone would be futile and frustrating; actions alone would be circular, exhaustive, and meaningless. Words and actions, however, each contain a mystery which can be appreciated only by the other; together they release an extraordinary power of the living God. This combination of word and action rests at the heart of the liturgical assembly. As today in the case of the Eucharist: bread and wine by themselves would remain bodily food, nothing more; the words, "This is my body...my blood," spoken in isolation without the bread and wine would be meaningless. Together they announce the presence of Jesus, renewing and actualizing the mysteries of his death and new glorious life in our midst.

Vv. 10-19, history prolongs creation and reveals more fully God's justice in remembering his promises of steadfast love. The meaning which God placed within the created world becomes ever clearer for us through the religion of Israel, *the people whom he has chosen as his heritage* (v. 12). While vv. 4-7 refer to God's *word* and vv. 8-12 to God's *plans and counsel*, vv. 10-19 speak of *eye of the Lord* (v. 18), looking down from heaven with interest, steadfast love and powerful protection. God keeps busy in his heavenly home!

Vv. 20-22, conclusion. The final verse is also the end of ancient hymn, *Te Deum*.

(IV) While pagan religions supplied the motif of God's creative word, the religion of Israel perceived that word to be personal, dependable, loving and faithful, fulfilling all the potential of the created universe through Israel, God's chosen people. The personal character of God's word in the Old Testament evolves into the Person of Jesus Christ, the Word who is God, through whom all things are made (John 1:1-3), the word who is the image of the invisible God through whom and for whom all things were created (Col 1:15-16), the Word re-creating our lives today, particularly through the consecrating words of Scripture, heard again in the liturgical assembly.

Psalm 34
A Psalm Of David, When He Feigned Madness Before
Abimelech, So That He Drove Him Out, And He Went
Away.

I

¹I will bless the Lord at all times;
  his praise shall continually be in my mouth.
²My soul makes its boast in the Lord;
  let the afflicted hear and be glad.
³O magnify the Lord with me,
  and let us exalt his name together!

II

⁴I sought the Lord, and he answered me,
  and delivered me from all my fears.
⁵Look to him, and be radiant;
  so your faces shall never be ashamed.
⁶This poor man cried, and the Lord heard him,
  and saved him out of all his troubles.
⁷The angel of the Lord encamps
  around those who fear him, and delivers them.
⁸O taste and see that the Lord is good!
  Happy is the man who takes refuge in him!

III

¹¹Come, O sons, listen to me,
  I will teach you the fear of the Lord.

¹⁸The Lord is near to the brokenhearted,
  and saves the crushed in spirit.

²⁰He keeps all his bones;
  not one of them is broken.

IV

²²The Lord redeems the life of his servants;
  none of those who take refuge in him will be condemned.

(I) This alphabetical psalm, almost identical in structure
with Ps 25 but thematically different, emphasizes thanksgiving and instruction. Structurally both psalms begin each

new line with the succeeding letter of the Hebrew alphabet,
except that the letter *waw* is overlooked and an extra line is
added at the end of the series, repeating the letter *pe* (see Ps
25). In the second part of Ps 34 (vv. 11-22) a didactic style
and vocabulary become ever more visible. The entire psalm,
moreover, evolves around the principle of retribution — the
good are rewarded and evil people punished — common in
sapiential literature like the Book of Proverbs. From the
constant way that the psalmist returns to troubles, affliction
and helplessness, we conclude that he probably experienced
more than life's normal share of problems. Yet the psalm
always concludes to the Lord's fidelity towards *the one who
takes refuge in him* (vv. 8 and 22).

(II) The strophic division is evident enough: vv. 1-3,
hymnic introduction; vv. 4-10, grateful witness to the Lord's
care for those who seek him; vv. 11-21, didactic instruction;
v. 22, a liturgical conclusion/addition, lest the psalm end
too negatively.

(III) The long title provides an opportunity for us to see
how scribes of the late postexilic age looked for incidents in
Israel's early history, not only to provide an interpretive
setting, but also to form an integral unity in Israel's long
religious development. Similarly the New Testament will
call upon the Old Testament, often enough by an association of words, to enlighten the history and theology of Jesus
and to show that "you are all one in Christ Jesus," as "there
is neither Jew nor Greek, neither slave nor free, neither male
nor female" (Gal 3:28). Ps 34 contains two Hebrew words,
ta'amu (*taste*, in v. 8) and *tithhallel* (*make a boast*, in v. 2),
which occur with only a slight variation in spelling but a
significant difference of meaning in the story of David. 1
Sam 21:13 states that in the presence of the Philistine king
Achish "David changed his behavior [in Hebrew, *ta'mo*, his
perception, sense, taste or behavior] and feigned himself
mad [in Hebrew, *hithholel*]." Because of the word similar-
ity, *ta'amu* and *ta'mo, tithhallel* and *hithholel*, the psalm
could now be associated with David. Later another scribe
confused Achish, king of Gath (in Hebrew, *'akish melek-
gath*) with a king of Gerar named Abimelek (Gen 20 and 26).

It seems that *'akish-melek* was read, or better was heard in the oral means of transmission, as *'abi-melek;* in Hebrew the letters "b" and "k" are almost identical in shape and the sound is very close. Out of respect for the sacred text, the confusion was never corrected. Moreover, in the psalms much more attention is paid to the role of history for knowing God's ways than for its details.

The phrase, *the angel of the Lord* (v. 7), in Hebrew, "angel of Yahweh," can be a reverential way of speaking about Yahweh, similar to "name" or "face" of Yahweh. Actually this angel frequently merges into the person of Yahweh, as in Gen 16:9, 13; Exod 3:2-6. It is often associated with Yahweh's help in serious danger and warfare (Exod 23:20-33). The recommendation in v. 8, *taste and see that the Lord is good*, implies knowledge by experience rather than by any didactic process; it can be identified with what the scholastics called "knowledge by connaturality," knowledge that comes from being the kind of person we are. This verse is incorporated into 1 Pet 2:3, "You have tasted the kindness of the Lord," and so became a standard piece in the eucharistic prayers of the church. First Peter is probably reflecting an early Christian ritual that combined baptism with Eucharist.

In the sapiential instruction of vv. 11-21, we meet words and phrases at home within the Book of Proverbs. V. 10 is quoted in the Passion narrative of John's gospel, that not a single bone of Jesus' body was to be broken. With the fuller background of Ps 34 John is implying that God will *redeem the life of his servant* (v. 22), and that Jesus will surely be raised to a new, glorious life.

(IV) When everything seems lost and we feel at the end of our endurance, we need Ps 34. It will encourage us to persevere to the end, and like the great saints mentioned in the Epistle to the Hebrews, chap. 11, we will eventually *taste* (fully realize by long experience) *and see* (as though by a vision of all that is in store for us) *that the Lord is good!* Then we can anticipate our heavenly song of thanksgiving on earth. As we *take refuge* now *in him*, the Lord, we will have a foretaste of eternal peace.

Psalm 35
A Psalm Of David.

> [11]Malicious witnesses rise up;
>   they ask me of things that I know not.
> [12]They requite me evil for good;
>   my soul is forlorn.
> [13]But I, when they were sick—
>   I wore sackcloth,
>   I afflicted myself with fasting.
>   I prayed with head bowed on my bosom,
> [14] as though I grieved for my friend or my brother;
>   I went about as one who laments his mother,
>   bowed down and in mourning.
>
> [15]But at my stumbling they gathered in glee,
>   they gathered together against me;
>   cripples whom I knew not
>   slandered me without ceasing;
> [16]they impiously mocked more and more,
>   gnashing at me with their teeth,
> [17]How long, O Lord, wilt thou look on?
>   Rescue me from their ravages,
>   my life from the lions!

(I) From a textual and literary viewpoint Ps 35 may receive a poor rating, at least at first reading. The Hebrew text is overloaded with glosses and corrections, suspicious and even incomprehensible words; many phrases seem to have been borrowed from other psalms of lament. In a monotonous way it repeats its theme three times. However, upon closer reading we find many redeeming qualities: a) a rapid, direct address (*draw the spear / Lord, who is like thee? / How long, O Lord? / they open their mouths and say, "Aha, Aha!"*); b) vigorous images (*draw the spear and the javelin / dark and slippery way / my life from the lions*); c) strong emotions (*I grieved for my brother / as one who laments his mother / thou hast seen it, O Lord; be not silent*). The psalmist is falsely accused and is caught in a trap of intrigue within the judiciary system; he can only take the case immediately to Yahweh. Personal details fade away and must be read in between the lines. The psalmist has preserved his privacy quite well, and so the loneliness is all the more harrowing. It seems impossible to date the psalm, probably because it did not reach full canonical status within Israel without a long existence in private prayer and only later expanded and adapted to public worship — something like the Book of Jeremiah, in whose tradition it stands (*cf.,* Jer 18:18-23; 20:10-31).

(II) The three sections of Ps 35 follow a similar pattern: a manifesto of persecution and calumny; imprecation against the deceivers and traitors (see Ps 69); petition for God's intervention; final word of gratitude. Because each strophe ends with thanksgiving, some consider Ps 35 to be a Prayer of Thanksgiving, particularly as used with the public liturgy; others point to the long supplication and classify the psalm as an Individual Lament. With much hesitation we favor the latter classification. About the only aspect of the psalm that is immediately clear is its division: Vv. 1-10, with images from warfare and the hunt of wild animals, against those secretly planning evil; vv. 11-18, with images from family and friendship, against ingrates who turn against an innocent friend; vv. 19-28, with images from the criminal court, against perfidious people.

(III) We restrict our comments to the second strophe. Vv. 11-18 provide us with a setting of public mourning. *Sackcloth* was worn against the skin, leaving a person no peace. References are frequent enough in the Bible: Gen 37:34, when Jacob hears about the "death" of Joseph; 2 Sam 3:31, when news is brought to David about the death of Abner, commander-in-chief of Saul's army; Joel 1:13, "Gird on sackcloth and lament, O priests...Go in, pass the night in sackcloth"; also Pss 30:11; 69:11. *Fasting* was undertaken during dangerous or sorrowful situations (2 Sam 12:16, when David's child was dying). Fasting accompanied a desire to unite with the needs of the poor (Isa 58:6-7, "Is not this the fast that I choose...to share your bread with the hungry and bring the homeless poor into your house; [to] cover the naked and not to hide yourself from your own flesh?"). Fasting purified the person as they awaited a divine communication (Exod 34:28, Moses "for forty days and forty nights. . . neither ate bread nor drank water"). Fasting, of course, became an important feature of Yom Kippur, *the day* (as the Rabbis called it) of at-one-ment, seeking purification from personal and collective sin in Lev 16:29, 31. In fact, from the last reference, we see that the phrase "to afflict yourselves" became a stereotyped reference to fasting. *Pray with bowed head* (literally, "my prayer returns to my bosom") was interpreted by the rabbis to mean: my prayer returned to my heart and entrails, as bodily motion and interior agony unite before God (*cf.,* Luke 18:13, "the tax collector, standing far off, would not even lift up his eyes to heaven"). The general phrase in v. 14, *in mourning,* means "with body unwashed and soiled clothes," a person is too distraught to attend even to bodily care (*cf.,* Ps 38:5-6, "my wounds grow foul and fester. . . I go about mourning"; Esth 4:1, "Mordecai. . . rent his clothes and put on sackcloth and ashes, and went out into the midst of the city, wailing with a loud and bitter cry"). The Hebrew text of vv. 15-16 is the most difficult in the entire psalm. The word, *cripples,* is sometimes read (with a slight emendation of the Hebrew) as "strangers." The Hebrew, *nekim,* refers to people beaten down or "contrite in spirit" (Isa 66:2) or to someone physically disabled (2 Sam 4:4; 9:3 — but here the text explicitly adds "feet," where Jonathan's son was "crippled"). The psalm is probably stating that even those people who shared the psalmist's misery and affliction cared not to console him; rather they *slandered me without ceasing.*

(IV) We must never program deceit and treachery — neither does God — yet when it happens, we find ourselves in a mystic moment, out in a spiritual desert, alone with God, whom we experience to be the supreme source of fidelity and strength. Public expressions of sorrow are not intended to win favor from God or from our neighbors; it is profane to "use" sorrow, our own or others, and it is hideous to put our naked children on display to win help. We do not atone for sins, and merit pardon, if we happen to be guilty, simply by fasting and sackcloth. We are required to make restitution (Num 5:5-10) and to be sincerely sorry. As is clear in Isa 58, external forms of penance are meant to unite us with the poor and sorrowing, to form a larger congregation that rallies around the unfortunate, and to learn from the hungry and mistreated how to look towards God as the ultimate source of life, strength, faithfulness and perseverance.

Psalm 36
To The Choirmaster. A Psalm Of David, The Servant Of The Lord.

I

¹Trangression speaks to the wicked deep in his heart;
   there is no fear of God
     before his eyes.

⁴He plots mischief while on his bed;
   he set himself in a way that is not good;
   he spurns not evil.

II

⁷How precious is thy steadfast love, O God;
   The children of men take refuge in
     the shadow of thy wings.
⁸They feast on the abundance of thy house,
   and thou givest them drink from the
     river of thy delights.
⁹For with thee is the fountain of life;
   in thy light do we see light.

III

¹⁰O continue thy steadfast love to those who know thee,

¹²There the evildoers lie prostrate,
   they are thrust down, unable to rise.

(I +II) It is difficult to grasp, at least at first, the unity and form of this psalm. An initial reading will detect three distinct sections: vv. 1-4, a description of the bold, self-confident evil person which, in style and vocabulary, is close to the sapiential literature; vv. 5-9, a hymn to Yahweh, the covenant God of Israel; vv. 10-11, a prayer that Yahweh's covenant love protect the upright; v. 12, a final curse against the wicked, an awkward down-beat for the conclusion (see Ps 34:22). Serious textual problems, moreover, plague the interpreter. A more careful study of Ps 36 detects a partial explanation by means of its gradual development within the liturgy. (1) An initial poem of lament (vv. 1-4) described the wicked who scheme secretly in their heart, as though God does not realize it, and *plot mischief* [securely and comfortably] *while on their bed*. Such a section could have been spoken in the liturgy, as we saw was the case in Ps 12:4. (2) A hymn was added to offset this vain boasting (vv. 5-9). The Lord's *steadfast* [covenantal] *love extends to the heavens* [and across] *the great deep* [of the oceans], therefore, none of the plans of the wicked are hidden from the Lord, so we sing confidently, *in thy light do we see light*. (3) The liturgy closes with a prayer in vv. 10-11 for all persecuted people, that *you, O God, continue thy steadfast love to those who know thee*. (4) The final liturgical line in v. 12 turns out to be up-beat after all. The priest promises that *the evildoers* [will] *lie prostrate. The upright of heart* will be vindicated.

(III + IV) We confine our comments to a few passages. V. 1, *Transgression speaks to the wicked deep in his heart:* The Hebrew is puzzling, for the word, *speaks* is a technical word for a divine oracle, *ne'um*, the word that also introduces Ps 110. A substitute translation would be: "An Oracle: In the heart of the lawless there is revolt!" From the very beginning God knows the schemes of the wicked. The hymn in vv. 5-9 is studded with covenant vocabulary: *steadfast love* (2 times), *faithfulness, righteousness, judgments*. In v. 7, *shadow of thy wings* refers to Yahweh's presence over the ark of the covenant, between the wings of the cherubim (see Ps 17:8). V. 9 speaks of life-giving water and light; it fits well the blessing of the baptismal font in the Christian ritual. In the liturgy, therefore, both of temple and of church, God's faithful people already have a pledge that every insidious evil will be revealed by the light of God's fidelity and every faithful person is already drinking from *the river of thy delights* (v. 8). The Hebrew word for *delight* comes from the same root as "Eden," the name for the garden of paradise. This verse has been interpreted by the rabbis and the church as a pledge of eating in the messianic banquet of paradise (*cf.*, Isa 25:6-8; 55:1-2). With the development of Israel's doctrine of future life, the final verse began to express the lifeless, immobile existence of the wicked, as secretly lost in the dark earth as once their schemes were hidden in their dark heart. The unity of Ps 36 is beginning to emerge! We recognize the power of the liturgy to unite what seems very diverse!

Psalm 37
A Psalm Of David.

I

¹Fret not yourself because of the wicked,
   be not envious of wrongdoers!
²For they will soon fade like the grass,
   and wither like the green herb.

³Trust in the Lord, and do good;
   so you will dwell in the land, and enjoy security.
⁴Take delight in the Lord,
   and he will give you the desires of your heart.

⁵Commit your way to the Lord;
   trust in him, and he will act.
⁶He will bring forth your vindication as the light,
   and your right as the noonday.

⁷Be still before the Lord, and wait patiently for him;
   fret not yourself over him who prospers in his way,
   over the man who carries out evil devices!

⁸Refrain from anger, and forsake wrath!
   Fret not yourself; it tends only to evil.
⁹For the wicked shall be cut off;
   but those who wait for the Lord shall possess the land.

II

¹⁰Yet a little while, and the wicked will be no more;
  though you look well at his place, he will not be there.
¹¹But the meek shall possess the land,
  and delight themselves in abundant prosperity.

¹²The wicked plots against the righteous,
  and gnashes his teeth at him;
¹³but the Lord laughs at the wicked,
  for he sees that his day is coming.

¹⁴The wicked draw the sword and bend their bows,
  to bring down the poor and needy,
  to slay those who walk uprightly;
¹⁵their sword shall enter their own heart,
  and their bows shall be broken.

III

¹⁶Better is a little that the righteous has
  than the abundance of the many wicked.
¹⁷For the arms of the wicked shall be broken;
  but the Lord upholds the righteous.

¹⁸The Lord knows the days of the blameless,
  and their heritage will abide for ever;
¹⁹they are not put to shame in evil times,
  in the days of famine they have abundance.

²⁰But the wicked perish;
  the enemies of the Lord are like the glory
    of the pastures,
  they vanish—like smoke they vanish away.

²¹The wicked borrows, and cannot pay back,
  but the righteous is generous and gives;
²²for those blessed by the Lord shall possess the land,
  but those cursed by him shall be cut off.

²³The steps of a man are from the Lord,
  and he establishes him in whose way he delights;
²⁴though he fall, he shall not be cast headlong,
  for the Lord is the stay of his hand.

²⁵I have been young, and now am old;
  yet I have not seen the righteous forsaken
  or his children begging bread.
²⁶He is ever giving liberally and lending,
  and his children become a blessing.

IV

²⁷Depart from evil, and do good;
  so shall you abide for ever.
²⁸For the Lord loves justice;
  he will not forsake his saints.

The righteous shall be preserved for ever,
  but the children of the wicked shall be cut off.
²⁹The righteous shall possess the land,
  and dwell upon it for ever.

³⁰The mouth of the righteous utters wisdom,
  and his tongue speaks justice.
³¹The law of his God is in his heart;
  his steps do not slip.

³²The wicked watches the righteous,
  and seeks to slay him.
³³The Lord will not abandon him to his power,
  or let him be condemned when he is brought to trial.

V

³⁴Wait for the Lord, and keep to his way,
  and he will exalt you to possess the land;
  you will look on the destruction of the wicked.

³⁵I have seen a wicked man overbearing,
  and towering like a cedar of Lebanon.
³⁶Again I passed by, and lo, he was no more;
  though I sought him, he could not be found.

³⁷Mark the blameless man, and behold the upright,
  for there is posterity for the man of peace.
³⁸But transgressors shall be altogether destroyed;
  the posterity of the wicked shall be cut off.

³⁹The salvation of the righteous is from the Lord;
  he is their refuge in the time of trouble.
⁴⁰The Lord helps them and delivers them;
  he delivers them from the wicked and saves them,
  because they take refuge in him.

(I) We have already met alphabetical psalms (Ps 9-10; 25 and 34) but none as long or as elaborate as this one, nor as completely in stride with the sapiential movement. In Ps 37 each letter of the alphabet has two verses for reflecting upon the overall motif of retribution: God rewards the just and allows the wicked to be punished, each by their good or evil deeds. It is best to date the psalm in the early postexilic age, sometime after 537 B.C. and the return from Babylon. We are in the long silent years about which the Bible tells very little (except for the building program of Nehemiah and the reform of Ezra, 445-420 B.C.). An old man (v. 25), possibly a teacher, draws upon well seasoned maturity to adapt to individual Israelites the ideas which Deuteronomy once delivered to the nation within the major sanctuaries. The conditions for possessing the land as well as the ramifications of curses and blessings now become a program for private meditation and individual morality.

Ps 37 can be compared and contrasted with other biblical books. Though it shares with Proverbs and Job a basic theology of retribution, still there are other important differences. Unlike Proverbs, it does not seek to gather and preserve the major collections of Israel's wisdom, nor to entrust its own sage remarks to a "school" or community of followers. Unlike the Book of Job, the psalmist is not struggling for an answer and fighting "the system" represented by other sages. The author of Ps 37 is at peace with what he knows. Neither does the psalmist attempt magnificent poetic essays and emulate the elegance and versatility in a book like Job. He in content with a calm, cool approach. His is a book of silent contemplation, of peaceful reflection, of sustained prayer. It seeks nothing more than what the last line declares, copying from Israel's liturgical tradition: *take refuge in the Lord* (*cf.,* Ps 2:12). Ps 37 strikes us as a piece for private piety, not liturgical prayer. Yet we may be overlooking the long silent moments in Israel' liturgy during its octaves and vigils when people came on pilgrimage, remained several days, intent to learn as well as to worship, to instruct the youth and to console the worried and anxious.

(II) Ps 37 does not intend to go anywhere but rather to help us become more deeply rooted in Israel's traditional theology. Ps 37 is not to be read but to be memorized and subconsciously to be repeated for strong integral guidance. Despite this lack of movement we can detect at least an introduction (vv. 1-9) and a conclusion (vv. 34-40) where most of the strophes are introduced with the imperative: fret not, trust, commit your way... wait, mark the blameless. The long section in between (vv. 10-33) proceeds with declarative sentences in the indicative mood. This central part clusters around three main areas: vv. 10-15, ruin of the impious; vv. 16-26, prosperity as Yahweh's gift; vv. 27-33, a return to fidelity.

(III + IV) The lines of this psalm do not need explanation so much as our prolonged, contemplative reflection. We need to memorize a poem like this one (one of the reasons for the alphabetical style) and then to allow its words and sentences to seep into many segments of our thought and conversation. Fortunately this type of contemplation does not wisk us off to the clouds. Typical of the sapiential movement, the whole realm of reward and punishment remains within the parameters of life on earth. Even such lines as *Take delight in the Lord* employs a Hebrew verb, *'anag*, here in its intensive, reflective form (technically called the *hithpael*), that seeks a joy that is delicate and dignified yet always of this earth: *i.e.,* Isa 55:2, "Why do you spend your money for that which is not bread and your labor for that which does not satisfy? Hearken to me... and *delight* in rich fares." The wicked are not said to be punished by hell but by their own sins (v. 15). Ps 37 expects what the oriental can do very well but modern people find very difficult — to take the time to *wait for the Lord* during one's earthly pilgrimage.

Ernesto Cardenal has retranslated and paraphrased sections of Ps 37 with a defiant, prophetical thrust:

> Do not be disturbed if you see them making millions
> Their stocks are but straw from the fields
> Do not envy millionaires nor the superstars of the movies
> or those with eight-column headlines in the newspapers
> or those who live in luxury hotels
> and eat at four-star restaurants
> because soon their names will not appear in any
>   newspaper
> and not even the scholars will remember their names
> Because they soon will be cut down like straw in the fields
> (*Psalms of Struggle and Liberation*, foreword by Thomas
> Merton, New York: Herder and Herder, 1971, p. 45)

Psalm 38
A Psalm Of David, For The Memorial Offering.

I

¹O Lord, rebuke me not in thy anger,
  nor chasten me in thy wrath!
²For thy arrows have sunk into me,
  and thy hand has come down on me.

II

³There is no soundness in my flesh
  because of thy indignation;
 there is no health in my bones
  because of my sin.
⁴For my iniquities have gone over my head;
  they weigh like a burden too heavy for me.

⁵My wounds grow foul and fester
  because of my foolishness,
⁶I am utterly bowed down and prostrate;
  all the day I go about mourning.
⁷For my loins are filled with burning,
  and there is no soundness in my flesh.

⁸I am utterly spend and crushed;
  I groan because of the tumult of my heart.

⁹Lord, all my longing is known to thee,
  my sighing is not hidden from thee.
¹⁰My heart throbs, my strength fails me;
  and the light of my eyes—it also has gone from me.

III
¹¹My friends and companions stand aloof from my
  plague,
  and my kinsmen stand afar off.

¹²Those who seek my life lay their snares,
  those who seek my hurt speak of ruin,
  and meditate treachery all the day long.

¹³But I am like a deaf man, I do not hear,
  like a dumb man who does not open his mouth.
¹⁴Yea, I am like a man who does not hear,
  and in whose mouth are no rebukes.

¹⁵But for thee, O Lord, do I wait;
  it is thou, O Lord my God, who wilt answer.
¹⁶For I pray, "Only let them not rejoice over me,
  who boast against me when my foot slips!"

¹⁷For I am ready to fall,
  and my pain is ever with me.
¹⁸I confess my iniquity,
  I am sorry for my sin.
¹⁹Those who are my foes without cause are mighty,
  and many are those who hate me wrongfully.
²⁰Those who render me evil for good
  are my adversaries because I follow after good.

IV
²¹Do not forsake me, O Lord!
  O my God, be not far from me!
²²Make haste to help me,
  O Lord, my salvation!

(I) We are entering the final section (Pss 38-41) of Book One of the Psalter which concentrates on sin and sickness; with Ps 38 we are also meeting another of the seven penitential psalms (see Ps 6). Three personal conditions heighten the agony in Ps 38: serious sickness which dominates every other concern of the psalm (vv. 5-8); abandonment by even one's closest friends (vv. 11-14, 19-20); a sense of being a sinful person, already forgiven one's guilt by God (v. 18) yet suffocating from silence and doubt (vv. 13-14). The author never despairs of God, yet serious personal doubt and prolonged isolation make the psalmist wonder if God has really forgiven.

The sickness would seem to correspond to biblical "leprosy" (serious, contagious skin disease) according to Lev 14 and from what we know of the disease: decomposition of the flesh (vv. 3, 5, 7); bones twisted and mashed together (vv. 3b, 6a); eyelids weakened, eyebrows falling out, and one's vision dimmed (v. 10b). We cannot be sure of this diagnosis, for these and other symptoms might indicate other kinds of serious debilitation, or the psalmist may be writing figuratively. Another aspect of leprosy also surfaces in the agony of the psalmist. Leprosy deprived a person of their humanity, their family relationship, their identification as an Israelite and therefore their right to claim the Lord's covenant love and loyalty. In Luke 17:11, 16, lepers who haunted the fringes of civilization included Israelites and Samaritans indiscriminately. It is not only the isolation from friends, themselves fearful of coming under the same curse, but also the excruciating doubts about one's relation with Yahweh, that made the psalmist feel as if God's *arrows have sunk into me* (v. 2).

(II) Stylistically, the psalm shows vigor and sincerity; a person as close to death as the psalmist with no one to turn to but Yahweh cannot afford to be anything else but totally honest, and with elemental strength to speak out abruptly. The Hebrew interjection, *ki*, occurs seven times, an unusually high occurrence; basically it means "indeed," "look," "surely," "therefore." There are many other repetitions, a phenomenon somewhat common in Hebrew poetry, yet usually with more elegance as in Pss 8 and 29. Accordingly, we may not classify Ps 38 among the better poems, but the psalmist gets high rating not only for sincerity and a strength that comes from near-panic, but also for a type of personal piety, devoted to sacred traditions. There are many citations from or comparisons with Pss 6; 22; 35; Isa 1 and 53; Jer 10:24, to name a few. These references may reflect a pensive, contemplative person, ruminating the traditions even when isolated from Israel; or they may be due to later liturgical additions. At times the lines of the psalm appear heavy, due either to the psalmist's mediocre skills or to interference from liturgy and popular devotions.

The division into strophes is not easily reached, but the following schema may be helpful:

vv. 1-2, call for help	vv. 11-20, abandoned by all, even by God
vv. 3-10, serious sickness	vv. 21-22, final call for help

(III) The title has been expanded in the Aramaic Targum to a daily memorial offering (*cf.,* Lev 6:7-16), while the Greek Septuagint refers to the Sabbath memorial offering (Lev 24:5-9). Evidently with the passage of time Ps 38 featured frequently in Israel's liturgy.

Vv. 1-2, in the call for help, the psalmist does not dispute God's prerogative to punish sin; he only asks God *not* [to] *rebuke me in thy anger* [and] *wrath,* but with covenantal mercy (Exod 34:6-7). The psalmist is at peace through an instinctive faith in Yahweh. The opening verse is almost identical with Ps 6:1.

Vv. 3-10, these verses are summarized in the twice repeated phrase, *no soundness in my flesh* (*cf.,* Isa 1:6, "from the sole of the foot even to the head there is no soundness . . . but bruises and sores and bleeding wounds"). *no health:* the Hebrew word is *shalom,* that state of perfect, complete wholesomeness and vitality. The words for *sin* and *iniquity* have already been discussed with Ps 32. V. 8, *I groan:* the Hebrew verb, *sha'ag,* denotes the roar of a lion (*cf.,* Ps 22:1 and 13, the same word for the psalmist's groaning and the lion's roar). Every Israelite knew the refrain, quoted with slightly different meaning in Amos 1:2; Jer 25:30 and Joel 3:16, "The Lord roars from Zion" and the land mourns, the earth quakes and the inhabitants of the earth are judged.

Vv. 11-20, a terrifying silence descends. *Friends* [literally, *those loving me*] *and companions stand aloof from my plague:* a line that can be pictured in its terrifying force by a similar reading in Luke 23:49, "Jesus' acquaintances... stood at a distance and saw these things." Another insight comes from the fourth Song of the Suffering Servant, where the Lord's beloved absorbs everyone's attention yet is mentioned by name only at the beginning and end, is referred to in the third person by contrast with ourselves, "he has borne our griefs," and who "opened not his mouth, like a lamb that is led to the slaughter" (Isa 53:7). Like the psalmist this servant too "had no form or comeliness... no beauty that we should desire him" (53:2b). V. 18, *I confess my iniquity*, reads literally: "Indeed [another use of *ki*] my iniquity I [*publicly*] announce," mortal sickness has reduced the psalmist to basic honesty in the elemental striving for human existence. The psalmist does not fear the false charges of the adversaries, but he absolutely needs recognition and trust, in order to belong to Israel and to be rid of his own doubts about himself, possibly about God.

Vv. 21-22. The final call begs God, *be not far from me*, a key word in Ps 22:1, 11, 19. *Make haste*, also in Ps 22:19, signals alarm and urgency.

(IV) For the Ashkenazi Jews of Eastern European origin, Ps 38 belongs to the evening prayer of the third day of the week. As night descends... we descend into desolation and are racked with doubts. While still surrounded by darkness, its howling voices and nightmares, we need Ps 38. The psalmist has not yet seen the least dash of color on the horizon to announce a new day, and yet he can pray, *for thee, O Lord, do I wait* (v. 15). Only God can break the silence. When we are deprived of human dignity (such seems the case with many forms of sickness and old age) we arrive at our basic dignity in prayer, prayer that lasts through the night before relief is in sight, prayer that brings us into a most private audience with God, even in our leprosy we enter the Holy of Holies.

Psalm 39
To The Choirmaster: To Jeduthun. A Psalm Of David.

I

¹I said, "I will guard my ways,
    that I may not sin with my tongue;
I will bridle my mouth,
    so long as the wicked are in my presence."
²I was dumb and silent,
    I held my peace to no avail;
my distress grew worse,
³ my heart became hot within me.
As I mused, the fire burned;
    then I spoke with my tongue:

II

⁴"Lord, let me know my end,
    and what is the measure of my days;
    let me know how fleeting my life is!
⁵Behold, thou hast made my days a few handbreadths,
    and my lifetime is as nothing in thy sight.
Surely every man stands as a mere breath!   *Selah*

⁶ Surely man goes about as a shadow!
Surely for nought are they in turmoil;
    man heaps up, and knows not who will gather!

III

⁷"And now, Lord, for what do I wait?
    My hope is in thee.
⁸Deliver me from all my transgressions.
    Make me not the scorn of the fool!
⁹I am dumb, I do not open my mouth;
    for it is thou who hast done it.
¹⁰Remove thy stroke from me;

I am spent by the blows of thy hand.
¹¹When thou dost chasten man
  with rebukes for sin,
  thou dost consume like a moth what is dear to him;
    surely every man is a mere breath!   *Selah*

IV

¹²"Hear my prayer, O Lord,
  and give ear to my cry;
  hold not thy peace at my tears!
For I am thy passing guest,
  a sojourner, like all my fathers.
¹³Look away from me, that I may know gladness,
  before I depart and be no more!"

(I) As a lament for an individual, suffering person, still in the prime of life, weighed down with a sense of sin and especially with the shadowy impermanence of human existence, Ps 39 struggles for an answer. It would seem that this psalmist cannot accept the calm reply of Ps 37, to "trust in the Lord, and do good: so you will dwell in the land, and enjoy security." The psalmist tried the prudent remedy of silence but had to admit that *I held my peace to no avail; my distress grew worse...*[I must speak] *with my tongue* (vv. 2-3). The attitude of the psalmist resembles that found in the Book of Job: "How forceful are honest words!" (Job 6:25). Quiet submission was not a major priority in the psalmist's spirituality! If someone were to suggest that whatever happens, because it happens, is God's will and therefore the best, the psalmist would blurt out: *my heart became hot within me...the fire burned* [in my bones]! Unlike Ps 38, this psalm evinces healthy creativity in vocabulary and style. The author does not rely on quotations and stereotypes. All the elements of a lament are here, but shall we say, somewhat mixed-up! Unfortunately, the Hebrew text is not well preserved; the ancient translations have many, serious variations. The meter is quite irregular. Most scholars refuse to hazard a date for the psalm!

(II) For appreciating Ps 39 the following outline is suggested:

vv. 1-3, Introduction: Silence is not sufficient.	vv. 7-11, Prayer for Deliverance.
vv. 4-6, Impermanence of human life.	vv. 12-13, Supplication that this prayer be heard.

(III) *The title* of the psalm refers to *Jeduthun*, an ancestor to one of three groups of temple cantors (1 Chron 16:41-42; 25:1) and associated also with Pss 62:1 and 77:1. This group of levites may have introduced an individual private lament like Ps 39 into temple liturgy. If it did originate in the realm of private devotion, then we have a plausible explanation for the poor condition of the Hebrew text, neglected for many decades or too easily adapted to private devotional practice. To this origin in private piety we may also attribute the flashing intuitions of life after death, at least for the righteous, a doctrinal position which the temple priests never quite accepted (see Ps 6) but which took root among lay groups like the Pharisees or among a fringe priestly group like the Qumran sectarians.

Vv. 1-3, *Silence is not sufficient*, therefore not golden! Perhaps the psalmist at first was afraid to speak, not so much for fear of providing ammunition to the adversaries who ridiculed the religious person for useless devotion to Yahweh (Ps 14:1; Ps 73:11), but principally lest he be held responsible for his own foolish words, once he falls into the hands of Yahweh. To suppress his reaction, however, meant that like Jeremiah "there is...a burning fire shut up in my bones, and I am weary with holding it in, and I cannot"(Jer 20:9). The introduction ends dramatically and firmly: *I spoke with my own tongue.*

Vv. 4-6, *Impermanence of human existence.* These lines *could* have destroyed any basis, however fragile it might have been, for further hope and prayer, but precisely by insisting on the impermanence of all life, the psalmist will come to the most profound basis of human existence, beyond words and even beyond the accepted, orthodox theology: *my hope is in thee* (v. 7) and what is implied, *in thee alone*, even when human life passes away *like a shadow* (v. 6). This lovely section, surprisingly calm after the *distress* and pent up, fiery feelings in vv. 2-3, begins with a prayer for insight (v. 4), continues with a confession that life is indeed *fleeting* (v. 5a), and then in v. 5b, 6a and 6b, concludes with a triple, *Surely* the emphatic Hebrew particle *'ak: Surely everyone stands as a mere breath! Surely...as a shadow! Surely just a breath their turmoil!* This final section is so true, that it is expressed in the impersonal third person with its universal ring.

Vv. 7-11, *Prayer for deliverance,* dominated by an opening confession of confidence: *And now, Lord* [the Hebrew language here is very emphatic], *for what do I wait? My hope is in thee.* This prayer weaves in and out of the preceding section and its conviction that life is as short-lived as *a moth...a mere breath.* In fact, *breath* (in Hebrew, *hebel,* prominent in Jer 2:5 where it is translated "worthless" and in Eccles 1:2, translated "vanity") is one of the key words in Ps 39. The psalmist cannot attest to a clear sense of forgiveness from the compassionate covenant God (Exod 34:6-7). The psalmist is staring into the sun and feels lost —lost in Yahweh, *my* [*only*] *hope.* His own words can seem like a transgression, not that they are sinful, only so inadequate, once the psalmist is led beyond their reach of meaning: *I am dumb, I do not open my mouth* (v. 9).

Vv. 12-13, Supplication that the prayer be heard. The statement about *passing guest* and *sojourner* link the conclusion with vv. 4-6; and the seemingly contradictory request, *look away from me,* actually finds its truest meaning in v. 7b, *my hope is in thee,* and thee alone. The psalmist, like the levite in Ps 16, does not want to base security on property, which for most Israelites was as basic as the covenant (*cf.,* Lev 25:23-55), and asks God to look away from all these common ingredients and supports. The passage from Lev 25, along with others (Gen 23:4, Num 35:15; especially 1 Chron 29:14-15), insists that every Israelite is a *sojourner* and *passing guest:* sojourner is the word for an overnight lodger; passing guest is a resident alien with rights bestowed by the good will of the citizens. The psalmist is begging God to *look away from me, that I may know gladness, i.e.,* do not look at me as someone to last forever amid the fleeting joys of this land, for then when *I depart* [I will] *be no more.* Not in the security of land, nor in generations of time, but *in thee* alone does the psalmist find *hope.*

(IV) If this interpretation seems too mystical, or theologically too advanced, such at least may have been the judgment of the Jeduthun-cantors who may have rearranged the original order and placed vv. 12-13 last, in order to bring the psalm more in line (so they thought) with orthodox theology of the Sadducee priesthood. For our part we see the important contribution from private piety in Israel and for that matter from non-Israelite religions in Egypt and Mesopotamia which had already developed officially an advanced doctrine about the future life. We read in an ancient Babylonian lamentation to the goddess Ishtar:

> O deity of men, goddess of women, whose designs no one can conceive;
> Where thou does look, *one who is dead lives;* one who is sick rises up;
> The erring one who sees thy face goes aright.
> I have cried to thee, suffering, wearied, and distressed, as thy servant.
> See me, O my Lady; accept my prayers.
> Faithfully look upon me and hear my supplication.
> Promise my forgiveness and let thy spirit be appeased.
> Pity! For my wretched body which is full of confusion and trouble. (*ANET*, 384)

Such non-Israelite piety permeated the ranks of Israel's laity and left them unsatisfied with the very restricted view of the future life at the temple (see Pss 6 and 16). Ps 39 witnesses not only to their vision beyond the limits of theology but also to the importance of settling deeply within themselves, beyond the reach of words, even their best words, where they seemed but a *shadow* (v. 6). The Hebrew word for

shadow, *selem*, occurs in Gen 1:27 where it means *the image
of God* according to which we were created. Ps 39 takes us
behind the shadow or image of God into the blinding and
silencing vision of God.

Psalm 40 (+ Psalm 70)
To The Choirmaster. A Psalm Of David.

I

¹I waited patiently for the Lord;
    he inclined to me and heard my cry.

II

²He drew me up from the desolate pit,
    out of the miry bog,
    and set my feet upon a rock,
    making my steps secure.
³He put a new song in my mouth,
    a song of praise to our God.
Many will see and fear,
    and put their trust in the Lord.

III

⁴Blessed is the man who makes
    the Lord his trust,
    who does not turn to the proud,
    to those who go astray after false gods!
⁵Thou hast multiplied, O Lord my God,
    thy wondrous deeds and thy thoughts toward us;
    none can compare with thee!
Were I to proclaim and tell of them,
    they would be more than can be numbered.

IV

⁶Sacrifice and offering thou dost not desire;
    but thou hast given me an open ear.
Burnt offering and sin offering
    thou has not required.
⁷Then I said, "Lo, I come;
    in the roll of the book it is written of me;

⁸I delight to do thy will, O my God;
   thy law is within my heart."

V

⁹I have told the glad news of deliverance
   in the great congregation;
  lo, I have not restrained my lips,
   as thou knowest, O Lord.
¹⁰I have not hid thy saving help within my heart,
   I have spoken of thy faithfulness and thy salvation;
  I have not concealed thy steadfast love and
   thy faithfulness
  from the great congregation.

VI

¹¹Do not thou, O Lord, withhold thy mercy from me,
   let thy steadfast love and thy faithfulness
      ever preserve me!

VII

¹²For evils have encompassed me without number;
  my iniquities have overtaken me,
   till I cannot see;
  they are more than the hairs of my head;
   my heart fails me.

VIII (= Ps 70)

¹³Be pleased, O Lord, to deliver me!
   O Lord, make haste to help me!
¹⁴Let them be put to shame and confusion altogether
   who seek to snatch away my life;
  let them be turned back and brought to dishonor
   who desire my hurt!
¹⁵Let them be appalled because of their shame
   who say to me, "Aha, Aha!"

¹⁶But may all who seek thee
   rejoice and be glad in thee;
  may those who love thy salvation
   say continually, "Great is the Lord!"
¹⁷As for me, I am poor and needy;

but the Lord takes thought for me.
Thou art my help and my deliverer;
do not tarry, O my God!

(I) Even a cursory reading of Ps 40 causes the signals to flash on our exegetical control system: a) the sequence from thanksgiving (vv. 1-11 or 12) to lament (vv. 13-17) is unusual, for as Franz Delitzsch wrote, "All at once the *magnificat* becomes a most plaintive *de profundis*"; b) the second part (vv. 13-17) is repeated almost verbatim as a separate psalm in Ps 70; c) the lines which we recognize most easily, vv. 6-8, are quoted differently in the NT (Heb 10:5-7), and in the psalm they interrupt the congregational prayer in vv. 5 and 9.

Ps 40 gradually came together for liturgical purposes. A preexisting lament was joined with a prayer of thanksgiving to produce *a new song* (v. 3) for a special feastday or celebration (*cf.,* Ps 33:3). The ensemble was incorporated into the first book of the psalter. The same lament was employed for a different liturgy, "the memorial offering" as the addition to the title of Ps 70 tells us, and was associated with a different group of psalms now within Book Two of the psalter. When the lament was joined to a prayer of thanksgiving to create Ps 40, other changes were undertaken. Some instructional or prophetical lines were added in vv. 4 and 6-8, and for smoothing the transition between vv. 1-11 and 13-17, v. 12 was blended in. Continual use and adaptation within the liturgy has smoothed out any personal or historical references for dating the psalm. A calculated guess would be the time between the destruction of the temple in 587 B.C. and its reconstruction in 520-515 B.C. During this stretch of years Israel realized that the covenantal Lord accepted prayers and obedience even if not accompanied by ritual sacrifices. Such a date would also allow for a prophetical impact upon the psalm.

(II) The division of Ps 40 has become complicated from changes within its long use:

v. 1 introduction	(vv. 6-8 Interruption; different
vv. 2-3 details about	meter)
deliverance	vv. 9-10 Gratitude within the
vv. 4-5 instruction and praise	assembly
	v. 11 Conclusion
v. 12 Transitional verse	
vv. 13-17 Individual Lament (= Ps 70)	

(III) V. 1, *an introduction to the thanksgiving prayer*. The words *I waited patiently* are very emphatic, by way of their position and their grammatical form (literally, *waited I waited*). "Waiting" appears with a great variety of meaning in the Bible, most often it implies that a sorrowful period is almost ended: Isa 25:9, "Lo, this is our God; we have waited for him, that he might save us. This is the Lord; we have waited for him; let us be glad and rejoice in his salvation"; or Isa 40:31, If those who faint and are weary "wait for the Lord [they] shall renew their strength; they shall mount up with wings like eagles."

Vv. 2-3, *a description of danger and deliverance*, mostly in stereotype or liturgical language, but with some prophetical influence. The *desolate pit* brings to mind Ps 69:1-2 or the prison into which Jeremiah was lowered (Jer 38). The reference here to both *pit* and *rock* makes us think of the large temple enclave with its cisterns as well as its rock of sacrifice (Ps 27:5). These lines are contrasting life and death, temple and sheol (see Ps 6 and 16), sickness and health (1 Sam 2:6), security and tumultuous danger (Jon 2:2-4, a reference that contrasts the tumultuous depths of the angry sea with the peaceful temple).

Vv. 4-5, *a combination of instruction and praise*, flowing from God's strong assistance in vv. 2-3. The instructional verse seems heavy, even forced; only here is there any mention of *false gods*, otherwise Ps 40 is dealing with more internal or more personal problems. V. 4 then has the marks of an intrusion or addition from sapiential circles, as the opening word, *blessed*, indicates (see Ps 1:1). The word *proud*, literally "people of Rahab," probably refers to idolators (*cf.*, Ps 89:11; Isa 51:9-10). V. 5 situates us fully within sanctuary worship. For the goodness of God beyond compare, see Ps 89:6; also Sir 43:27, 30, "Though we speak much we cannot reach the end, and the sum of our words is, 'He is all in all,'. . . do not grow weary, for you cannot praise him enough."

Vv. 6-8, *Faith and obedience*, the soul of the liturgy. These lines echo a continuous prophetical stance, particularly strong in the north, whether it be the Deuteronomic tradition of 1 Sam 15:22, or the prophets Hos 6:6 and Jer 6:20, but spilling over into the south with prophets like Amos 5:21-25; Mic 6:6 and Isa 1:11-17. The prophets are not condemning ritual outright, for the Deuteronomic tradition in the Books of Samuel and Kings centers around the Jerusalem temple. Even in Ps 40, these lines are surrounded by ritual texts, not to cancel them out but to instil the proper spirit within them. V. 6 spans the circuit of ritual acts: sacrifice (*zebeh*, animal offering, like the paschal lamb, part of which was returned to the offerer for a sacred meal in the family); offering (*minhah*, a general word, but generally consisting of grain); burnt offering (*'olah*, entirely consumed by the fire on the altar out of homage and adoration); sin offering (*hata'ah*, mostly returned to the priest for their upkeep). The phrase, *thou has given me an open ear* (literally, "ears that you have dug for me") reflects an early practice according to which the earlobe of a slave was pierced at the temple, if out of love for the master and his household, the slave did not opt for freedom but for continued bondage (Exod 21:5-6). Here the idea is spiritualized into an attitude of obedient listening to God's will, just as Jer 6:10 and 9:25 speaks of "uncircumcised ears," not disciplined to hear the covenant correctly and to respond sincerely. A similar idea, expressed positively, occurs in Isa 50:4-5, where the Suffering Servant declares: "morning by morning Yahweh wakens my ear to hear as those who are taught." *Thy law is within my heart:* words that clearly resonate Jer 31:31-34, who was attempting to revive Deut 6:4-9 as the new covenant; *cf.,* Ezek 36:22-32, where these ideas are closely associated with a reformed ritual of sacrifice. The Greek Septuagint made a slight but significant messianic adaptation, reading "thou has given to me [not an open ear but] a body," which is then reinterpreted by Heb 10:5-7 of Jesus' incarnation and obedience upon death.

Vv. 9-10 celebrate *the glad news* (the Hebrew word, *basar*, lies at the base of our word "gospel") *in the great congregation* (using the northern, Deuteronomic word, *qahal*), therefore with ritual sacrifice and a series of covenant phrases like faithfulness and steadfast love (Exod 34:6-7). V. 11 concludes the prayer of thanksgiving; v. 12 acts as a transitional verse, somewhat repeating the sorrow in v. 2 and also preparing for the following lament. The powerlessness of the psalmist in v. 12 makes us think of Paul's words in Rom 7:14-16, "sold under sin, I do not understand my own actions. For I do not do what I want, but I do the very thing I hate."

Vv. 13-17, *a sincere, well constructed lament*, beginning and ending with urgency: *make haste...do not tarry*. These verses are almost identical with Ps 70. The first verse in the Latin Vulgate of Ps 70 has been used for centuries as an invitation to prayer in the Divine Office: "Deus in adiutorium meum intende; Domine, ad adiuvandum me festina —God, come to my assistance; Lord, make haste to help me." V. 16, *may all who seek thee:* the psalmist is seeking Yahweh more directly and earnestly than he is seeking deliverance!

(IV) A patchwork psalm like Ps 40 may disturb us at first. To proceed from thanksgiving back again to lament may annoy us for getting nowhere or even for falling backward. The ambiguous attitude towards liturgy — celebrating *in the great congregation* (v. 9), yet declaring that God has *not required sacrifice and offering* (v. 6) — may please no one! Here as always we need to remind ourselves that the canonical editor or final redactor of the psalms was a reasonable person, actually an inspired person, cooperating with the Holy Spirit in producing a part of the Bible. We must presume by faith that there is an important message here and beg God to *give me an open ear* (v. 6) to hear that message. As the Servant of Isaiah (50:4) advises, we must persevere in prayer "morning by morning" and gradually the integrity of the psalm will be perceived. The diversity of the psalm, moreover, mirrors differences in any family or congregation and alerts us to be aware of our brother and sister, who may be sorrowing as we celebrate, or vice versa.

Psalm 41
To The Choirmaster. A Psalm Of David.

I

¹Blessed is he who considers the poor!
  The Lord delivers him in the day of trouble;
²the Lord protects him and keeps him alive;
  he is called blessed in the land;
  thou dost not give him up to the will of his enemies.
³The Lord sustains him on his sickbed;
  in his illness thou healest all his infirmities.

II

⁴As for me, I said, "O Lord, be gracious to me;
  heal me, for I have sinned against thee!"
⁵My enemies say of me in malice:
  "When will he die, and his name perish?"
⁶And when one comes to see me, he utters empty words,
  while his heart gathers mischief;
  when he goes out, he tells it abroad.
⁷All who hate me whisper together about me;
  they imagine the worst for me.

⁸They say, "A deadly thing has fastened upon him;
  he will not rise again from where he lies."
⁹Even my bosom friend in whom I trusted,
  who ate of my bread, has lifted his heel against me.
¹⁰But do thou, O Lord, be gracious to me,
  and raise me up, that I may requite them!

III

¹¹By this I know that thou art pleased with me,
  in that my enemy has not triumphed over me.

¹²But thou hast upheld me because of my integrity.
and set me in thy presence for ever.

IV
¹³Blessed be the Lord, the God of Israel,
from everlasting to everlasting!
Amen and Amen.

(I) We come to the last psalm in the First Book of the
Psalter and according to the titles of the psalm the last in the
first major series of Psalms of David. The ending does not
come in any spectacular way, for Ps 41 is not a brilliant
psalm from a literary or liturgical viewpoint, but there is a
comprehensiveness of mood as it catches many moments in
earlier psalms: didactic (vv. 1-3); prayer for help and healing
(v. 4) and for the downfall of the enemy (v. 10); confidence
(v. 1-3) and thanksgiving (vv. 11-12). The final verse, 13,
actually a conclusion not to the psalm but to the entire First
Book of the Psalter, resonates praise. The comprehensiveness also spans the history of Israel; some words or phrases
are very ancient and stereotyped, like *be gracious* or *have
mercy* (vv. 4 and 10; also in Pss 4:1; 26:11; 27:7; 30:10; 31:9)
while the opening lines of Ps 41 conform to the didactic
movement of the postexilic age. This eclectic spirit of drawing from many sources makes it difficult to type the psalm,
except to say that the psalmist was once very sick (vv. 3, 6,
8), surrounded with whispering and rumors (vv. 6-7), and
restored to the full community in temple worship (v. 12).

(II) At an earlier stage the psalm may have been an
individual lament; this element continues prominently in vv.
4-10. In its present, canonical form it seems to have been
adapted for a thanksgiving ceremony in the temple, quite
evident in vv. 11-12. The introductory section (vv. 1-3) is
heavily didactic but also well adapted to the instructional
part of the temple liturgy. The following division is pro-
posed for appreciating Ps 41:

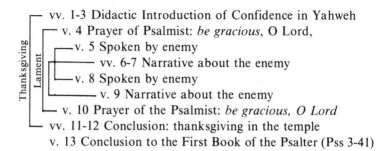

vv. 1-3 Didactic Introduction of Confidence in Yahweh
v. 4 Prayer of Psalmist: *be gracious*, O Lord,
v. 5 Spoken by enemy
vv. 6-7 Narrative about the enemy
v. 8 Spoken by enemy
v. 9 Narrative about the enemy
v. 10 Prayer of the Psalmist: *be gracious, O Lord*
vv. 11-12 Conclusion: thanksgiving in the temple
v. 13 Conclusion to the First Book of the Psalter (Pss 3-41)

(III) Vv. 1-3, *Didactic Introduction*, beginning like Ps 1 with the word *blessed, 'ashre* (see Ps 1:1). These opening lines gather confidence from the long experience and the faith position of Israel (see Ps 37). The sick person is assured of healing, a doctrinal stand that brought many questions, as in the Book of Job or Ps 39, yet somehow or other remains fundamentally true if sickness is seen in its community and timeless perspective (see Pss 13 and 31). One answer of Wisdom was: "The Lord reproves the one whom he loves, as parents the child in whom they delight" (Prov 3:12, quoted in Heb 12:6).

V. 4, *prayer*, very eloquent in its Hebrew form — as though what more can a person do who has shown sincere compunction and confessed their sin.

Vv. 5-9, in the liturgy a special choir could have taken the part of the wicked (see Ps 12), so that these verses constitute a dramatic contrast between the sly, lying approach of the false friends (vv. 5 and 8) and the congregational response to them (vv. 6-7 and 9). The last phrase, *ate my bread*, probably indicates friendly hospitality, but in the final context of temple liturgy, it may also refer to the sacred meals that were part of a thanksgiving sacrifice (Ps 22:25-26, "...in the great congregation...the afflicted shall eat and be satisfied [and] praise the Lord!"). V. 10, *that I may requite them:* these words, like many others in the psalter of personal revenge, are very human yet still remain very difficult to accept within the inspired word of the Bible. Many explanations can be offered: that the psalmist will not personally seek revenge but let the ways of life converge against the enemy; or that the psalmist's own healing is itself a rebuke and humiliation to the enemy. Somehow or other, none of these edifying answers hold up! See Ps 69 for further discussion.

Vv. 11-12 reflect *a thanksgiving ceremony* in the temple where the congregation feels that God has *set me in thy presence for ever*. The phrase, however, can simply mean to live peacefully in the promised land (*cf.,* Ps 11:7) but the liturgical ambience of the psalms favors a more cultic explanation.

V. 13, *conclusion* to the First Book of the Psalter, similar to Pss 72:20; 89:52; 106:48 and the entire Ps 150, which mark a formal closing of the other four books of the psalter. *Amen and Amen* simply transliterate a Hebrew stative verb, to be firm, reliable, consistent with one's person, calling, responsibility and hopes, to be openly and fully what one is, particularly what one is in God's call and plans.

(IV) Ps 41 is not among the great poetic achievements of the psalter, nor is it a great clarifier of theology, not even a favorite psalm to which many turn in sickness, calumny or gratitude. In God's wisdom, however, we need an ordinary psalm for ordinary persons to express their feeling! If the psalm was collated from laments and thanksgiving, it certainly claimed a steady place in temple piety and was popular among the people generally. Sometimes our day or even our year ends with no fanfare, just with the quiet falling of the sun over the horizon; Ps 41 is made for such times.

BOOK II
(PSALMS 42-72)

Psalm 42
To The Choirmaster. A Maskil Of The Sons Of Korah.

I

[1]As a hart longs
  for flowing streams,
so longs my soul
  for thee, O God.
[2]My soul thirsts for God,
  for the living God.
When shall I come and behold
  the face of God?
[3]My tears have been my food
  day and night,
while men say to me continually,
  "Where is your God?"

[4]These things I remember,
  as I pour out my soul:
how I went with the throng,
  and led them in procession to the house of God,
with glad shouts and songs of thanksgiving,
  a multitude keeping festival.

⁵Why are you cast down, O my soul,
    and why are you disquieted within me?
Hope in God; for I shall again praise him
    my help ⁶and my God.

II

My soul is cast down within me,
    therefore I remember thee
from the land of Jordan and of Hermon,
    from Mount Mizar.
⁷Deep calls to deep
    at the thunder of thy cataracts;
all thy waves and thy billows
    have gone over me.

⁸By day the Lord commands his steadfast love;
    and at night his song is with me,
    a prayer to the God of my life.

⁹I say to God, my rock:
    "Why hast thou forgotten me?
Why go I mourning
    because of the oppression of the enemy?"
¹⁰As with a deadly wound in my body,
    my adversaries taunt me,
while they say to me continually,
    "Where is your God?"

¹¹Why are you cast down, O my soul,
    and why are you disquieted within me?
Hope in God; for I shall again praise him,
    my help and my God.

Psalm 43

III

¹Vindicate me, O God, and defend my cause
    against an ungodly people;
from deceitful and unjust men deliver me!
²For thou art the God in whom I take refuge;
    why hast thou cast me off?

Why go I mourning
because of the oppression of the enemy?

³Oh send out thy light and thy truth;
let them lead me,
let them bring me to thy holy hill
and to thy dwelling!
⁴Then I will go to the altar of God,
to God my exceeding joy;
and I will praise thee with the lyre,
O God, my God.

⁵Why are you cast down, O my soul,
and why are you disquieted within me?
Hope in God; for I shall again praise him,
my help and my God.

(I) It is generally agreed that Pss 42-43 constitute a *single* poem or lament. This fact becomes clear, not only from some very early Hebrew manuscripts which indicate no break between the two psalms but also from the absence of a title for Ps 43 (the only instance of such an omission in Book Two of the psalter except Ps 71), from the identical rhythm in both poems, and especially from the recurring refrain (42:5, 11; 43:5). We also note below a number of other features favoring a developmental unity.

As the title indicates, the author belonged to a group of levites called *The Sons of Korah*, who are responsible for two series of psalms, Pss 42-49 and Pss 84-85 + 87-88. Each series begins with a lament or a nostalgic longing for the sanctuary, as though the psalmist had been banished from the temple. References to Korah in the First Book of Chronicles indicate a serious demotion in rank: in 1 Chron 9:31, they are reduced to the "charge of making the flat cakes" for the liturgy; in 1 Chron 9:19, to the "charge of the work of the service [and] keepers of the entrance." However, by contrast in another series of passages the Korahites appear in an earlier more prominent position, as in 2 Chron 20:19, "the Korahites stood up to praise the Lord, the God of Israel, with a very loud voice." The plot thickens when we turn to

Num 16, a long story about a revolt of the Korahites against the authority and prestige of other levites and their severe punishment; Num 26:11 adds that "notwithstanding, the sons of Korah did not die." Our facts are too scattered and fragmentary to reach a certain conclusion, yet they raise strong suspicions that the Korahites lost out in a serious struggle for rank and power. Some of them could have been banished, all of them were excluded from any prominent role in the liturgy. We ask if Pss 42-43 and 84 reflect the nostalgic pain over the loss? Or were the Korahites suffering from the common lot of all Israelites, captured in war and exiled in a foreign country?

(II) The single poem of Pss 42-43 is divided into three strophes. The meter of lamentation (3 + 2) is maintained throughout, along with a series of significant developments:

(I)	42:1-4	*past* is recalled	timid & afraid	yearning for God	water, life-giving	desert terrain
	v. 5, refrain					
(II)	42:6-10	*present* suffering	affirmed	deserted by God	water, destructive	mountainous terrain
	v. 11, refrain					
(III)	43:1-4	*future* hopes	triumphant	petition and hope	light, life-giving	sanctuary terrain
	v. 5, refrain					

In the three-fold repetition of the refrain, it is possible that the emphasis after the first strophe was on the first line: after the second strophe, on the second line; and after the final strophe, on the third and fourth lines of the refrain:

strophe 1 stresses *Why are you cast down, O my soul,*
strophe 2 stresses *and why are you disquieted within me?*
strophe 3 stresses *Hope in God; for I shall again praise him,*
        my help and my God.

From the above outline we see that the psalm develops at least five motifs which are summarized at the end of each stanza by one or two of the lines. The rich interlacing of emotions and themes also becomes evident from the various dialogues or poles of tension within Pss 42-43:

God's distance	& presence	rock	& sea
water (food)	& water (destructive)	with oneself	& with outsiders
downcast	& worship	mourning	& joy
desert	& abundant water	scorned	& reaching out

We are impressed by the numerous times, 22 altogether, that God is mentioned. Except for one instance (v. 8, in a context of the covenant) the divine name is always God or *'elohim*. With Ps 42 we have left behind the "Yahwist Psalms," and from here to Ps 83 we are in the midst of the "Elohist collection." If these details, drawn particularly from L. Alonso Schökel and L. Jacquet, are burdensome, they can be overlooked; this psalm will carry itself by its emotional depth, strong sincerity, and evident piety. The reading is not impeded even by the many textual problems along the way of the Hebrew text.

(III) Vv. 1-4, *nostalgic remembrance.* In this elegy the psalm dialogues with God and with itself over the deprivation of attending temple liturgy. In fact, the psalmist will sometimes call upon ritual language to express this separation and longing. *As a hind* (female, from the feminine gender of the verb) *longs for flowing streams.* The verb, *longs*, occurs in only one other place of the Hebrew Bible, the liturgical Book of Joel 1:20, "Even the wild beasts *cry* to thee [O God,] because the water brooks are dried up, and fire has devoured the pastures of the wilderness." *behold the face of God:* the Hebrew makes a theological correction and reads in a passive form, "that I may be seen [in] the presence of God." The correction represents a later Old Testament stage when only the high priest came into the Holy of Holies, just once a year, amid a cloud of incense; in quoting this passage, Rev 22:4 recalls the original form, "they shall see his face." In any case the phrase was a technical term for entering the temple precincts (Deut 31:11, "when all Israel comes to appear before the face of the Lord your God at the place which he will choose"). In many parts of the Bible, God is the source of living water, an image of life in its purity and strength (Jer 2:13; Ps 36:9); ritual texts see this water symbolically flowing from the altar of sacrifice (Ps 46:4; Ezek 47). *my tears have been my food,* substituting for the sacred meal at the sanctuary (Ps 22:26); somehow or other sorrowful tears, discipline and nourish the psalmist! *day and night:* it is difficult to know if the text refers to night vigils (see Ps 1:2). *as I pour out my soul:* the words recall a double image of water, sorrowfully missing in this time of spiritual drought, also the image of water poured out sacrificially in temple ritual (1 Sam 7:6; Is 57:6).

V. 5, *refrain,* to be sung by the community, once the psalm was incorporated into temple liturgy. *Why are you cast down:* the Hebrew verb (*shaḥaḥ*) is almost identical in spelling with *shaḥah,* "to bow in worship," a word where the final "h" is less forceful. Somehow or other the psalmist's prostrating in sorrow has turned into adoration. *hope in God:* the verb is also used of a pregnant mother, waiting and hoping for what she already possesses.

Vv. 6-10, *elegy over present sorrows* + v. 11, *the refrain.* The setting changes from the desert wilderness to the marshy land, north of the Lake of Galilee, extending to Mount Hermon, a snow-capped, three-summit peak, 9200'. *Mount Mizar* is unknown; the Hebrew word means "small." Some will translate: "from the country of Jordan and [Mount] Hermon, O small mountain," small, that is, compared with the dignity and wonder of Mount Zion, Jerusalem (*cf.,* Ps 68:16-17, where a similar comparison is made). The physical grandeur of Hermon is no match for the elevated spiritual wonder of Jerusalem. *Deep calls to deep:* the word *deep,* in Hebrew *tehom,* frequently refers to mythological sea monsters, the goddess *tiamat* in the Babylonian creation story, the primeval oceans in Gen 1:2; Ps 77:16; Isa 51:9-10. The psalmist expresses himself like the prophet Jonah 2:5, "The waters closed in over me, *the deep* was round about me." V. 8 is the one verse where God is called Lord or *Yahweh* and the covenant word, *steadfast love* occurs. The verse is snarled with many textual and rhythmic problems, yet clearly the covenant bond is strong enough to overcome demonic forces in v. 7, even to outride religious jealousy and problems, if our explanation of the Korahites is correct. V. 9, *God, my rock:* see Ps 18:2; 95:1. V. 10 raises the question of the psalmist's or levite's physical health, a serious blow for those who direct the worship of the *living* God.

Ps 43:1-4, *Prayer for the future* + v. 5, *refrain.* The geographical imagery modulates from the mountains around Hermon in the preceding strophe to the sanctuary of Mount Zion; the physical imagery, from water to light; the spirit from sorrow and distress to triumphant hope. *vindicate me:* the prayer asks God to fulfill his promises fully and so justify or vindicate himself as the covenant God of Israel. V. 4, *Then I will go to the altar of God, to God my exceeding joy:* reads in the Greek and ancient Latin, "...to the altar of God, the God who gives joy to my youth," a verse formerly spoken at the foot of the altar at the beginning of every Catholic mass.

(IV) Pss 42-43 have occupied a prominent place in various liturgical approaches towards God: 1) as mentioned already, as the priest began to mount the altar for the Eucharist; 2) in the Office of the Dead, as the deceased person begins a final journey into the heavenly sanctuary; 3) on Holy Saturday after the blessing of the baptismal water and during the procession to the baptistry. On the walls of some ancient baptistries a deer was sculptured, standing beside running water, holding a serpent in its mouth, to symbolize the defeat of the devil and the return to paradise where the four rivers of abundant, life-giving water flow (Gen 2-3). The spirituality of Pss 42-43 centers then around thirst and longing, a reaction all the more painful and poignant the closer anyone may be to the source of living water. The double imagery of water in the psalms —life-giving and destructive — reflects the twofold aspect of baptism, sharing in the death of Jesus, "so that the life of Jesus may be manifested in our mortal flesh" (2 Cor 4:11). While Pss 42-43 always have liturgical worship primarily in view, they apply very well to the personal, mystical experience, whether on earth or in purgatory, where the nearness of God and the brilliance of divine light blind and striken our senses and leave us with only an abyss of longing. Mystics, in fact, have interpreted 42:7 to mean that the "depth [of human weakness and sinfulness] is calling out to the depth [of divine strength and goodness]."

Psalm 44
To The Choirmaster. A Maskil Of The Sons Of Korah.

I

¹We have heard with our ears, O God,
  our fathers have told us,
  what deeds thou didst perform in their days,
    in the days of old:
²thou with thy own hand didst drive out the nations,
    but them thou didst plant;
  thou didst afflict the peoples,
    but them thou didst set free;
³for not by their own sword did they win the land,
    nor did their own arm give them victory;
  but thy right hand, and thy arm,
    and the light of thy countenance;
  'for thou didst delight in them.

⁴Thou art my King and my God,
  who ordainest victories for Jacob.
⁵Through thee we push down our foes;
  through thy name we tread down our assailants.
⁶For not in my bow do I trust,
  nor can my sword save me.
⁷But thou hast saved us from our foes,
  and hast put to confusion those who hate us.
⁸In God we have boasted continually,
  and we will give thanks to thy name for ever. *Selah*

II

⁹Yet thou hast cast us off and abased us,
  and hast not gone out with our armies.

¹⁰Thou hast made us turn back from the foe;
   and our enemies have gotten spoil.
¹¹Thou hast made us like sheep for slaughter,
   and hast scattered us among the nations.
¹²Thou hast sold thy people for a trifle,
   demanding no high price for them.

¹³Thou hast made us the taunt of our neighbors,
   the derision and scorn of those about us.
¹⁴Thou hast made us a byword among the nations,
   a laughingstock among the peoples.
¹⁵All day long my disgrace is before me,
   and shame has covered my face,
¹⁶at the words of the taunters and revilers,
   at the sight of the enemy and the avenger.

III

¹⁷All this has come upon us,
   though we have not forgotten thee,
   or been false to thy covenant.
¹⁸Our heart has not turned back,
   nor have our steps departed from thy way,
¹⁹that thou shouldst have broken us in the place of jackals,
   and covered us with deep darkness.

²⁰If we had forgotten the name of our God,
   or spread forth our hands to a strange god,
²¹would not God discover this?
   For he knows the secrets of the heart.
²²Nay, for thy sake we are slain all the day long,
   and accounted as sheep for the slaughter.

IV

²³Rouse thyself! Why sleepest thou, O Lord?
   Awake! Do not cast us off for ever!
²⁴Why dost thou hide thy face?
   Why dost thou forget our affliction and oppression?
²⁵For our soul is bowed down to the dust;
   our body cleaves to the ground.
²⁶Rise up, come to our help!
   Deliver us for the sake of thy steadfast love!

(I) Every religious person, and religion itself, shall come to the agony and darkness of Ps 44 when credal statements, ritual actions and family traditions seem like pious generalities that collapse before the onslaught of massive, useless suffering. This psalm belongs to the tradition of Jeremiah, Habbakuk and Job, when our human questions become the word of God to us and when the dark, mystic experience of God is more sustaining than the clear articulation of faith, yet it is the strength of this articulated faith in God's fidelity and compassion that precipitates the agony and leads to the final word, as in this psalm, of God's *steadfast love.*

It is generally recognized that the closest biblical parallel is located in 2 Chron 20:1-19. In the days of King Jehoshaphat (873-849 B.C.), as Judah was invaded by Moabites and Ammonites, the king proclaimed a fast and prayed:

> O Lord, God of our ancestors, art thou not God in heaven?. . . Didst thou not, O our God, drive out the inhabitants of this land before thy people Israel, and give it for ever to the descendants of Abraham thy friend (2 Chron 20:6-7).

In 2 Chron 20:22-23 the enemy turned upon one another and defeated themselves without Israel risking a single life. God was truly Israel's savior! Yet in Ps 44 Israel has suffered a severe military defeat. The psalm then is closer in spirit to Pss 42-43, also composed by the "sons of Korah," in which happy memories make the present sorrow all the more painful. As to date and occasion, it seems impossible to be more exact than to think of the late pre-exilic age, before the destruction of the temple (a trauma never mentioned in Ps 44), contemporaneous perhaps with the prophet Jeremiah (627-587) when the revival of the Deuteronomic law proved insufficient and the people must prepare for still greater suffering and purification. The influence of Jeremiah and Deuteronomy, northern traditions like the Elohist Psalter in Book Two of the psalms, show up in Ps 44.

(II) This communal lament shows a clear enough structure, yet as Ps 44 is read carefully some intricate or delicate interaction of voices is detected:

vv. 1-8	*Hymnic Introduction*	vv. 9-16	*Community Lament*
vv. 1-2	Call to praise, sung by everyone	v. 15	individual cantor or choir
v. 3	Motivation by large choir	vv. 17-22	Reflection, in which different choirs
v. 7	Confidence		
vv. 4&6	individual cantor or special choir	vv. 17-19	speak to God
		vv. 20-21	speak about God
v. 8	choral refrain by everyone	v. 22	speak to God

vv. 23-26, *Prayer of Petition*

(III) Ps 44 opens in hymnic style (vv. 1-8). It may have followed a liturgical proclamation, either in the sanctuary, or in family worship if we see a strong influence of Deuteronomy here (*cf.,* Deut 4:9, "Only take heed, and keep your soul diligently, lest you forget the things which your eyes have seen... make them known to your children and your children's children"; also 6:7, 20-25). A classic example of Israel's creed would be Deut 26:1-11, again celebrated in the extended family unit ("Your house, the Levite and the sojourner among you"). The hymn reflects the "Holy War" tradition in proclaiming Yahweh as the warrior who battles for Israel, as in Josh 1-6 in which Israel's part consisted in reciting the Torah, trusting in Yahweh, and obediently complying with liturgical prescriptions. Therefore, Yahweh calls it "my land" (Josh 22:19; Jer 16:18). While first referring to "days of old" (vv. 1-3), the psalm confidently actualizes the past in the present moment (vv. 4-8, "through thee *we* push down our foes...").

Vv. 9-16. A communal lament picks up identical words or at least similar motifs from the preceding strophe, only to reverse them: in v. 7, the foes were *put to confusion,* now in v. 9, *thou has abased us;* in v. 7, *thou hast saved us from our foes,* yet in v. 10, *thou hast made us turn back from the foe.* Present reality is denying the glorious statements of Israel's ancient faith. Yet the psalmist remains closely in touch with Israel's traditions, this time those of community lament: *cast us off* (Pss 43:2; 74:1; etc.); *not gone out with our armies* (Num 10:35; Jos 6:6; 1 Sam 4:3; 7:5-11); *sheep for slaughter* (Jer 11:19; 12:3; Isa 53:7); *laughingstock* (literally, wagging or shaking one's head, Pss 22:7, 64:8; Job 16:4).

Vv. 17-22, as in the case of Jeremiah or Job, the innocent sufferers still need to separate the precious from what is worthless in their hearts (Ps 12:6; Jer 15:19). V. 21, *Would not God discover this?* almost as though God has forgotten or made a mistake! V. 22, *For thy sake we are slain all the day long:* this verse is quoted in Rom 8:36 where death and every other trial is overcome "because of him who has loved us," the same appeal to be found at the end of Ps 44.

Vv. 23-26. desperate petitioning of God, consisting of imperative calls, agonizing questions, statement of helplessness but ending with the covenant word, *thy steadfast love. Why sleepest thou?:* it seems as though Yahweh is classified with gods like Baal whose prophets were taunted by Elijah on Mount Carmel: "Cry aloud, for he is a god; either he is musing, or he has gone aside . . . or perhaps he is asleep and must be awakened" (1 Kgs 18:27). Yet this is Yahweh, who according to Ps 121:4 "will neither slumber nor sleep." The psalmist is faced with an experience most dreadful for a just person, the silence of God (*cf.,* Pss 10:1; 22:1). V. 25, *bowed down*, see comments on Ps 42:5, where the same Hebrew word is translated, "cast down." V. 26, *rise up:* a call associated with the ark of the covenant and its faithful journeys with Israel (Num 10:35; Ps 68:1). From beginning to end, the psalm remains within the faith tradition of Israel. Because the psalmist took the faith this seriously, the people were being purified ever more thoroughly. None of the psalmist's questions are answered, yet to speak them before God and for them to become the word of God in the Bible means that God and the people were communicating at a depth beyond words.

(IV) This psalm enables us to deal with the silence of God, with hopes and ideals that reach even beyond the sacred words of tradition, with the need for the "just" to be purified still further in their motivation, with the strength of faith and credal formulas to lead us into a mystic experience of God, too intimately personal for the legal formulations of the covenant yet approached and discovered through the promises of the covenant. The repetition of the word and idea of *shame* in Ps 44 enables us to deal with a personal reaction that can be destructive of human dignity and therefore of human morals, but can also lead to the purest motives for love and fidelity — not for anyone else's sake but for "thy steadfast love," O God!

Psalm 45
To The Choirmaster: According To Lilies. A Maskil Of The Sons Of Korah; A Love Song.

I
¹My heart overflows with a goodly theme;
  I address my verses to the king;
    my tongue is like the pen of a ready scribe.

II
²You are the fairest of the sons of men;
  grace is poured upon your lips;
    therefore God has blessed you for ever.
³Gird your sword upon your thigh, O mighty one,
  in your glory and majesty!

⁴In your majesty ride forth victoriously
  for the cause of truth and to defend the right;
    let your right hand teach you dread deeds!
⁵Your arrows are sharp
  in the heart of the king's enemies;
    the peoples fall under you.

⁶Your divine throne endures for ever and ever.
  Your royal scepter is a scepter of equity;
⁷ you love righteousness and hate wickedness.

Therefore God, your God, has anointed you
  with the oil of gladness above your fellows;
8 your robes are all fragrant with myrrh and aloes
  and cassia.
From ivory palaces stringed instruments make you glad;
9 daughters of kings are among your ladies of honor;
  at your right hand stands the queen in gold of Ophir.

III

10Hear, O daughter, consider, and incline your ear;
  forget your people and your father's house;
11 and the king will desire your beauty.
Since he is your lord, bow to him;
12 the people of Tyre will sue your favor with gifts,
  the richest of the people 13with all kinds of wealth.

The princess is decked in her chamber
  with gold-woven robes;
14 in many-colored robes she is led to the king,
  with her virgin companions, her escort, in her train.
15With joy and gladness they are led along
  as they enter the palace of the king.

IV

16Instead of your fathers shall be your sons;
  you will make them princes in all the earth.
17I will cause your name to be celebrated
  in all generations;
  therefore the peoples will praise you for ever and ever.

(I) Liturgical texts and patristic writers in early Christianity consistently interpreted this psalm symbolically of the marital bond between Christ and the church, and to this extent completed a cycle of exposition found in late Judaism among the rabbis and in the Aramaic translation, the Targum, who saw in the psalm the figure of David, his messianic son and the eschatological Israel. Modern scholars are not at all this certain. Some, like Raymond Tournay, O.P., and Alphons Deissler position themselves close to late Judaism and consider the psalm the product of a temple scribe in the 4th century who drew heavily upon prophetical texts and the Song of Songs, to sustain faith in Israel's messianic hope. Others, like Artur Weiser, explain Ps 45 as the single example of a profane lyric in the Book of Psalms; A. Maillot and A. Lelièvre tilt towards a marriage song, honoring and consecrating marital love and its joys. E. Beaucamp argues strongly that it was composed for the marriage of King Ahab and Queen Jezebel of the northern kingdom (@ 869 B.C.). Another writer, L. Jacquet, prefers to see the wedding of King Hezekiah of Judah (@ 715 B.C.).

Undoubtedly the psalm represents a long interpretive tradition. It was originally composed, in my opinion, for a royal marriage within the northern kingdom with its ivory palace (v. 9; *cf.,* 1 Kgs 22:39), its relations with Tyre and Sidon (v. 12; *cf.,* 1 Kgs 16:31), and the name of its king Ahab (=one who loves) possibly reflected in v. 7, *you love righteousness.* Later the psalm was adapted to the southern royalty, especially for King Hezekiah with its reference to the king as *"God"* (*cf.,* Isa 7:14, to be called "Immanuel" or "God with us"), *mighty one* or hero (*cf.,* Isa 9:6, "mighty hero," literally, God-hero). The psalm also interacted with the prophetic tradition by which Israel (as in Hos 1-3 or Jer 2:1-3) or Zion (as in Isa 61:10-11; 66:7-14) are addressed as the spouse of the Lord who will give birth to the messianic people. The evolution of the psalm possibly began with the marriage of an Israelite king with a foreign, pagan princess and extended all the way to the mystical marriage between Christ and the church or between Christ and the saints.

(II) This royal psalm can be easily subdivided: v. 1, solemn introduction; vv. 2-9, eulogizing the royal bridegroom, in a stately, dignified style; vv. 10-15, acclaiming the bride, yet like a teacher who imparts instruction, in the midst of which the bridal procession with musical accompaniment approaches the palace; finally vv. 16-17a, final words for the king. The liturgical conclusion in v. 17b breaks the meter and may be a late addition.

(III) V. 1, *the introduction,* is similar to Pss 49 and 78 and provides a dignified setting in which to begin the marriage ceremony. *a goodly theme* reads literally "a good word," and may allude to Joshua's farewell to Israel: "and you know in your heart and souls, all of you, that not one thing (lit., one word) has failed of all the good things (lit., good words) which the Lord your God promised." The psalmist prays that Joshua's promise for Israel find its fulfillment in the royal marriage. *I address:* the Hebrew emphasizes the personal privilege which *I myself* have received in announcing these good words. The style of this introduction is more "private" or "sapiential" (see also v. 10a) than is appropriate for public liturgy. V. 1 may represent the final editing by the Sons of Korah (see the title to this psalm and to Ps 42 + commentary), after they had been demoted within the priestly ranks and could no longer lead the worship.

Vv. 2-9, eulogizing the royal bridegroom. The language is stately and traditional, not obsequious nor demeaning. It draws upon memories that are the substance of hope for the future — from the royal protocol of 2 Sam 7 and David's perpetual dynasty (v. 6); from royal etiquette in Egypt and other foreign countries. *Your divine throne:* reads in the Hebrew, "Your throne, O God." This use of the word "God" is not common today; in Israel *'elohim* could apply to members of Yahweh's heavenly court (Pss 29:1; 82:1) and to important persons like Moses whom scripture declares will be to Aaron "as God" (Exod 4:16).

Vv. 10-15 acclaim the bride, but carefully instruct her to *forget your people and your father's house;* the psalmist was fearful lest the foreign princess contaminate the religion of Israel. His fears were legitimate, as we see in the case of Solomon (1 Kgs 11) and Ahab (1 Kgs 16:31-32).

(IV) We spoke already of the adaptation of the psalm to an ever more spiritual meaning. In the Epistle to the Hebrews vv. 6-7 are quoted to establish the superiority of Jesus over the angels as "God's first born"; Jesus is proclaimed Son of God in full divinity. St. Augustine wrote lyrically of Jesus as *the fairest* [or most beautiful] *of the sons of men* (v. 2): "He is beautiful in the heavens as the Word with God; beautiful on earth, robed with human nature; he is beautiful within the womb and beautiful in the arms of his parents; he is beautiful in miracles, and beautiful in his flagellation; he is beautiful in conferring life and beautiful in not refusing to die; he is beautiful in giving up his soul and in taking it back; he is beautiful on the cross, beautiful in the sepulchre, beautiful in his return to heaven." Thomas Aquinas takes advantage of this passage to extol the excellence of Jesus, physically, emotionally, spiritually — in every aspect of his being human as well as divine. Both writers seem to recapitulate the history of Ps 45, from the physical-emotional joys of marriage to the glory of the mystical marriage of God and Israel, Christ and the church.

Psalm 46
To The Choirmaster. A Psalm Of The Sons Of Korah. According To Alamoth. A Song.

I

¹God is our refuge and strength,
  a very present help in trouble.
²Therefore we will not fear though the
    earth should change,
   though the mountains shake in the heart of the sea;
³though its waters roar and foam,
   though the mountains tremble with its tumult. *Selah*

II

⁴There is a river whose streams make glad the city of God,
  the holy habitation of the Most High.
⁵God is in the midst of her, she shall not be moved;
  God will help her right early.
⁶The nations rage, the kingdoms totter;
  he utters his voice, the earth melts.
⁷The Lord of hosts is with us;
  the God of Jacob is our refuge.   *Selah*

III

⁸Come, behold the works of the Lord,
  how he has wrought desolations in the earth.
⁹He makes wars cease to the end of the earth;
  he breaks the bow, and shatters the spear,
  he burns the chariots with fire!

¹⁰"Be still, and know that I am God.
   I am exalted among the nations,
   I am exalted in the earth!"
¹¹The Lord of hosts is with us;
   the God of Jacob is our refuge.   *Selah*

(I) As a people of faith, we are invited into the center of God's presence, into the holy city of Jerusalem, the symbol of God's absolute fidelity and unassailable strength. Here Christians form the assembly of the church, the new Jerusalem. Ps 46 is the first of the Zion Songs in the psalter and is close in spirit with Pss 48 and 76. While Ps 76 may reflect the period of David with little or no shadow of serious difficulty, we associate Ps 46 with the reign of King Hezekiah, and the devastating invasion of Sennacherib (701 B.C.), and Ps 48 with the still more sombre epoch of King Josiah (640-609 B.C.), Judah's last chance at survival and reconstruction.

During King Hezekiah's reign most of Judah had been burnt to the ground and only Jerusalem remained intact. The Assyrian king Sennacherib arranged a treaty of survival for Jerusalem (2 Kgs 18:13-16). The withdrawal of Sennacherib gradually became a major symbol of God's intervention to save Jerusalem at all costs. There developed the notion of Jerusalem's inviolability, even to the point of being miraculously preserved (Isa 37:30-36). This ever greater enhancement of Jerusalem is seen in the prophecy of Isaiah — Zion can be seriously threatened but never completely destroyed. The Isaian double symbolism of peaceful waters that bring life and raging waters that sweep destruction before them (Isa 8:5-8), linked with the name of *Immanuel — God with us* (Isa 7:14) and the title, "God of Jacob" (Isa 2:3), are interwoven into Ps 46: raging waters in v. 3, life-giving waters in v. 4, God with us and God of Jacob in the refrain of vv. 7 and 11. Ps 46 reminds us of the time when Philistia was thrown into a panic yet "The Lord has founded Zion, and in her the afflicted of his people find refuge" (Isa 14:31-32).

(II) This canticle of Zion began as a hymn of praise, prophetically influenced in many of its motifs and even in its style of oracle in v. 10. Once Jerusalem was actually destroyed in 587 B.C., the psalm had to be reinterpreted and in the postexilic age it announced the new Jerusalem which will emerge out of the ashes and the titanic struggles of the eschatological age. Vv. 1-3 praise Yahweh with mythological language and imagery of eruptions across the universe; vv. 4-7 praise Yahweh within the Jerusalem temple where the mythological references in vv. 1-3 have been historicized for victory over foreign nations; vv. 8-11 praise Yahweh in the midst of sanctuary song and ritual. We note several simultaneous developments in the three strophes: the setting modulates from the universe to the Jerusalem temple and finally to its liturgical action; mythology about shaking mountains and raging oceans evolves into historical action of armies beseiging the holy city and then to theological reflection on universal peace. The refrain after vv. 4-6 and 8-10 also belongs after the first strophe, vv. 1-3.

(III) Vv. 1-3 draw upon mythological imagery, common across the ancient Near East: roaring and destructive waters and the shaking of mountains: see comments on Ps 29; also Ps 89:9-12 where the mythology in the earlier verses is also historicized in the later stanza of vv. 19-37. The phrase, *a very present help* in v. 1, is translated "infallible" by L. Jacquet, in that God will never permit our basic community of faith and its external manifestation to disappear — even if Israel and the church must go through excruciating moments of death and resurrection, they always emerge stronger and purer.

Vv. 4-7 focus the cosmic imagery upon the Holy City, a mountain that never collapses into the sea, a home where water sustains life rather than destroys it. Words that were used of the raging waters and the tottering mountains in vv. 1-3 are now employed of foreign nations that rage and totter before the voice of the Lord. Not only has the raging water been pacified into a gentle fresh stream (we think of "the waters of Shiloah that flow gently" from the base of Zion into the Holy City — Isa 8:6) but these life-giving waters are "relocated" liturgically at the altar, the rock from which they now flow as in Joel 3:18, "a fountain shall come forth from the house of the Lord." The abundant streams of water in the first paradise (*cf.,* Gen 2:10-14) are also associated with the temple in Ps 46 and in a series of texts like Ezek 47;

Isa 33:21; Zech 14:8 and most clearly of all in Sir 24 where "the book of the covenant" comes to rest at Zion where it "fills people with wisdom like the Pishon and the Tigris ...understanding like the Euphrates...instruction shines forth like the Gihon" (Sir 24:24-27). V. 7, the refrain, strongly redolent of Isaiah, whose ministry began with a vision of the Lord of hosts (Isa 6:3) and could be summarized and capped with the enthronement of "the God of Jacob" on "the mountain of the house of the Lord [to which] all the nations shall flow" (Isa 2:2-3).

Vv. 8-11 are in the style of a vision: *Come, behold*, climaxed in v. 10, *Be still and experience how I am God!*

(IV) This vision of universal peace, centering at Jerusalem or in the church but reaching through the earth, is as certain as God's faithfulness, but it must be received in faith — that is, as reaching beyond our apparent human ability and limited ideals, as conditioned only by our willingness to share peace with all peoples. If such a hope is abused by selfish or narrow interests, then "I have hewn them by the prophets, I have slain them by the words of my mouth" (Hos 6:5). Ps 46 features prominently in the liturgy for the feast of the Epiphany which celebrated universal salvation, the baptism of the Lord and the transformation of water into wine at Cana — motifs of water and nations, prominent also in the psalm. Ps 46 is part of the ceremony for the dedication of a church. It inspired Martin Luther's famous hymn, *Ein feste Burg is unser Gott — A Mighty Fortress is our God.*

Psalm 47
To The Choirmaster. A Psalm Of The Sons Of Korah.

I-a

¹Clap your hands, all peoples!
  Shout to God with loud songs of joy!

-b-

²For the Lord, the Most High, is terrible,
  a great king over all the earth.
³He subdued peoples under us,
  and nations under our feet.

-c-

⁴He chose our heritage for us,
    the pride of Jacob whom he loves.   *Selah*

⁵God has gone up with a shout,
    the Lord with the sound of a trumpet.

II-a

⁶Sing praises to God, sing praises!
    Sing praises to our King, sing praises!

-b-

⁷For God is the king of all the earth;
    sing praises with a psalm!

⁸God reigns over the nations;
    God sits on his holy throne.

-c-

⁹The princes of the peoples gather
    as the people of the God of Abraham.
For the shields of the earth belong to God;
    he is highly exalted!

(I) We need to visualize and hear this psalm (not just read it) in conjunction with other biblical passages which speak of processions with the ark and so to reconstruct its setting within festival moments at Jerusalem: (a) as the ark approaches the Holy City, the people break into song and dance: 1 Sam 4-6; 2 Sam 6; (b) a procession with the ark around the city walls: Ps 48:12-14; (c) at the city gate, a ceremony of purification and reconciliation: Ps 15:3-6, "Who shall ascend the hill of the Lord?. . . the one with clean hands and a pure heart"; (d) the gates are swung open: Ps 24:7, 9; (e) the people march through the outer courtyard: Ps 100; (f) the ark is carried into the Holy of Holies: Ps 47; (g) Yahweh is once again proclaimed King: Pss 93 or 95. See E. Otto and T. Schramm, *Festival of Joy* (1980) 59-65.

The universalism of Ps 47 makes us think of the reign of King David, when Israel's kingdom extended from Egypt to the Euphrates. Even though the military might by which the empire was established collapsed, still the memory of a "world empire" imparted an important substance within Israelite religion, which would re-emerge in the postexilic psalms about Yahweh's eschatological kingdom.

(II) We disregard the *selah* at the end of v. 4 and divide Ps 47 into two sections which enable us to see the transfer from a political emphasis to a more religious-cultic reign of God:

v. 1,	Call to praise from all peoples	v. 6,	Call to praise *our* God, Israel
vv. 2-3,	Motivation: God, the Most High has sub- dued peoples under us.	vv. 7-8,	Motivation: God reigns over the nations and is enthroned.
vv. 4-5,	Conclusion: election of Israel; God mounts his throne.	v. 9,	Conclusion: election is shared by all nations.

(III) Vv. 1-5, the first section of this processional hymn is more nationalistic and patriotic. The clap of hands and particularly the shout had a strong political and even military character: Num 23:21; Josh 6:16, 20: 1 Sam 10:24; Ezra 3:12. The epithet, *Most High* (in Hebrew, *'elyon*) recalls Melchizedek "priest of God Most High" (Gen 14:18-20); it is frequently associated with Jerusalem in the Psalms and carries a universal connotation, here more noticeable than usual. There may be a play on words in the Hebrew between *the Lord 'elyon* and *God* [who] *has gone up* (v. 5; in Hebrew *'alah*).

Vv. 6-9, here the religious character is more pronounced. V. 7, *with a psalm:* the Hebrew word, *maskil,* implies beauty, artistic quality, appropriateness. V. 8, *God reigns:* the phrase is similar to the enthronement of kings in ancient times (2 Sam 15:10; 2 Kgs 9:13), yet God is considered as continuing in the role always his, only actualizing it anew *as though* for the first time. *God sits on his holy throne:* God was invisibly present above the ark, between the cherubim in the Holy of Holies (Exod 25:22). V. 9, *shields of the earth:* reference to princes.

(IV) This biblical "Marseillaise" or national anthem is still recited by Jewish people, seven times before sounding the trumpet which signals the new year on the eve of *Rosh HaShanah*. Christian liturgy associates it with the feasts of Epiphany and Ascension, when Christ is acclaimed king of all the earth. For us it provides an excellent example not only of spiriting religion with new enthusiasm but also of remembering our hopes of a universal kingdom. This psalm calls us to transfer the political or economic success of our lives into Christ's kingdom where everyone worships "in spirit and in truth" (John 4:23).

Psalm 48
A Song. A Psalm Of The Sons Of Korah.

I

¹Great is the Lord and greatly to be praised
  in the city of our God!
 His holy mountain, ²beautiful in elevation,
  is the joy of all the earth,
 Mount Zion, in the far north,
  the city of the great King.
³Within her citadels God
  has shown himself a sure defense.

II

⁴For lo, the kings assembled,
  they came on together.
⁵As soon as they saw it, they were astounded,
  they were in panic, they took to flight;
⁶trembling took hold of them there,
  anguish as of a woman in travail.
⁷By the east wind, thou didst shatter
  the ships of Tarshish.
⁸As we have heard, so have we seen
  in the city of the Lord of hosts,
 in the city of our God,
  which God establishes for ever.   *Selah*

III

9We have thought on thy steadfast love, O God,
　in the midst of thy temple.
10As thy name, O God,
　so thy praise reaches to the ends of the earth.
　Thy right hand is filled with victory;
11 let Mount Zion be glad!
　Let the daughters of Judah rejoice
　because of thy judgments!

IV

12Walk about Zion, go round about her,
　number her towers,
13consider well her ramparts,
　go through her citadels;
　that you may tell the next generation
14 that this is God,
　our God for ever and ever.
　He will be our guide for ever.

(I) The origin of Ps 48 is similar to that of Ps 46. After Jerusalem was preserved from destruction before Sennacherib's army (701 B.C.), the doctrine of its invincible strength became so firmly rooted in Judah, that even its destruction by the Babylonians in 587 B.C., only served to solidify the idea of its continuous rebirth. There emerged such texts as Ezek 38-39 which proclaim Jerusalem's preservation from all attacks, even from the onslaught of Gog, or Isa 54 which sees the repopulation of the Holy City.

(II) This hymn in praise of Zion can be subdivided:

vv. 1-3, Call to praise Jerusalem, city of our God, fairest of heights.

vv. 4-8, Motivation: Jerusalem invincible.

vv. 9-11, New Call to praise and to rejoice.

vv. 12-14, Solemn procession. (see Ps 47, introduction)

(III) This psalm is a gold mine of titles for Jerusalem: city of our God, holy mountain, beautiful in elevation (or better, "fairest of heights," NAB), Joy of all the earth, in the far north (or better, "Recesses of the north," NAB; *cf.,* Isa 13:14), city of the great King. Some of these titles originated in pagan mythology and served to communicate the mysterious meaning of Jerusalem.

(IV) What began politically and then continued for a time in a religious guise in Ps 48, underwent a death-and-new-life experience and was totally reinterpreted. This type of rereading is found in Jesus' statement about the temple which must be destroyed and rise again in his own body, a fulfillment never anticipated in the earlier Scriptures and understood by Jesus' disciples only after "he was raised from the dead" (John 2:19-22). The fulfillment of Scripture then often implies a death to what had been expected. It is interesting to note that Ps 48 ends in the Hebrew, *'al-muth,* "unto or beyond death," an enigmatic phrase, sometimes corrected to *'olamoth,* "forever." The new life, once it comes forth, will be seen in continuity with the earlier passages of the Bible. By faith the ancient Scriptures lead us to an understanding beyond the immediate sense of the Word of God.

Psalm 49
To The Choirmaster. A Psalm Of The Sons Of Korah.

I

¹Hear this, all peoples!
  Give ear, all inhabitants of the world,
²both low and high,
  rich and poor together!
³My mouth shall speak wisdom;
  the meditation of my heart shall be understanding.
⁴I will incline my ear to a proverb;
  I will solve my riddle to the music of the lyre.

II

⁵Why should I fear in times of trouble,
  when the iniquity of my persecutors surrounds me,
⁶men who trust in their wealth

and boast of the abundance of their riches?
⁷Truly no man can ransom himself,
   or give to God the price of his life,
⁸for the ransom of his life is costly,
   and can never suffice,
⁹that he should continue to live on for ever,
   and never see the Pit.
¹⁰Yea, he shall see that even the wise die,
   the fool and the stupid alike must perish
and leave their wealth to others.
¹¹Their graves are their homes for ever,
   their dwelling places to all generations,
   though they named lands their own.
¹²Man cannot abide in his pomp,
   he is like the beasts that perish.

III

¹³This is the fate of those who have foolish confidence,
   the end of those who are pleased with their portion.
                                        Selah

¹⁴Like sheep they are appointed for Sheol;
   Death shall be their shepherd;
straight to the grave they descend,
   and their form shall waste away;
   Sheol shall be their home.
¹⁵But God will ransom my soul from the power of Sheol,
   for he will receive me.   *Selah*

¹⁶Be not afraid when one becomes rich,
   when the glory of his house increases.
¹⁷For when he dies he will carry nothing away;
   his glory will not go down after him.
¹⁸Though, while he lives, he counts himself happy,
   and though a man gets praise
      when he does well for himself,
¹⁹he will go to the generation of his fathers,
   who will never more see the light.
²⁰Man cannot abide in his pomp,
   he is like the beasts that perish.

(I) The first group of psalms from the "Sons of Korah" ends with Ps 49 (see Pss 42-43, introduction), again on a melancholy note, once more with a flash of hope as in the extraordinary line, v. 15, that *God will ransom my soul from the power of Sheol [and] receive me.* This psalm asserts that wealth and in fact every human resource pass away and cannot give true wisdom and absolute security. The thought remains within Israel's traditional view that rejected personal immortality (see Pss 6; 16; and 39). Yet because this psalm is composed in the style of proverbs — for that matter, like Ps 1 — it could risk: 1) contradictory statements: compare vv. 8-9 that no one *can live for ever and never see the Pit,* with v. 15, *God will ransom my soul from the power of Sheol;* or compare v. 14b, *Death shall be their shepherd* with Ps 23:1, "The Lord is my shepherd...though I walk through the valley...of death, I fear no evil"; 2) contrasting statements: compare v. 15, above, with v. 7, *no one can ransom themselves;* 3) unorthodox statements, especially in the refrain, vv. 12 and 20, *humankind...is like the beasts that perish, cf.,* Eccl 3:19; Job 18:3. With such an enigmatic style the psalmist risked a flashing insight, reaching towards personal immortality: *God will ransom my soul [and] receive me* (v. 15). The verb, *receive,* is the same used in Gen 5:24 about Enoch who "was not [seen on earth] for God *took* him" and also in 2 Kgs 2:3, 5, 9-11 about Elijah who was "*taken* from you...and went up by a whirlwind into heaven."

(II) This wisdom psalm is generally divided between: vv. 1-4, the long introduction; vv. 5-12 and 13-20, the discussion of transitory wealth, the inevitability of death and the baffling refrain.

(III-IV) The long, solemn introduction of this psalm, with even the summons for musical accompaniment (*I will solve my riddle to the music of the lyre* — v. 4b), seems to lead nowhere. The final line endorses the orthodox theology of Israel: that death and Sheol lie beyond the presence and power of Yahweh: each human being is like the beasts that perish (v. 20b, see Ps 16). One of the key words in the psalm, *to ransom* one's life from death, reminds us of Jesus's statement: "The Son of Man also came not to be served but to serve, and to give his life as a ransom for many" (Mark 10: 45); the inspired commentary also comes to mind: "You were ransomed from the futile ways inherited from your ancestors, not with perishable things such as silver or gold, but with the precious blood of Christ, like that of a lamb without blemish or spot" (1 Pet 1:18-19). The solution to wealth and the false hopes which it engenders, is not more silver and gold, but the bond of love that unites in family, "not to be served but to serve," which includes even the one flow of blood that makes God through Jesus one with us in a most intimate way.

Psalm 50
A Psalm Of Asaph.

I

¹Mighty One, God the Lord,
   speaks and summons the earth
   from the rising of the sun to its setting.
²Out of Zion, the perfection of beauty,
   God shines forth.

³Our God comes, he does not keep silence,
   before him is a devouring fire,
   round about him a mighty tempest.
⁴He calls to the heavens above
   and to the earth, that he may judge his people:
⁵"Gather to me my faithful ones,
   who made a covenant with me by sacrifice!"
⁶The heavens declare his righteousness,
   for God himself is judge!   *Selah*

II

⁷"Hear, O my people, and I will speak,
   O Israel, I will testify against you.
   I am God, your God.
⁸I do not reprove you for your sacrifices;
   your burnt offerings are continually before me.
⁹I will accept no bull from your house,

nor he-goat from your folds.
10For every beast of the forest is mine,
   the cattle on a thousand hills.
11I know all the birds of the air,
   and all that moves in the field is mine.
12If I were hungry, I would not tell you;
   for the world and all that is in it is mine.
13Do I eat the flesh of bulls,
   or drink the blood of goats?
14Offer to God a sacrifice of thanksgiving,
   and pay your vows to the Most High;
15and call upon me in the day of trouble;
   I will deliver you, and you shall glorify me."

III

16But to the wicked God says:
   "What right have you to recite my statutes,
   or take my covenant on your lips?
17For you hate discipline,
   and you cast my words behind you.
18If you see a thief, you are a friend of his;
   and you keep company with adulterers.
19You give your mouth free rein for evil,
   and your tongue frames deceit.
20You sit and speak against your brother;
   you slander your own mother's son.
21These things you have done and I have been silent;
   you thought that I was one like yourself.
   But now I rebuke you, and lay the charge before you.

IV

22"Mark this, then, you who forget God,
   lest I rend, and there be none to deliver!
23He who brings thanksgiving as his sacrifice honors me;
   to him who orders his way aright
   I will show the salvation of God!"

(I) While the preceding psalms of Korah (Pss 42-49) manifested delicacy and restraint, melancholy and hope, this psalm of Asaph appears vigorous and direct, confident and regal. While Korah was demoted (see introduction to Ps 42), Asaph was not only put in charge by David and "prophesized under the direction of the king" (1 Chron 25:1-2) but remained among the upper echelon of temple singers all the way into the postexilic era (Ezr 3:10). The temple singers of Asaph must have inherited a strong character to interact with prophets like Amos, Hosea, Isaiah and Micah — or their disciples — and yet maintain their own dignity, self-respect and control over the renewal of temple liturgy. In Ps 50 we detect an interaction with such prophetic pieces as Am 5:21-22; Hos 6:1-6; Isa 1:2-20; Mic 6:1-8.

Ps 50 belongs to the pre-exilic period, when Zion existed in "the perfection of beauty," and to be more specific, it may come from the reform of King Hezekiah (715-687) or of King Josiah (640-609). We prefer the former, corresponding with the early ministry of the prophet Isaiah and a prosperous condition at Jerusalem. Ps 50 is not condemning liturgy but mediating the prophetic challenge to sacrifice and other liturgical actions.

(II) This prophetic psalm opens with a majestic theophany (vv. 1-6), and continues with two main sections: vv. 7-15, centering on the proper understanding of worship; and vv. 16-21, on the moral expectations of worship. It ends, vv. 22-23, with warning and hope.

(III) Vv. 1-6, *hymnic introduction*, blends the style of a prophetic lawsuit, in which heaven and earth are summoned as witnesses (*cf.,* Isa 1:2; Mic 6:1-2; Deut 32:1), with a theophany which resonates with majestic temple liturgy and distantly echoes pagan ritual. Blended into this account are memories of Sinai, the people's march through the desert and the installation of the ark at Jerusalem (Exod 19; Judg 5; Hab 3; Ps 68). Liturgy attempted to communicate to later generations the great redemptive acts which gave birth to Israel in the days of Moses, Joshua and David.

Vv. 7-15, *correct appreciation of sacrifice*. This section opens with an introduction in v. 7 which emphasizes that the speaker is *God, your God,* [*yes*] *I myself* (v. 7). The principal types of sacrifice are mentioned: communion sacrifice, in which most of the animal was eaten in a sacred meal by the worshiping family; holocaust or "burnt offering," consumed totally on the altar out of adoration and union with the God of life; thanksgiving sacrifice, at the end of fulfilling a vow (*cf.,* Leviticus, chaps. 1, 3, 6, 7). These were not offered to God as though God stood in need of food, like pagan gods in Deut 32:38 or Dan 14. Rather their purpose and symbolism lie in a covenant of life with one another and with God, who chose Israel out of all other creatures and nations.

Vv. 16-21 insist that sacrifice and religion not become, in the words of Maillot-Lelievre, an alibi for sinning! Just as sacrifice symbolized a communion between God and worshiper, there must also be a communion between ritual and morality. In v. 17, *discipline* is a rich Hebrew word, *musar,* which implies the disciplinary power of suffering and training, an important word with prophecy (Isa 53:5, "*chastisement* that made us whole"; Jer 31:18, "Thou hast *chastened* me, and I was *chastened*") and with the sapiential literature (Prov 5:23, "He dies for lack of *discipline* and because of his great folly he is lost"). In v. 18, thief and adulterer may refer to someone who condones these offenses or gains from the sins of others (*cf.,* Hos 4:8, "They feed on the sin of my people; they are greedy for their iniquity"). V. 21, *silent . . . one like yourself:* God was in danger of being formed to the image and likeness of selfish people!

Vv. 22-23, the conclusion reminds us of the warning in Hos 6:5, "Therefore I have hewn them by the prophets, I have slain them by the words of my mouth." The final words, *I will show the salvation of God,* means not only to perceive the true meaning of God's great redemptive acts in Israel's history but also to relive their wondrous impact through the renewal of the covenant. Israel thus became a people purified, chastened and more fully alive: *cf.,* Ps 95:7-8, "*Today* you would hearken to his voice! Harden not your hearts."

(IV) If a religion is strong, it can afford to be humble and open to further purification. If it is endowed with divine promises, it must be reminded not to make its ritual and its authority a cloak for covering its shortcomings. If it is endowed with splendid ritual, it is in still greater danger of confusing its ritual for divinity! Ps 50 shows a healthy interaction between prophet and priest, between the secular and the sacred, between the real and the symbolic.

Psalm 51
To The Choirmaster, A Psalm Of David, When Nathan
The Prophet Came To Him, After He Had Gone In To
Bathsheba.

I
[1]Have mercy on me, O God, according
 to thy steadfast love;
 according to thy abundant mercy
 blot out my transgressions.
[2]Wash me thoroughly from my iniquity,
 and cleanse me from my sin!

II
[3]For I know my transgressions,
 and my sin is ever before me.
[4]Against thee, thee only, have I sinned,
 and done that which is evil in thy sight,
 so that thou art justified in thy sentence
 and blameless in thy judgment.
[5]Behold, I was brought forth in iniquity,
 and in sin did my mother conceive me.

[6]Behold, thou desirest truth in the inward being;
 therefore teach me wisdom in my secret heart.

III
[7]Purge me with hyssop, and I shall be clean;
 wash me, and I shall be whiter than snow.
[8]Fill me with joy and gladness;
 let the bones which thou hast broken rejoice.
[9]Hide thy face from my sins,
 and blot out all my iniquities.

IV

¹⁰Create in me a clean heart, O God,
   and put a new and right spirit within me.
¹¹Cast me not away from thy presence,
   and take not thy holy Spirit from me.
¹²Restore to me the joy of thy salvation,
   and uphold me with a willing spirit.

V

¹³Then I will teach transgressors thy ways,
   and sinners will return to thee.
¹⁴Deliver me from bloodguiltiness, O God,
   thou God of my salvation,
   and my tongue will sing aloud of thy deliverance.

¹⁵O Lord, open thou my lips,
   and my mouth shall show forth thy praise.

¹⁶For thou hast no delight in sacrifice;
   were I to give a burnt offering, thou
     wouldst not be pleased.
¹⁷The sacrifice acceptable to God is a broken spirit;
   a broken and contrite heart, O God,
     thou wilt not despise.

VI

¹⁸Do good to Zion in thy good pleasure;
   rebuild the walls of Jerusalem,
¹⁹then wilt thou delight in right sacrifices,
   in burnt offerings and whole burnt offerings;
   then bulls will be offered on thy altar.

(I) One of the seven penitential psalms (see Ps 6) and possibly the most known of all 150 psalms, at least during penitential seasons like Lent, the *Miserere*, as Ps 51 is known from the opening word of the ancient Latin translation, derives from a contemplative re-reading of Isaiah, Jeremiah and Ezekiel and a blending with temple traditions. Like Ps 50 it brings a strong, positive prophetical impact to the ritual worship of temple sacrifice, and because of its highly personal character (written emphatically in the first person singular) it has guided popular piety over the centuries from sin and collapse to a newly created purity and joy.

Some of the prophetical texts reflected in the psalm would be:

vv. 3-4, *cf.,* Isa 59:12-13, "For our transgressions are multiplied before thee...conceiving and uttering from the heart lying words";

v. 4, *cf.,* Jer 14:7, "Though our iniquities testify against us, act, O Lord,...we have sinned against thee"; 14:20, "We acknowledge our wickedness, O Lord...for we have sinned against thee";

v. 5, *cf.,* Jer 3:25, "we have sinned against the Lord our God, we and our ancestors, from our youth even to this day";

vv. 6 and 10, *cf.,* Ezek 36:25-26, "I will sprinkle clean water upon you....A new heart I will give you, and a new spirit I will put within you";

v. 11, *cf.,* Isa 63:10-11, "But they rebelled and grieved his holy Spirit....Where is he who put in the midst of them his holy Spirit."

Therefore, we place the composition of the psalm sometime after the ministry of these prophets (therefore, after the exile) and before the rebuilding of the city walls by Nehemiah (v. 18; Neh 2:17), between 539 and 445 B.C. To appreciate sin's heinous seriousness and to acquire a profound depth of sorrow over sin and a hope for re-created goodness, Ps 51 was associated with David's sin of adultery with Bathsheba and the murder of her husband, Uriah (*cf.,* 2 Sam 11-12).

Ps 51 is carefully structured: sin or sinner are mentioned 6 times in the first part (vv. 1-9), only 1 time in the second part (vv. 10-17); God is named 1 time in the first part, 6 times in the second part. The verbs, blot out, wash and cleanse (vv. 1-2) occur in the reverse order in vv. 7 and 9b. (See R.A.F. MacKenzie, *Old Testament Reading Guide.*)

(II) With E. R. Daglish, we divide this penitential psalm of lament accordingly:

vv. 1-2, Introductory call for mercy;

vv. 3-6, Confession of sinfulness:

   v. 3, sin-consciousness

   v. 4, confession

vv. 5-6, moral impotence

vv. 7-9,   Prayer for forgiveness

vv. 10-12, Prayer for Moral Renewal

vv. 13-17, Thanksgiving

vv. 18-19, Addition

(III) Vv. 1-2, *Call for mercy.* The entire psalm, but particularly the opening lines, are rich in a vocabulary of sin and forgiveness (see Ps 32). We must hear these words as they blend one with the other:

have mercy (in Hebrew, *ḥanan*) implies graciousness beyond expectation, certainly beyond one's dignity or merits;

steadfast love (*ḥesed*): bond of covenant, family or at least treaty (*cf.,* Ps 12);

abundant mercy (*raḥamim*): from the Hebrew word for a mother's womb;

blot out (*maḥah*): *cf.,* Neh 13:14, "Wipe not out my good deeds that I have done for the house of my God and for her service";

transgressions (*pesha‘*): rebellious action against legitimate authority;

wash me (*kabas*): very vigorous action of washing clothes in cold water, beating against rocks, hammering with wood, laying out in the sun to bleach;

iniquity (*'awon*): malformed, crooked, bent;

cleanse me (*tahar*): usually reserved for ceremonial purity but basically means that a person will not spread contagious diseases;

sin (*ḥaṭṭa'*): offend community relationships, and metaphorically to miss the mark or target, go astray in traveling.

As typical of Hebrew style, these lines mix their metaphors, perhaps deliberately to show how sin disrupts human harmony and physical integrity. More than anything else, sin distorts and perverts (not in the narrow, sexual sense but in the total complexity of human/community life); it violates the intimate bonds of love.

Vv. 3-6, *Confession of sin*. V. 3 stresses the individual, personal poignancy of sin: literally: "Indeed, *my* rebelliousness, yes *mine, I myself* experience; and *my* going astray [is] ever before *me*. V. 4a makes us Christians think of Jesus' words: "As you did it to one of the least of these my brothers and sisters, you did it to me" (Matt 25:40). V. 4b has been subjected to profound and unending scrutiny: how is God to be justified in his sentence [literally, his word]? *Justified* must be understood in the sense of being true to the divine promise of compassion and to disciplinary punishment, as announced in Exod 34:6-7, "The Lord, a God merciful and gracious... abounding in steadfast love... forgiving iniquity... yet not declaring the guilty innocent." In this sense God is *justified* by listening to the cry for mercy in vv. 1-2, living up to his covenantal promise in Exod 34, and assuring both forgiveness and the disciplinary transformation of the sinner through the suffering induced by wilful sin. Vv. 5-6, from the suggestion of Maillot-Lelièvre, ought to be read together: while v. 5 stresses the a-rational, yet almost universal sense of shame and guilt associated with sex, v. 6 emphasizes the positive side of sexuality, particularly if it is translated: "Indeed, you take pleasure in fidelity amid [conjugal] intimacy; in such secret acts you impart the experience of [wondrous] wisdom." Biblically, sexual intercourse has been blessed by God from the moment of creating humankind "male and female," with the direction to "be fruitful and multiply, and fill the earth" (Gen 1:27-28). Yet from biblical passages like Leviticus, chap. 15, we learn that Israel shared with all humankind an a-rational sense of shame in association with sex. Shame varies from culture to culture, so that there is no single norm even for dress and behavior. Such shame, frequently surrounded with strange and awkward inhibitions, is due, at least in part, to a strong determination to safeguard the sacredness of sex, always fragile and easily betrayed with serious, lasting consequences. In any case v. 5 is not referring to original sin, not only because the sin of Adam and Eve is never again mentioned in the Hebrew Scriptures (unless in Sir 25:24 and

Wis 2:22-25; 10:1) but also because the father is not mentioned here, the one in biblical times thought to transmit life
into the passive receptacle of the womb.

Vv. 7-9, *prayer for forgiveness.* The word, *purge*, in v. 7 is
intriguing. The root, in its simple meaning, indicates "to sin"
by splintering relationships and missing the mark (see *ḥaṭṭa'*
in v. 2); yet in its intensive or "piel" form, it means, "to be
free(d) from sin," almost as though the poignant, trenchant
sense of sin will force a person to reject sin; in the Bible, such
purification is God's exclusive work or "creation." *Purge* [or
better, *sprinkle*] *me with hyssop* certainly implies ritual
action. Although God alone purifies, the healing of any
contagious condition and the full amends of sin must be
certified by a temple priest in case anyone had been harmed
(Lev 6:1-7; Num 5:5-10). V. 8, *joy and gladness:* this phrase
is found five times in Jeremiah (Jer 7:34; 15:16; 16:9; 25:10;
33:11), another indication of interaction with the prophetic
movement.

Vv. 10-12, *moral renewal.* The use of the word *create,
bara',* clearly testifies to the faith that only God can achieve
this new state of innocent vitality of life. *right spirit:* also
includes one of the principal "creation" words of the
Hebrew Bible (Isa 45:8; Ps 24:2) and implies not so much
"right" as sturdy and deep security (Job 21:8; 2 Kgs 2:12).
The newly created righteous person is integrally complete,
well balanced, sturdy and secure.

Vv. 13-17, *thanksgiving.* The psalmist asks to be freed of
whatever is destructive of this newly created life; thus we
interpret "bloodguiltiness." V. 16, *no delight in sacrifice:*
such is the case only when ritual acts are not closely associated with moral reform and faith in God's re-creative
forgiveness (see the discussion with Ps 50), for the psalmist
uses cultic imagery to describe the interior renewal.

Vv. 18-19, *addition,* fully reintegrating the psalm with
temple liturgy.

(IV) Ps 51 summarizes a rich liturgical and prophetical
tradition; it must be reflected upon as long and seriously as
the psalmist contemplated the great prophets and the cultic
heritage of Israel in the Priestly Tradition ("P") of the

Pentateuch. It reaches beyond temple and prophecy into cultural practices and secular styles. It seeks a total re-creation.

Psalm 52
To The Choirmaster. A Maskil Of David, When Doeg, The Edomite, Came And Told Saul, "David Has Come To The House Of Ahimelech."

I

¹Why do you boast, O mighty man,
　of mischief done against the godly?
All the day ²you are plotting destruction.
　Your tongue is like a sharp razor,
　you worker of treachery.
³You love evil more than good,
　and lying more than speaking the truth.　　　*Selah*
⁴You love all words that devour,
　O deceitful tongue.

⁵But God will break you down for ever;
　he will snatch and tear you from your tent;
　he will uproot you from the land of the living. *Selah*
⁶The righteous shall see, and fear,
　and shall laugh at him, saying,
⁷"See the man who would not make
　God his refuge,
　but trusted in the abundance of his riches,
　and sought refuge in his wealth!"

II

⁸But I am like a green olive tree
　in the house of God.
I trust in the steadfast love of God
　for ever and ever.
⁹I will thank thee for ever,
　because thou hast done it.
I will proclaim thy name, for it is good,
　in the presence of the godly.

(I + II) The problem besetting this psalm offers a clue to its original meaning and present application! 1) While the psalm principally condemns the *deceitful tongue* (v. 4b), the long title refers to Doeg, an informer, who told the truth to Saul and so was responsible for the execution of Ahimelech and the other priests at Nob who had given food to David and his soldiers (1 Sam 21-22); 2) the Hebrew text and the structuring of the psalm have been poorly preserved; 3) it is difficult to determine the literary form of the psalm, as it combines sapiential elements (like Ps 1) contrasting the good and the wicked and their retribution, with prophetical elements of a judgment speech: the reproaches or evidence (vv. 1-4), the verdict (v. 5), and mockery of the wicked (v. 7) — see Isa 1:2-20; 22:15-25, where sapiential features are also visible; part of the psalm corresponds with an individual lament (vv. 1-7) and part with a prayer of thanksgiving or confidence (vv. 8-9). The psalm, therefore, represents a confrontation of loyal but persecuted priests against other priests or temple personnel who have turned their religious authority and the ritual to their own advantage. Therefore, an editor added to the title the reference to Doeg the Edom- ite who took advantage of his position close to King Saul to improve his own lot at the expense of the priests at Nob. Particularly in the pre-exilic age, prophets combated cor- ruption in temple personnel and priestly ranks, as we read in Hos 4:4, 6 — "With you is my contention, O priest...I reject you from being a priest," *cf.,* Jer 28; Amos 7:10-17. Never used in the sanctuary, so far as our documentation testifies, the psalm was not carefully preserved. In fact, Pss 52-55, each called *a maskil* (*or instruction*) *of David,* have been thoroughly eclipsed in popularity by Ps 51. While temple priests preserved this latter psalm — and for that we must credit them — nonetheless, they would not be anxious to publicize this serious division and even corruption in their own midst!

(III) We interpret *tent* in v. 5 as a reference to the temple (*cf.,* 2 Sam 7:4, where God says, "I have been moving about in a tent for my dwelling"; Lev 1:1, "meeting tent"; Ps 15:1,

"O Lord, who shall sojourn in thy tent. . . on thy holy hill?")
— In v. 8, *green olive tree* can refer to priests (*cf.,* Zech 4:3;
Sir 40:10, where Simon the high priest is "like an olive tree").

(IV) Not only is Ps 52 a warning against (ab-)using religion for selfish motives and manipulating its power to suppress criticism, but its link with Doeg and the killing of the
priest Ahimelech reminds us of an incident in the preaching
of Jesus (Mark 2:25-28). Jesus refers to the common sense
judgment of the priests who broke the law and gave to
David and his hungry soldiers what "was not lawful for any
but the priests to eat." Religion and priesthood, sabbath and
laws are "made for the human family, not the human family
for the sabbath." This is not a complete statement about the
origin and nature of relgion, but coming from Jesus it is not
only a healthy challenge for religion and religious people
but an appropriate way to reread the individual lament in
Ps 52.

Psalm 53

See Ps 14, with which it is almost identical. Ps 14 belongs to
the Yahwist collection, Ps 53 to the Elohist collection.

Psalm 54
*To The Choirmaster: With Stringed Instruments. A
Maskil Of David, When The Ziphites Went And Told
Saul, "David Is In Hiding Among Us."*

I
¹Save me, O God, by thy name,
and vindicate me by thy might.
²Hear my prayer, O God;
give ear to the words of my mouth.

II
³For insolent men have risen against me,
ruthless men seek my life;
they do not set God before them.   *Selah*

III

⁴Behold, God is my helper;
  the Lord is the upholder of my life.
⁵He will requite my enemies with evil;
  in thy faithfulness put an end to them.

IV

⁶With a freewill offering I will sacrifice to thee;
  I will give thanks to thy name, O Lord, for it is good.
⁷For thou hast delivered me from every trouble,
  and my eye has looked in triumph on my enemies.

(I-II) A lament for the individual, this psalm is ordinary in every sense of the word. Its structure is easily discernible: vv. 1-2, call for help; v. 3, motivation of sorrow; vv. 4-5, expression of confidence in God; vv. 6-7, a spontaneous thanksgiving sacrifice. The language, particularly in the Hebrew, is quite stereotyped: *i.e., save me:* Pss 3:7; 6:4; 7:1; etc.; *vindicate me:* Pss 7:8; 26:1; 35:24; etc.; *hear my prayer:* Pss 4:1; 17:1; 39:12; etc.; *give ear:* Pss 3, 5:1; 17:1; 39:12; etc. The entire v. 3 is repeated again in Ps 86:14. It is difficult, therefore, to attach the psalm to any particular moment. Possibly its highlighting of God's *name* in vv. 1 and 6, forming an "inclusion," a device to note the beginning and end, would point to a period after the Deuteronomic reform of King Josiah (621-609 B.C.), responsible for the important role of the Lord's name in such passages as Deut 12:5, "But you shall seek the place which the Lord your God will choose out of all your tribes to put his name and make his habitation there."

(III-IV) While the structure and vocabulary reflect little originality, still a strong, urgent note is heard. The psalmist's life is at stake for *ruthless people seek my life,* (v. 3), but the Lord is *the upholder of my life* (v. 4). In this latter phrase the Hebrew grammar employs what is called "*beth essentiae.*" The preposition *beth* or "b" is used in the Hebrew phrase *b + someke naphshi* (= "b" + "upholder of my life") to point out that the Lord is to be known in the "essense" of his character and person as our Savior, one who upholds our basic existence. For us, as Maillot-Lelièvre point out, the Lord is God not in some abstract or ideal concept of power but in the practical manner of sustaining us with life now and with hope for our future. The "name theology" turns our attention to the Acts of the Apostles and the Gospel of John where the name of the Lord Jesus is invoked as the essence of salvation, the source of miracles and peace (Acts 2:21, 38; 3:6; 4:10; John 1:2; 12:13; 14:13; etc.). At times "name" may be a circumlocution to avoid saying Jesus or Yahweh; it is also and more truly a personal way of realizing the continuing, life-giving, protecting presence of our Immanuel, God with us.

Psalm 55
To The Choirmaster: With Stringed Instruments. A
Maskil Of David.

I

¹Give ear to my prayer, O God;
    and hide not thyself from my supplication!
²Attend to me, and answer me;

II

I am overcome by my trouble.
I am distraught ³by the noise of the enemy,
    because of the oppression of the wicked.
For they bring trouble upon me,
    and in anger they cherish enmity against me.

⁴My heart is in anguish within me,
    the terrors of death have fallen upon me.
⁵Fear and trembling come upon me,
    and horror overwhelms me.
⁶And I say, "O that I had wings like a dove!
    I would fly away and be at rest;
⁷yea, I would wander afar,
    I would lodge in the wilderness,   *Selah*
⁸I would haste to find me a shelter
    from the raging wind and tempest."

⁹Destroy their plans, O Lord, confuse their tongues;

III

for I see violence and strife in the city.
¹⁰Day and night they go around it on its walls;
   and mischief and trouble are within it,
¹¹ ruin is in its midst;
oppression and fraud
   do not depart from its market place.

¹²It is not an enemy who taunts me—
   then I could bear it;
   it is not an adversary who deals insolently with me—
      then I could hide from him.
¹³But it is you, my equal,
   my companion, my familiar friend.
¹⁴We used to hold sweet converse together;
   within God's house we walked in fellowship.
¹⁵Let death come upon them;
   let them go down to Sheol alive;
   let them go away in terror into their graves.

IV

¹⁶But I call upon God;
   and the Lord will save me.
¹⁷Evening and morning and at noon
   I utter my complaint and moan,
   and he will hear my voice.
¹⁸He will deliver my soul in safety
   from the battle that I wage,
   for many are arrayed against me.
¹⁹God will give ear, and humble them,
   he who is enthroned from of old;
because they keep no law,
   and do not fear God.   *Selah*

V

²⁰My companion stretched out his hand against his friends,
   he violated his covenant.
²¹His speech was smoother than butter,
   yet war was in his heart;
his words were softer than oil,
   yet they were drawn swords.

VI

22Cast your burden on the Lord,
  and he will sustain you;
he will never permit
  the righteous to be moved.

23But thou, O God, wilt cast them down
  into the lowest pit;
men of blood and treachery
  shall not live out half their days.
But I will trust in thee.

(I) If by comparison with the preceding psalm, Ps 55 shows more creativity, action and depth of feeling, it has also suffered in the process. The Hebrew text is badly preserved, at least so it seems to us who live centuries away; Aramaic expressions point to a redactional history into the later postexilic period. What may seem to the modern reader to be repetitious doublets (compare vv. 3-5 and 16-17; vv. 9-15 and 20-21; v. 15 and 23), may actually have been acceptable style in biblical times. While the ancient rabbis linked the psalm with David's betrayal by his counselor Ahithophel (*cf.,* 2 Sam 16:15-22; 1 Chron 27:33), modern interpreters tend to see closer parallels with Jeremiah, who longed to have "in the desert a wayfarers' lodging place, that I might leave my people" (Jer 9:2), who was betrayed by his own family (Jer 12:6) and suffered from a fellow priest, "Pashhur [who] beat Jeremiah the prophet, and put him in the stocks" (Jer 20:2). We place this lament of the individual within a Jeremian tradition.

(II) A complicated psalm like this one cannot be easily divided into strophes, but for convenience sake we suggest:

vv. 1-2ab	Call for help	vv. 16-19	Prayer
vv. 2c-9a	Lament and temptation to flee	vv. 20-21	Lament and betrayal
vv. 9b-15	Lament: betrayal everywhere	vv. 22-23	Trust in thee, God.

(III) Vv. 1-2ab, Introductory call for help, begin with the fearful silence of God (see Ps 10:1; 13:2; etc.).

Vv. 2c-9a, the first lamentation, include one of the most delicate yet frightening images in the psalms: *like a dove I would fly away*. We think of Jeremiah's words, already quoted (9:2; *cf.,* 48:28), of David in flight from Saul (1 Sam 23:4), of Israel fearful of being delivered like "the soul of thy dove to the wild beasts" (Ps 74:19), or of the beloved, "my dove, in the clefts of the rock" (Song 2:14).

Vv. 9b-15 continue the lament, with the plaintive words in vv. 13-14a, translated literally: "But you are that one, a man like myself, my companion, my bosom-friend, together we have faced the experience of life, sweet as our sharing of secret counsel."

Vv. 16-19 refer to prayer *evening, morning and at noon* and have influenced synogogal and church prayer: the rabbinical midrash linked the verse with Gen 19:27, "*Abraham* went *early in the morning* to the place where he had stood before the Lord"; with Gen 24:63, "*Isaac* went out to meditate in the field in the evening" which the rabbis understood as *noonday prayer;* and Gen 28:11, *Jacob* "stayed there *that night*...and he dreamed that there was a ladder" from earth to heaven. We recall the Christian practice of ringing the "angelus" for prayer at 6 AM, noon, and 6 PM.

Vv. 22-23, *cast your burden on the Lord* — words that echo again in the New Testament: Matt 6:25-34; 10:19; Luke 12:22-31; 21:34. The psalm ends magnificently: *I will trust in thee.*

(IV) Ps 55 has been a traditional lenten prayer; its opening lines are repeated in prayers for the sick. If the psalm is broken and mixed up, tender like a dove and violent against the enemy, such is the spirit of Lent and such too is the physical condition of the sick.

Psalm 56
To The Choirmaster: According To The Dove On
Far-off Terebinths. A Miktam Of David, When The
Philistines Seized Him In Gath.

¹Be gracious to me, O God,
   for men trample upon me;
   all day long foemen oppress me;
²my enemies trample upon me all day long,
   for many fight against me proudly.
³When I am afraid,
   I put my trust in thee.
⁴In God, whose word I praise,
   in God I trust without a fear.
   What can flesh do to me?

⁸Thou hast kept count of my tossings;
   put thou my tears in thy bottle!
   Are they not in thy book?
⁹Then my enemies will be turned back
   in the day when I call.
   This I know, that God is for me.
¹⁰In God, whose word I praise,
   in the Lord, whose word I praise,
¹¹in God I trust without a fear.
   What can man do to me?

¹²My vows to thee I must perform, O God;
   I will render thank offerings to thee.
¹³For thou hast delivered my soul from death,
   yea, my feet from falling,
   that I may walk before God
   in the light of life.

(I) From the title we learn that the next five psalms are a "miktam," a very obscure word, possibly from an Akkadian root, "to cover," and associated with covering or atoning for sin (*cf.,* Ps 51:1). The obscurity continues into the Hebrew text of Ps 56 which is particularly corrupt. A typical, explanatory addition (technically, a gloss) is seen in v. 8, in which an earlier word (*sapar,* to count) is picked up and repeated differently (*seper,* book): *Thou has kept count [sapar] of my tossings; put thou my tears in thy bottle* [or wineskin — an unusual metaphor, now to be clarified] *are they not in thy book [seper].* Ancient translators found difficulties in the title, so that the enigmatic phrase, *according to The Dove on Far-Off Terebinths,* has been changed to read in the Greek "concerning the people removed from the sanctuary," and in the Aramaic Targum, "for the community of Israel, compared to a silent dove in the time of the distant deportation from their cities." Beneath the obscurities a common consensus of thought would be distance or separation: from the temple or homeland; from friends; from life's security. The title sees an example of that in David, exiled among the Philistines (1 Sam 21:10-15; 27:12; Ps 34, title).

(II) When this individual lament was accepted into the liturgy, it is possible that the refrain (vv. 4 and 10-11) would also have been repeated after vv. 6c-7 and at the very end.

1) v. 1a	call for help/ mercy	3) vv. 8-9	lament
vv. 1b-3	lament and confidence	vv. 10-11	refrain
v. 4	refrain	4) vv. 12-13	thanksgiving offering
2) vv. 5-6ab	lament		(+ refrain in vv. 10-11)
vv. 6c-7	curse upon enemy (+ refrain in v. 4)		

The reference in v. 8, that the psalmist's sufferings are written in God's book, corresponds with a long tradition: Ps 69:28; Exod 32:32; Job 19:23; Mal 3:16; Dan 7:10; Rev 20:12; 21:27.

(IV) The refrain in v. 4 that no human being can harm us because of our trust in God may have inspired Paul's statement in Rom 8:31-39 that nothing "will be able to separate us from the love of God in Christ Jesus our Lord." The final line that we *walk before God in the light of life* reminds us of

John's gospel where Jesus declares, "I am the light of the world; the one who follows me... will have the light of life" (John 8:12; *cf.,* 1:4).

Psalm 57

¹In the shadow of thy wings I will take refuge,
    till the storms of destruction pass by.

³God will send forth his steadfast love
    and his faithfulness!

⁵Be exalted, O God, above the heavens!
    Let thy glory be over all the earth!

⁶They set a net for my steps;
    my soul was bowed down.
  They dug a pit in my way,
    but they have fallen into it themselves.   *Selah*

⁸ Awake, my soul!
  Awake, O harp and lyre!
  I will awake the dawn!

¹⁰For thy steadfast love is great to the heavens,
    thy faithfulness to the clouds.

¹¹Be exalted, O God, above the heavens!
    Let thy glory be over all the earth!

(I) What originally may have been two separate psalms (vv. 7-11 are repeated almost verbatim in Ps 108:1-5), has been structurally unified around covenant and temple as well as by a common refrain (vv. 5 and 11). Seriously harassed by calumniators whose "tongues [are] sharp swords" (v. 4), the psalmist takes refuge "in the shadow of thy wings" (v. 1c) near the ark of the covenant (see Ps 17:8, relying on Exod 25:20, where the ark of the Lord and the mercy-seat or throne of the invisible God are surrounded by the cherubim's wings). Here too Isaiah saw a vision of the Lord, as the cherubim or seraphim proclaimed the Lord's glory extending over the universe (Isa 6:3), similar to the refrain, *thy glory be over all the earth* (vv. 5 and 11). The second part of the psalm also locates the poet within the temple, awaking the dawn with temple *harp and lyre* (v. 8). The covenant language of the Lord's *steadfast love and faithfulness* (in Hebrew, *ḥesed* and *'emeth*; see Ps 12) resounds in both parts of the psalm (vv. 3 and 10).

(II) The psalm was prepared for people, slandered and persecuted by other Israelites, that they might find peace and new confidence. It is principally an individual lament but with an exceptionally strong emphasis upon confidence. A. A. Anderson's division is helpful:

vv. 1-4,	individual lament	vv. 7-10,	Hymnic expression
v. 5,	refrain		of confidence
v. 6,	transitional verse	v. 11,	refrain

(III—IV) If the transitional v. 6 sounds inappropriate for temple prayer, it is good to recall, first, that the language is very stereotyped across the religious literature of the ancient Near East, and second, that God does not remain an idle onlooker, helplessly bemoaning the sad lot of the persecuted people.

Not only does Ps 57 bring a new tranquility to us in times of persecution and calumny, but it secures our faith in God's covenantal protection and personal concern. When we are "down," we stand in need of the exciting upbeat in: *I will sing and make melody! awake...awake...awake the dawn!* When our small world is beset with fears and persecution, we break out of this imprisonment by singing anew the refrain that God's glory fills all the earth and will be effective in our own individual lives upon this earth.

Psalm 58
To The Choirmaster: According To Do Not Destroy. A Miktam Of David.

I
¹Do you indeed decree what is right, you gods?
  Do you judge the sons of men uprightly?

²Nay, in your hearts you devise wrongs;
your hands deal out violence on earth.

II

³The wicked go astray from the womb,
they err from their birth, speaking lies.
⁴They have venom like the venom of a serpent,
like the deaf adder that stops its ear,
⁵so that it does not hear the voice of charmers
or of the cunning enchanter.

III

⁶O God, break the teeth in their mouths;
tear out the fangs of the young lions, O Lord!
⁷Let them vanish like water that runs away;
like grass let them be trodden down and wither.
⁸Let them be like the snail which dissolves into slime,
like the untimely birth that never sees the sun.
⁹Sooner than your pots can feel the heat of thorns,
whether green or ablaze, may he sweep them away!

IV

¹⁰The righteous will rejoice when he sees the vengeance;
he will bathe his feet in the blood of the wicked.
¹¹Men will say, "Surely there is a reward for the righteous;
surely there is a God who judges on earth."

(I) A collective lament and curse psalm against wicked judges who use their high office and religious dignity for their own advantage against the poor or defenseless. Like many of the oracles against the nations, particularly in the prophecies of Isaiah (chaps. 13-23) and Jeremiah (chaps. 46-51), this psalm excels in literary excellence: there is strength, vigor, color, action, striking imagery. Unfortunately, the Hebrew text is badly preserved.

(II) After an introduction, summoning the unjust judges to trial (vv. 1-2), there follows a statement about their incorrigible wickedness (vv. 3-5) and a list of seven curses (vv. 6-9). The psalm ends with assurance for the righteous (vv. 10-11).

(III) In v. 1 the reference to *you gods* indicates dignitaries of the highest rank within Israel (see Pss 2, 8 and 82). In v. 3, the phrase, *wicked...from their womb...from their birth*, is not an allusion to original sin (see Ps 51:5), because only a select group are here condemned. The statement accords with a biblical tradition of being consecrated from the womb: Judg 13:7; Ps 22:10-11; Jer 1:5; Gal 1:15, except that these references are positive in scope and speak of consecration to God by one's parents or by personal choice.

(IV) For a further explanation of the "curse psalm" and its application for today, see Ps 69.

Psalm 59
To The Choirmaster: According To Do Not Destroy. A Miktam Of David, When Saul Sent Men To Watch His House In Order To Kill Him.

I

¹Deliver me from my enemies, O my God,
    protect me from those who rise up against me,
²deliver me from those who work evil,
    and save me from bloodthirsty men.

³For lo, they lie in wait for my life;
    fierce men band themselves against me.
For no transgression or sin of mine, O Lord,
⁴ for no fault of mine, they run and make ready.

Rouse thyself, come to my help, and see!

⁵ Thou, Lord God of hosts, art God of Israel.
Awake to punish all the nations;
    spare none of those who treacherously plot evil.

Selah

II

⁶Each evening they come back,
    howling like dogs
    and prowling about the city.
⁷There they are, bellowing with their mouths,

and snarling with their lips—
for "Who," they think, "will hear us?"

III
8But thou, O Lord, dost laugh at them;
thou dost hold all the nations in derision.
9O my Strength, I will sing praises to thee;
for thou, O God, art my fortress.
10My God in his steadfast love will meet me;
my God will let me look in triumph on my enemies.

(I) An innocent person, plagued by deceit and false charges from the ranks of friends and compatriots, drew upon traditional phrases within the ritual (*cf.*, vv. 1-2, 4-5, 8, 10) in composing this individual lament. It was easily adaptable, therefore, to becoming a collective lament for ritual use in times of national mourning, particularly when Israel was overrun by foreign armies.

(II) The Hebrew text is poorly preserved and the division into strophes or stanzas is awkward. We detect the following arrangement, based upon the repetition of two sets of refrains.

vv. 1-5	11-13	Call for help, lament and prayer
vv. 6-7	14-15	Refrain about dogs — one's enemies
vv. 8-10	16-17	Refrain about confidence in God

The title refers to David's flight from Saul and his betrayal as told in 1 Sam 19 and 24, and so sets up some interesting word-parallels between the psalm and these chapters of 1 Samuel:

to watch: in the title and in v. 9 of the psalm, where the Hebrew reads, "I will watch" instead of the RSV, "I will sing praises";
morning: in Ps 59:16. In 1 Sam 19:11-12 we read that "Saul sent messengers...that he might kill David in the morning";
innocence: in Ps 59:3-4 and in 1 Sam 19:4;
stray dogs: Ps 59:6-7, 14-15. In 1 Sam 24:14 David called out to King Saul: "After whom has the king come out?...after a dead dog?"

(III) In the Bible references to dogs (vv. 6-7, 14-15) are generally derogatory. They are unclean beasts, prowling on human corpses (1 Kg 14:11); even the references to watch-dogs are not complimentary (Isa 56:10-11; Ps 22:15). Male prostitutes were called by this name (Deut 23:19). For the phrase in v. 8, *God laughs at them,* see Pss 2:4; 37:13. The words in v. 16, *in the morning,* may indicate morning prayer, or it may state metaphorically that the night of sorrow and fear is over.

(IV) Even though the final line is fragmentary, still we note that the last word in this psalm is God's *steadfast love* or *hesed.* At first the psalmist found strength in an innocent conscience, but throughout the psalm and especially at the end emphasis is placed upon the bond of love and life, uniting Israel and Yahweh through the covenant (see Ps 12).

Psalm 60
To The Choirmaster: According To Shushan Eduth. A Miktam Of David: For Instruction: When He Strove With Aram-Naharaim And With Aram-Zobah, And When Joab On His Return Killed Twelve Thousand Of Edom In The Valley of Salt.

I

¹O God, thou hast rejected us, broken our defenses;
   thou hast been angry; oh, restore us.
²Thou hast made the land to quake,
    thou hast rent it open;
   repair its breaches, for it totters.
³Thou hast made thy people suffer hard things;
   thou hast given us wine to drink that made us reel.
⁴Thou hast set up a banner for those who fear thee,
   to rally to it from the bow.   *Selah*
⁵That thy beloved may be delivered,
   give victory by thy right hand and answer us!

II

⁶God has spoken in his sanctuary:
   "With exultation I will divide up Shechem

and potion out the Vale of Succoth.
⁷Gilead is mine; Manasseh is mine;
    Ephraim is my helmet;
    Judah is my scepter.
⁸Moab is my washbasin;
    upon Edom I cast my shoe;
    over Philistia I shout in triumph."

⁹Who will bring me to the fortified city?
    Who will lead me to Edom?

III

¹²With God we shall do valiantly;
    it is he who will tread down our foes.

(I-II) With the help of the *selah* after v. 4 (an ancient Hebrew indicator for a pause) and from the fact that vv. 5-12 are repeated again, with only minor variations, in Ps 108:6-14, we can disentangle the literary history of Ps 60.

vv. 1-4, a national lament, added last. It comes slightly before, if not after the exile, after a massive military defeat, perhaps the same one bemoaned by Israel in Pss 44 and 74, only these latter psalms seem still more bleak;
v. 5, a transitional verse, added at the same time as vv. 1-4;
vv. 6-9, an ancient oracle, affirming the Israelite settlement of their tribal portions and the conquests of King David (1000-961 B.C.);
vv. 10-12, prayer of petition, attached at the same time as vv. 1-4.

(III) The long title to this psalm reflects David's extended conquests from Edom in the south to the Euphrates river in the north, placed here as a pledge that the kingdom of David will rise again.

Vv. 1-5 recognize Israel's trauma over military defeat, which deprived the people of territory and even of their control of the promised land. It seemed as if God were reneging on his promises as these were recited in the great credal formulas, Deut 26 or Josh 24 (see Ps 44). The image of earthquake in v. 2 reminds us of texts like Amos 1:1-2 or

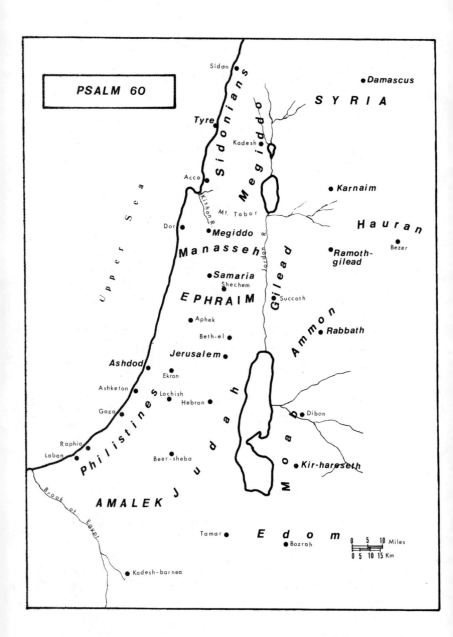

Jer 4:24; eventually it was a sign of the final day of the Lord: Is 13:13; 24:18-20; Matt 24:7. Wine imaged Israel, stagger-ing in stunned fright and agony, as in Is 51:17, 22 and Ps 75:8.

Vv. 6-9, an oracle, possibly of King David's time. Vv. 6-7 recall the settlement and division of the land; the event is associated with *Shechem*, some 40 miles north of Jerusalem in the center of the promised land, where Joshua made the initial covenant with the local inhabitants (Josh 8:30-35). *Succoth*, east of the River Jordan, is where Jacob built a sanctuary after his meeting with Esau and right before his return to Shechem (Gen 33:17-18); *Gilead*, also east of the Jordan between the brooks or wadis Arnon and Yarmuk; *Ephraim* indicates the northern tribes west of the Jordan, and *Judah* the southern tribes. If we make one slight change in the Hebrew text, reading Aram instead of Edom in v. 8, then the countries mentioned in vv. 8-9 follow the chrono-logical sequence of the Bible in their conquest or control by David: *Moab,* east of the Dead Sea, enslaved by David as "water carriers" (2 Sam 8:2); *Aram* (2 Sam 8:5-10); *Philistia* (2 Sam 8:12b); *Edom* (2 Sam 8:13-14). *The fortified city* is probably Tyre's mainland tributary (2 Sam 24:7). See the map.

Vv. 10-12, the final prayer for help, reflects the conviction that only God can relieve Israel of submission to foreign powers. Israel must continue to recite with unwavering faith her ancient creeds. The psalm, therefore, ends positively: *with God we shall do valiantly.*

(IV) If Ps 60 seems interlocked with the ancient history and geography of Israel and further distanced from us by its identification of Yahweh with Israel's wars, it also insists that religion does not subsist separately from politics, eco-nomics and armaments. Ps 60 is not dealing directly with military operations but with such religious questions as the fidelity of God in the midst of national defeat and with the necessity of hope during the collapse of one's homeland. Ps 60 remains somewhere in between the pacifist and the milit-arist, between the political question and religious response, between God who is immanently present and God who is illusive and transcendent.

Psalm 61
To The Choirmaster: With Stringed Instruments. A Psalm Of David.

I

¹Hear my cry, O God,
  listen to my prayer;

II

²from the end of the earth I call to thee,
  when my heart is faint.

Lead thou me
  to the rock that is higher than I;
³for thou art my refuge,
  a strong tower against the enemy.

⁴Let me dwell in thy tent for ever!
  Oh to be safe under the shelter of thy wings!   *Selah*

III

⁵For thou, O God, hast heard my vows,
  thou hast given me the heritage of
    those who fear thy name.

⁶Prolong the life of the king;
  may his years endure to all generations!
⁷May he be enthroned for ever before God;
  bid steadfast love and faithfulness watch over him!

IV

⁸So will I ever sing praises to thy name,
  as I pay my vows day after day.

(I) Sorrow and hope are expressed for a person separated from the sanctuary and communal worship, perhaps because of serious sickness. Yet, we cannot be sure; the evidence is too vague. The prayer for the king, moreover, in vv. 5-7 may not be the central concern either, for these lines may have been added later. However, in a culture where the king occupied a central religious position, it would be natural to join prayer for the king with one's own needs. The various liturgical phrases throughout this psalm enabled this individual lament to become part of the temple liturgy, ready at hand for others who wanted to offer thanksgiving or fulfill a vow after personal difficulty.

(II) The structure of the psalm is uncertain, due to the unevenness or uncertainty where the prayer for the king occurs. One possible division would be:

v. 1,	call for help	vv. 5-7,	prayer for the king
vv. 2-4,	motivation: separation from temple	v. 8,	Conclusion & thanksgiving

(III) V. 1. The psalm begins in a way similar to other individual laments: Pss 5:1-2; 17:1.

Vv. 2-4, motivation for calling out *from the end of the earth*. This phrase can be variously interpreted. Perhaps, like many liturgical phrases, it is left vague or general, so that it can be adapted to many individual needs. *Earth*, or in Hebrew *'eres*, can mean: the entire *earth*, as normally in Isa 40-55, or simply a particular country, as usually in Ezekiel (*cf.*, Isa 48:13; Ezek 14:13). Because the psalm was composed in the pre-exilic age, its vision would be more restricted; the Jewish diaspora living in foreign countries had not yet entered prominently into the literature. As in Pss 42-43, the author might be living in a distant part of Palestine. Yet, if the psalmist or one who prays is very sick, then *ends of the earth* might signify the edge of Sheol or the nether world. *Lead me to the rock:* that is, to the Jerusalem temple, as in Pss 27:4-5. *Dwell in thy tent...under the shelter of thy wings:* close to the ark of the covenant where God was invisibly enthroned surrounded by the wings of the cherubim: see Pss 17:8; 36:7; 57:1.

Vv. 5-7, prayer for the king, is rich in its allusions: a vow to make a thanksgiving offering; a reference to the promised land to which the king is devoted; a prayer for the fulfillment of the pledge of an everlasting dynasty in 2 Sam 7:16, 25-29:

"bless the house [or dynasty] of thy servant, that it may continue for ever before thee," linked up with the everlasting *fidelity and steadfast love* of the Mosaic covenant (Exod 34:6-7).

V. 8, the conclusion, provides for the fulfillment of the vow and the thanksgiving sacrifice: *cf.,* Lev 7:11-18; Jer 33:11.

(IV) Ps 61 reminds us of our obligation to pray for religious and civil leaders. We are made to realize that our individual, national and international welfare are closely knit together. Religion enables us to form this integral union. It sustains us in our separations, it draws us back to a common point where God's fidelity becomes the basis, inspiration and reward of our own fidelity. In our own personal bouts with isolation and sickness, we are no longer alone. We find our faith in God sustained by the magnificent promises for all the covenant community.

Psalm 62
To The Choirmaster: According To Jeduthun. A Psalm Of David.

I

¹For God alone my soul waits in silence;
    from him comes my salvation.
²He only is my rock and my salvation,
    my fortress; I shall not be greatly moved.

II

³How long will you set upon a man
    to shatter him, all of you,
    like a leaning wall, a tottering fence?
⁴They only plan to thrust him down from his eminence.
    They take pleasure in falsehood.
    They bless with their mouths,
    but inwardly they curse.   *Selah*

⁵For God alone my soul waits in silence,
    for my hope is from him.
⁶He only is my rock and my salvation,

my fortress; I shall not be shaken.
7On God rests my deliverance and my honor;
  my mighty rock, my refuge is God.

8Trust in him at all times, O people;
  pour out your heart before him;
  God is a refuge for us.   *Selah*

9Men of low estate are but a breath,
  men of high estate are a delusion;
 in the balances they go up;
  they are together lighter than a breath.
10Put no confidence in extortion,
  set no vain hopes on robbery;
  if riches increase, set not your heart on them.

III

11Once God has spoken;
  twice have I heard this:
 that power belongs to God;
12 and that to thee, O Lord, belongs steadfast love.
 For thou dost requite a man
  according to his work.

(I) Severe contrasts show up here, yet the spirit of Ps 62 remains tranquil, the tone one of confidence, the attitude one of meditation about God. There is, however, *no* prayer nor address *to* God. Twice the refrain floats over the surface: *my soul waits in silence*, or according to the better Hebrew reading in v. 5, the imperative, *wait, be silent.* Yet all the while one's acquaintances *take pleasure in falsehood,* as *they bless with the mouth but inwardly they curse.* These two kinds of silence — waiting upon God and tranquilly enduring curses — speak of heroic faith and exceptional strength within the psalmist. The author confesses that every human being is *but a breath,* only a *delusion* (it is not a case here of wickedness, only extended weakness, even powerlessness), yet the psalm ends with God's requiting each person *according to their work.* Evidently God's steadfast love, mentioned immediately before the conclusion, transforms weakness into confident strength. In vv. 4 and 10 the psalmist seems to be meditating upon Ezekiel, especially chap. 18, but moderating its strident note, and in vv. 9-10 and 12b to be reflecting upon the sapiential tradition, but surrounding it with sanctuary prayer. Although the psalm contains features of a lament, still there are no curses, no groaning, no supplication. The tone, as we have mentioned, is so quiet and confident, that many scholars conclude that the trial is over. Yet, this position of modern writers may be taking advantage of the psalmist's mild and trustful disposition!

(II) The reflective quality of this psalm of confidence or instructional meditation has allowed the structure to slip its moorings and to be difficult to determine. One would expect the refrain (vv. 1-2, 5-6) to conclude a major strophe, but it doesn't; the sapiential conclusion seems almost anticlimactic, like a later addition. With hesitation we offer the following division:

vv. 1-2, Introduction, about
         Yahweh
vv. 3-10, Motives for
      confidence
   vv. 3-4 + selah, falsehood
   vv. 5-8 + selah, trust in
   God
   vv. 9-10, human weakness

vv. 11-12, Conclusion
   vv. 11-12a, Divine oracle
     of God's steadfast love
   v. 12b, sapiential
    conclusion.

(III) Vv. 1-2. Although the introduction is dominated by contemplative silence, the words abound with strength and almost shout their message! Grammatically, these two opening verses (plus vv. 4, 5, 6, and 9) begin with the Hebrew particle, *'ak*, which demands attention and usually introduces a confident assertion. Besides divine epithets like *rock* and *fortress* (derived from the rock upon which Jerusalem and especially the temple were constructed — see Ps 95), the final word, *moved,* frequently refers to world cataclysms, as "mountains *tremble* with its tumult" (Ps 46:3), or "the foundations of the earth *are shaken*" (Ps 82:5). The psalmist presents an imposing figure of a strong contemplative person at the temple while the world round about is collapsing under deceit and extortion.

Vv. 3-10. Motivation for confidence is derived from the contrast between God and false friends. Even though they fall upon the psalmist like *a leaning wall, a tottering fence,* God is *my rock;* even though *they bless with their mouths, but inwardly they curse,* God remains *my honor* (from a Hebrew root to be heavy, secure, dignified, dependable). V. 8, *pour out your heart,* echoes Ps 42:4, "these things I remember as I *pour out* my soul: how I...led them in procession to the house of God." While the remembrance in Pss 42-43 induced sorrow, here it brings renewed confidence. V. 9, *people of low estate* [and] *of high estate are a delusion; in the balances* [scales] *they are lighter than a breath,* nothing human can be a source of ultimate stability, only God. The image of the scales occurs elsewhere in the Bible (*i.e.,* Prov 21:2, "the Lord weighs the heart") and in Egyptian murals and literature. If we challenge God, we will be taken seriously, weighed, and shown to be *lighter than a breath.* V. 10, such "bourgeoisie" morality, as reliance on sophisticated *extortion* and *robbery* — similar to *falsehood* and silent *curses* in vv. 4-5 — cannot provide stability and peace.

Vv. 11-12. The conclusion begins with a numerical saying: *first...second,* a style common in the sapiential literature (Prov 6:16-17; 30:15-21) but also among the prophets (Amos 1:3-2:16) and appropriate for this meditative psalm. The psalm originally concluded with the covenantal word, *steadfast love* (see Ps 12). Still later a sapiential statement was appended: God will *requite persons according to their work,* a phrase quoted frequently enough, Rom 2:6; 1 Cor 3:8; 2 Tim 4:14; Rev 22:12. God raises us up, once fragile as breath, to function in the covenant bond and participate in both the work and the reward. God thereby crowns *his* greatest work, humankind (A. Maillot-A. Lelièvre).

(IV) This psalm quietly insists that there are no easy, quick answers. At times by going nowhere but remaining silently in God's presence, we grow in dignity, strength and self-control. We thereby silence people of falsehood, we reveal the *vain hopes* (v. 10) of riches, especially those immorally obtained. At times by remaining still, we gradually realize that we are securing ourselves upon a Rock that is God within the fortress of prayer.

Psalm 63
A Psalm Of David, When He Was In The Wilderness Of Judah.

I
¹O God, thou art my God, I seek thee,
  my soul thirsts for thee;
  my flesh faints for thee,
    as in a dry and weary land where no water is.

II
²So I have looked upon thee in the sanctuary,
  beholding thy power and glory.
³Because thy steadfast love is better than life,
  my lips will praise thee.
⁴So I will bless thee as long as I live;
  I will lift up my hands and call on thy name.

⁵My soul is feasted as with marrow and fat,
  and my mouth praises thee with joyful lips,
⁶when I think of thee upon my bed,
  and meditate on thee in the watches of the night;

III
⁷for thou hast been my help,
  and in the shadow of thy wings I sing for joy.
⁸My soul clings to thee;
  thy right hand upholds me.

IV
⁹But those who seek to destroy my life
  shall go down into the depths of the earth;
¹⁰they shall be given over to the power of the sword,
  they shall be prey for jackals.

¹¹But the king shall rejoice in God;
   all who swear by him shall glory;
   for the mouths of liars will be stopped.

(I) The mystic tone of this psalm defies classification and explanation: the psalmist *thirsts* (v. 1) and yet *is feasted as with* [the delicacies of] *marrow and fat* (v. 5); at a distance the psalmist *faints for thee,* O God (v. 1), and yet *in the shadow of thy wings...my soul clings to thee* (vv. 7-8; see Ps 17:8). Yet for the true mystic contradictions melt away, for to such a person God's presence is most real in one's passionate desire, where love leaps beyond feeling and understanding. As in Ps 16, the bonds of God's *steadfast love* enable the psalmist to surpass the boundaries of orthodox theology and glimpse a life *that is better than* [*this*] *life*. Not until the very late postexilic age did Israel's theology accept personal immortality (Dan 12:3; 2 Macc 7), yet already in the pre-exilic age and the period of the monarchy (*cf.,* v. 11), the psalmist is anticipating immediate intimacy with God while keeping a night vigil before the ark, surrounded by the outstretched wings of the cherubim (Ps 17). Ps 63 is frequently compared with Pss 42-43, yet we notice that it is calmer in already possessing what it is thirsting to taste in its separation.

(II) The attitude of the psalmist is difficult to determine. Because the opening and final verses (vv. 1 and 9-11) reflect a sorrowful situation, we hesitantly consider the psalm a lament for the individual. The body of the psalm reflects joyful thanksgiving (vv. 2-6) and strong confidence (vv. 7-8).

(III) The title refers most likely to David's flight from Saul into the *wilderness of Judah*, the very barren, mountainous terrain between the central mountain ridge and the Dead Sea (1 Sam 23:14; 24:2). The psalm, however, seems to be post-Davidic as it refers to the Ark at Jerusalem within the temple of Solomon. The title introduces a mystic tonality. Even the later kings and devout worshipers who were present with the Lord at the temple, may still have felt alienated and distanced from God by many personal and national trials.

V. 1, introduction of lament, not only has a unique grammatical form (in fact the entire psalm is very original and creative) but the word *seek* is derived from the one for "dawn." It can be translated, "O God, you are my God, you I seek at the break of dawn." As if the psalmist had been fasting during a night vigil, we read: *my soul thirsts for thee; my flesh faints for thee.* The fasting induced by the *dry and weary land* is only symbolic of the greater, even more real thirst of the spirit for God. Yet, this thirst for God is caused by the remembrance of God (v. 6), or better, a remembrance of the wonderful covenant of *steadfast love* (v. 3) which God stirs within the psalmist. As Gregory of Nazianzen wrote: "Deus sitit, sitiri — God thirsts, to be thirsted for!"

Vv. 2-6, where the verbs are mostly in the incomplete tense, offer thanks to God for the experience of his *steadfast love.* The section begins from a strong position: *I have looked upon thee,* with a verb, *ḥazah,* that frequently refers to a prophetic vision, at least to an extraordinary insight. *Power and glory* remind us of the long history of the ark of the covenant, the glory of its presence (Exod 40:34-38), its loss when God's glory left Israel (1 Sam 4:21), or its symbolic departure and return in Ezek 10:2; 18-23; and 43:1-9. Though the psalmist may have fled into the temple to preserve life, still the covenant leads to a personal intimacy *better than life! I will bless:* the phrase carries the strong connotation of recognizing what God has done and therefore it is filled with joyful gratitude; it often is linked with a sacrificial meal of thanksgiving (*cf.,* Exod 18:10-12, where Jethro, Moses' father-in-law, declared: "Blessed be the Lord who has delivered you...; [then they] offered a burnt offering and sacrifices to God [and began to] eat bread..." *Marrow and* especially *fat* were considered a delicacy (Job 36:16), generally reserved for sacrifices to God (Lev 3-7); here we sense again a mystic union with God (*cf.,* Isa 55:2, "hearken diligently to me...and delight yourselves in fatness"). V. 6, while night can symbolize danger (Amos 5:18) and even the chaotic absence of God as in the age before creation (Gen 1:1-2), it also introduces one into God's overwhelming presence in wonder and goodness (Exod 12:42; *cf.,* Wis 18:1, "for thy holy ones [at darkness] there was a very great light").

Vv. 7-8. The psalmist, near the ark and like it enfolded within the outstretched wings of the cherubim (*cf.,* Exod 25:20-21), is carried into a mystic intimacy with God to whom *my soul clings.*

Vv. 9-11. These final lines combine lament with confidence; they so break the spirit of the preceding lines that they seem a later addition, adapting the psalm to the everyday problems of worshipers: those who seek to destroy the life of the devout will themselves be left in *the depths of the earth* (*i.e.,* Sheol, see Pss 6:5; 16:10), the corpses unburied (*cf.,* 2 Sam 21:10-14; 2 Kgs 1:9-10), so that the fate of the body represents the fate of the entire person. The final line of the psalm may have read originally: "all who swear by him shall praise him!"

(IV) Ps 63 passes from a night vigil in the temple to the dawn of a new day and to a new confidence, from a mystical intimacy with God in darkness to an ability to face the difficult trials of the day with renewed strength. Ps 63 enables us to live responsibly and confidently on earth, assured that we have the promise of something — indeed, Someone — *better than life* (v. 3). We can easily understand why this psalm quickly became the classic morning prayer of the early church. The Armenian church associates it with its eucharistic liturgy, especially because of v. 5, *my soul is feasted as with marrow and fat.* In the very early *Apostolic Constitutions,* the faithful are exhorted as "members of Christ" to attend daily morning and evening prayer at church: "Be not careless of yourselves, neither deprive your Savior of His own members, neither divide His body nor disperse His members, neither prefer the occasions of this life to the word of God; but assemble yourselves together every day, morning and evening, singing psalms and praying in the Lord's house: in the morning, saying the sixty-second psalm [our Ps 63 in the Hebrew enumeration]" (Book II, no. 59).

Psalm 64

This individual lament confidently looks to God for help against plots and intrigue which no one can see, much less search out (vv. 5-6). The text is poorly preserved, especially vv. 4-7, and the meaning of some phrases is uncertain. The structure, however, is clear enough:

vv. 1-2, call for help	vv. 7-9, Confidence in God's
vv. 3-6, narrative of dangers	help
	v. 10, Joyful conclusion

That evil people are eventually unmasked and punished is a theme this psalm shares with the sapiential movement (see Ps 1). The psalmist may be opposing those people who use religion for their own selfish motives, even as they attack others whom they fear or dislike. In that case the psalm resonates the prophetical movement (Isa 1:10-17; Hos 4:4-10; Mic 3). This latter motivation enables us to read Ps 64 in conjunction with Jas 2:2-9.

Psalm 65
To The Choirmaster. A Psalm Of David. A Song.

I

¹Praise is due to thee,
   O God, in Zion;
   and to thee shall vows be performed,
² O thou who hearest prayer!
 To thee shall all flesh come
³ on account of sins.
 When our transgressions prevail over us,
   thou dost forgive them.

⁴Blessed is he whom thou dost choose and bring near,
   to dwell in thy courts!
 We shall be satisfied with the goodness of thy house,
   thy holy temple!

II

⁵By dread deeds thou dost answer us with deliverance,
  O God of our salvation,
 who art the hope of all the ends of the earth,
  and of the farthest seas;
⁶who by thy strength hast established the mountains,
  being girded with might;
⁷who dost still the roaring of the seas,
  the roaring of their waves,
  the tumult of the peoples;
⁸so that those who dwell at earth's farthest bounds
  are afraid at thy signs;
 thou makest the outgoings of the
   morning and the evening
   to shout for joy.

III

⁹Thou visitest the earth and waterest it,
  thou greatly enrichest it;
 the river of God is full of water;
  thou providest their grain,
  for so thou hast prepared it.
¹⁰Thou waterest its furrows abundantly,
  settling its ridges,
 softening it with showers,
  and blessing its growth.
¹¹Thou crownest the year with thy bounty;
  the tracks of thy chariot drip with fatness.
¹²The pastures of the wilderness drip,
  the hills gird themselves with joy,
¹³the meadows clothe themselves with flocks,
  the valleys deck themselves with grain,
  they shout and sing together for joy.

(I) The unity and momentum of this psalm are detected in three key places: v. 2, *thou hearest prayer;* v. 5, *thou dost answer*; and v. 9, *thou visitest the earth.* From prayer to answer to action! A further development becomes apparent: in vv. 2-4, God hears our prayer and forgives our sins, drawing us closely to himself in the sanctuary; in vv. 5-8, God answers by quieting the roaring chaos of the world. The psalm modulates from personal forgiveness to universal peace, from the Jerusalem temple to its surrounding court- yard, the world. In vv. 9-13, God visits the world with life-giving water, which we are tempted to think originates within the sanctuary (*cf.,* Ezek 47; or Ps 46:4, "a river whose streams make glad the city of God, the holy habitation of the Most High"). This sequence reminds us of the high holydays in the month of Tishri (Sept-Oct), particularly from Yom Kippur on 10 Tishri to Tabernacles or Booths on 15-22 Tishri, from at-one-ment and forgiveness to thanksgiving for the year's harvest and prayer for rain to break the long dry season (*cf.,* Ps 67). During the octave of Tabernacles the pouring of water was a prominent feature of the ritual at the beginning of each new day. Ps 65 possibly occupied a promi- nent place in these pilgrimage festivals in the month of Tishri. This fact may explain why the title to the psalm links it with David in the Hebrew, but with Jeremiah and Ezekiel and the return from exile in the Greek, with David who first marched into Jerusalem after conquering the city and with the exiles who return to the Holy City to re-create their life. All three persons, David, Jeremiah and Ezekiel, are asso- ciated closely with sin and its forgiveness, Jeremiah also with new life (chaps. 30-31) and Ezekiel with the reconstruc- tion of the temple (chaps. 40-48).

(II) The structure of the psalm is clear: vv. 1-4, God hears prayers, forgives sin and by the beauty of his holy temple makes us happy; vv. 5-8, God as Creator overcomes chaos and settles the universe in secure and joyful peace; vv. 9-13, God as Giver of Rain makes the earth fertile, decked with grain and bounding for joy. The reference to sin in vv. 2-3 makes us think that this psalm is less a hymn of praise (the early hymns would not deal with sin) and much more a prayer of thanksgiving.

(III) Vv. 1-4. In accord with the ancient Greek and Syriac versions, the opening line is usually read, as in the RSV, "Praise is due to thee"; yet the Hebrew reads, "For you silence is praise, O God, in Zion," the attitude of ecstatic wonder over what God is about to do, coupling with the later line, Thou *dost still the roaring of the seas* (v. 7). This opening verse, according to the Greek (and RSV) has inspired the dialogue at the beginning of the Preface to the Eucharistic Prayer: "Let us give thanks to the Lord our God — it is right and just." In v. 2, *all flesh* may indicate the weakness of sinful Israel. V. 3, *transgressions prevail:* by ourselves we are unable to lift ourselves out of sin. V. 4 is rich in covenant and ritual allusions: *Blessed* (see Ps 1:1); *choose* (*cf.,* Deut 7:7-8, "the Lord chose you...because the Lord loves you"); *dwell in thy courts,* possible for all Israelites (*cf.,* Pss 15 and 24 which speak of entering the courts of the temple after a ritual of purification/forgiveness); *the goodness of thy house,* probably a reference to the sacred meals (*cf.,* Ps 22:26, "the afflicted shall eat and be satisfied" within the assembly of worship).

Vv. 5-8. These lines have the hallmark of Israel's great hymns, like Pss 29 or 89:5-18 (see also Ps 8), with the hymnic participle — establishing the mountains, quieting the roar of the sea — the Lord's magnificent, even fearful and awesome display of power over all chaotic forces, the shout of joy from morning till evening.

Vv. 9-13. Here the perfect tense of the Hebrew verb is employed, the narrative style of praise: if God visits the earth with rain and enriches it with new life, it is done so perfectly that the results continue from harvest to new planting, from the early rains in October-November to the late rains in March-April. Again there is a joyful shout to conclude the psalm.

(IV) By drawing upon pagan mythology in vv. 5-8, and linking the Jerusalem temple with the universe, by dwelling upon the blessings of the earth's harvest, Ps 65 enabled Israel to *glimpse* its world mission even from the beginning. Only at rare moments, as in the final poems of Second Isaiah (Isa 40-55), did a faithful Israelite begin to see the consequences of its mission and to break through the more narrow bonds of election that separated Israel from all other nations. Such flashes of insight are crucial for future development. Biblical religion is glimpsed as the center of world religions; the covenant God is the source of forgiveness and new life for everyone, whether "Jew or Greek, slave or free, male or female" (Gal 3:28).

Christian tradition has linked Ps 65 with the liturgy for the deceased. The dead are to receive full purification from sin, to be called into the blessedness of the heavenly sanctuary, and to find their entire world re-created and transformed.

Psalm 66
To The Choirmaster. A Song. A Psalm.

I

¹Make a joyful noise to God, all the earth;
² sing the glory of his name;
    give to him glorious praise!
³Say to God, "How terrible are thy deeds!
    So great is thy power that thy enemies
        cringe before thee.

⁴All the earth worships thee;
    they sing praises to thee,
    sing praises to thy name."   *Selah*

⁵Come and see what God has done:
    he is terrible in his deeds among men.
⁶He turned the sea into dry land;
    men passed through the river on foot.
    There did we rejoice in him,
⁷ who rules by his might for ever,
    whose eyes keep watch on the nations—
        let not the rebellious exalt themselves.   *Selah*

II

⁸Bless our God, O peoples,
    let the sound of his praise be heard,
⁹who has kept us among the living,
    and has not let our feet slip.
¹⁰For thou, O God, hast tested us;
    thou hast tried us as silver is tried.

11Thou didst bring us into the net;
   thou didst lay affliction on our loins;
12thou didst let men ride over our heads;
   we went through fire and through water;
   yet thou hast brought us forth to a spacious place.

III

13I will come into thy house with burnt offerings;
   I will pay thee my vows,
14that which my lips uttered
   and my mouth promised when I was in trouble.
15I will offer to thee burnt offerings of fatlings,
   with the smoke of the sacrifice of rams;
   I will make an offering of bulls and goats.   *Selah*

16Come and hear, all you who fear God,
   and I will tell what he has done for me.
17I cried aloud to him,
   and he was extolled with my tongue.
18If I had cherished iniquity in my heart,
   the Lord would not have listened.
19But truly God has listened;
   he has given heed to the voice of my prayer.

IV

20Blessed be God,
   because he has not rejected my prayer
   or removed his steadfast love from me!

(I) What is most effectively achieved in Ps 66 is the actualization or reliving of God's redemptive acts, particularly the exodus out of Egypt and the crossing of the River Jordan, within the *contemporary* situation of the Israelite nation and the individual worshiper. Unlike much of modern biblical study, the psalm does not attempt to recapture the historical setting of the past but rather enables the ancient act of God to become an important ingredient of the later age. We are reminded of the well known "today" passages in Deuteronomy, *i.e.,* "The Lord our God made a covenant *with us* at Horeb. Not with our ancestors...but

with us, who are *all of us* here *alive this day"* (Deut 5:2-3); or
we think of the answer given to the child who asks, "What is
the meaning" of this liturgical action: "*We* were pharaoh's
slaves...and the Lord brought *us* out of Egypt...showed
signs and wonders...before *our* eyes" (Deut 6:20-22). The
psalmist is not constrained to remain within ancient liturgical formulas and actions, but rather was creative enough to
adapt the community ritual of vv. 1-12 to personal, individual needs (vv. 13-20, where the plural changes to the singular
"I"). Important liturgical actions presume a right attitude
within each individual worshiper before God. While
remaining within the main lines of the ancient liturgy, we
find strong, personal conviction and individual consecration expressed through the sacrifices and holocausts.

The psalm is too general to determine what may have
been the serious trial for the nation (vv. 10-12) and for the
individual psalmist (vv. 18-19). The contact with Isaiah and
Jeremiah (vv. 10-11 and Isa 1:25; Jer 6:29; 9:6) and with
Second Isaiah's theme of the new exodus (v. 6 and Isa
43:16-21) inclines us to a date during the exile or immediately afterwards, but the reasons are not absolutely
compelling.

(II) The structure of Ps 66 is complex yet clear, as the
following division of Louis Jacquet shows:

	I	II	III
Praise	vv. 1-4	vv. 8-9	vv. 13-15
Thanksgiving	vv. 5-7 for past deliverance	vv. 10-12 for recent deliverance	vv. 16-19 for recent deliverance
Conclusion	v. 20		

(III) Vv. 1-4, an introductory hymn of praise, beginning
with four strong summons: *make a joyful noise* (or more
simply in the Hebrew, shout — cf., Ps 47:1), *sing, give to
him, say to God.* V. 1. To call upon *All the earth,* again in v.
4, is more hyperbole than realism, suited to enthusiastic
praise; yet the later reference to the exodus involves other
nations besides Israel and so may tilt the scale again towards

some general type of universal call. Israel's religion was so
rooted in world history, that sooner or later its covenant
election was bound to be thrown open to all nations. It is
interesting to note that this enlargement of the covenant did
not come principally from Israel's religious resources but
more from her international involvement.

Vv. 5-7. The hymn of praise is followed by a grateful
remembrance and a reliving of God's deliverance at the
exodus and the River Jordan. These two great acts are
associated in Pss 114 and 136; see also Isa 43:16-18. With
stylistic elegance, there is a second call to praise in v. 5, very
similar to Ps 46:8. Just as the heavens rejoiced in God's
giving birth to the universe (Ps 19:1), the peoples of the
world now acclaim God's life-giving act for Israel (E. Beaucamp). The psalm turns quickly from the past to the present
moment and the present place of worship: *there did we
rejoice in him who rules by his might for ever.* The emphasis
is surely on *there* where we assemble, *we* who worship and
rejoice, and the continuation *for ever;* this is similar to Isa
43:18-19, "Remember not the former things [about which he
has just spoken!]. . . Behold I am doing a new thing; now it
springs forth, do you not perceive it?" God's conquest of the
chaotic forces of the sea and river, derived from Canaanite
mythology, is folded into God's mighty act of saving Israel
(*cf.,* Isa 51:9-10).

Vv. 8-12, community thanksgiving. The people realize
that their trials have been a testing and a purification, to
establish for ever in their mind that *thou* [O God] *hast
brought us forth to a spacious place.* Without such suffering
and even frustration, we might attribute salvation to our
own enterprise. "Testing" is a common enough word in
Deuteronomy (*cf.,* Deut 6:16; 8:2, 16; 33:8) but the special
Hebrew word here (*bahan*) is more common in Jeremiah
(*cf.,* 8:27; 9:6; 11:20; 12:3; etc.) in which we learn that God
tests us and so explores the secrets of the heart (12:3). We are
close to the secret joys of the mystics in the midst of their
suffering (see Ps 63).

Vv. 13-20, individual thanksgiving. The abundant
thanksgiving offerings make us think of a prominent person

like a king or high priest. The confession of faith in vv. 16-19 reminds us of Ps 22:22-31. Liturgical words and cultic actions have centered Israel's entire redemptive history in the person of each worshiper. Vv. 16-19 are held together by the word *listen:* the psalmist asks *all who fear God* to *come and hear,* but at the source of the praise and gratitude is the fact that *truly God has listened . . . to the voice of my prayer.* Instruction is not a primary purpose of liturgy, but it happens in the midst of enthusiastic praise and gratitude. *Blessed be God,* means our recognition through faith and ritual of God's wondrous actions in our favor (*cf.,* Exod 18:10-12), as these actions are united with God's care for his people through the ages. Gratitude is capped with the covenant promise of God's *steadfast love* (Exod 34:6-7).

(IV) This psalm was linked very early with the resurrection of Jesus, as we learn from the title in the Latin Vulgate, *Canticum Psalmi resurrectionis.* This relationship is not surprising in view of the link between the paschal mystery of the exodus (v. 6) and Jesus' death and resurrection and because of v. 12 in the psalm: *thou hast brought us forth to a spacious place.* The references to *all the earth* (vv. 1 and 4) induced early patristic writers to associate the psalm with the feast of the Epiphany when foreigners came to worship the new born king (Matt 2:1-12). Mystics like St. Paul of the Cross considered Ps 66 their favorite on account of the transition from overwhelming sorrow and intense interior testing to a profound union with God and a new, secret peace.

Psalm 67
To The Choirmaster: With Stringed Instruments. A Paslm. A Song.

I

¹May God be gracious to us and bless us
   and make his face to shine upon us,   *Selah*
²that thy way may be known upon earth,
   thy saving power among all nations.

³Let the people praise thee, O God;
    let all the peoples praise thee!

II

⁴Let the nations be glad and sing for joy,
    for thou dost judge the peoples with equity
    and guide the nations upon earth.   *Selah*
⁵Let the peoples praise thee, O God;
    let all the peoples praise thee!

III

⁶The earth has yielded its increase;
    God, our God, has blessed us.
⁷God has blessed us;
    let all the ends of the earth fear him!

(I) Like Ps 65, this psalm turns gratefully to God after a bountiful harvest. The good fruits of the earth unite people of every race and background; a strong universal note is perceived here. In fact, future blessings, even messianic ones, are portrayed as an abundance of earthly produce. In Hos 14:5, God "will be as the dew to Israel, [who] shall blossom as the vine"; in Amos 9:13, "the plowman shall overtake the reaper, [and] the mountains shall drip sweet wine." We remember the classic text of Isa 45:8, "Shower, O heavens, from above, and let the skies rain down righteousness; let the earth open, that salvation may sprout forth.... I the Lord have created it." Gradually the messianic sweep of Israel's mission became associated with *the* harvest festival of the year, Tabernacles or Booths, 15-22 Tishri in our Sept-Oct (*cf.,* Ps 65; also Zech 14:16-17, "[On] the feast of booths, if any of the families of the earth do not go up to Jerusalem to worship the King, the Lord of hosts, there will be no rain upon them"). Again, the world mission of Israel was perceived more through God's action across the world in rain and fertility — or in international politics — than in purely religious sources! It is equally clear that the hidden presence of God in nature and politics would remain too obscure without an explicit revelation to Israel about her role of being God's elect people with a mission.

(II) The structure of this prayer of thanksgiving for bountiful crops is easily detectible in English translation: vv. 1-3, a general statement of God's way across the earth; vv. 4-5, a recognition by the nations of God's fidelity; vv. 6-7, the specific goodness of God in the harvest. The refrain (vv. 3 and 5) needs to be added after v. 7. The Hebrew text raises problems: the divisions, especially the *selah*, are placed awkwardly; some of the verbs might be translated as jussives: *i.e.*, v. 6, "Let the earth yield its increase," in which case the psalm is transformed into a lament, begging God for rain and fertility to break a long drought. Yet the tone and spirit of the psalm seem to militate against this latter interpretation.

The universal reach of Ps 67 is also evident in the large number of words (71% of the total according to Helen G. Jefferson) that parallel Ugaritic, a North West Semitic language. It is possible that a poem, strongly non-Israelite in influence was later introduced in v. 1 by the priestly blessing of Num 6:24-26, still later felt the impact of Second Isaiah's outreach of the nations, and during a peaceful period of the postexilic age reached its final form.

(III) The opening verse, taken from the priestly blessing of Num 6:24-26, would have been recited by the priest in attendance. God's blessing is most manifest in *life*, especially in the family (Ps 128) but also in food (Ps 132:15), dew (Ps 133:3), rain (Hos 6:3), etc. For God to shine his face on us means special delight in us and gracious generosity (Pss 4:6-7; 27:8; etc.). *thy saving power:* the Hebrew word is "thy salvation," and shows that God's blessings reach us first externally and physically, and then as we reflect upon our lives and world, they seep ever more deeply into our thoughts and judgments. We need the Scriptures for this reflective process.

(IV) God makes his face to shine upon us in Jesus, the eternal Word, who "reflects the glory of God and bears the very stamp of God's nature" (Heb 1:3). Jesus too manifests the abundant blessings of this earth, born as he was of a woman of earthly origin (Gal 4:4). We are further reminded that each earthly blessing should redound upon others and become a means of proclaiming salvation to all peoples. Our material generosity ought to become an instrument of the gospel to proclaim that Jesus is Lord and Giver of life.

Psalm 68
To The Choirmaster. A Psalm Of David. A Song.

I-a

¹Let God arise, let his enemies be scattered;
    let those who hate him flee before him!
²As smoke is driven away, so drive them away;
    as wax melts before fire,
    let the wicked perish before God!
³But let the righteous be joyful;
    let them exult before God;
    let them be jubilant with joy!

-b-

⁴Sing to God, sing praises to his name;
    lift up a song to him who rides upon the clouds;
    his name is the Lord, exult before him!

⁵Father of the fatherless and protector of widows
    is God in his holy habitation.

⁶God gives the desolate a home to dwell in;
    he leads the prisoners to prosperity;
    but the rebellious dwell in a parched land.

II-a

⁷O God, when thou didst go forth before thy people,
    when thou didst march through the wilderness,
                       Selah
⁸the earth quaked, the heavens poured down rain,
   at the presence of God;
  yon Sinai quaked at the presence of God,
   the God of Israel.
⁹Rain in abundance, O God, thou didst shed abroad;
    thou didst restore thy heritage as it languished;

¹⁰thy flock found a dwelling in it;
   in thy goodness, O God, thou didst
      provide for the needy.

-b-
¹¹The Lord gives the command;
   great is the host of those who bore the tidings:
¹²"The kings of the armies, they flee, they flee!"
The women at home divide the spoil,
¹³though they stay among the sheepfolds—
   the wings of a dove covered with silver,
      its pinions with green gold.
¹⁴When the Almighty scattered kings there,
   snow fell on Zalmon.

-c-
¹⁵O mighty mountain, mountain of Bashan;
   O many-peaked mountain, mountain of Bashan!
¹⁶Why look you with envy, O many-peaked mountain,
   at the mount which God desired for his abode,
      yea, where the Lord will dwell for ever?

¹⁷With mighty chariotry, twice ten thousand,
   thousands upon thousands,
      the Lord came from Sinai into the holy place.
¹⁸Thou didst ascend the high mount,
   leading captives in thy train,
   and receiving gifts among men,
      even among the rebellious, that the
         Lord God may dwell there.

-d-
¹⁹Blessed be the Lord,
   who daily bears us up;
      God is our salvation.   *Selah*
²⁰Our God is a God of salvation;
   and to God, the Lord, belongs escape from death.

²¹But God will shatter the heads of his enemies,
   the hairy crown of him who walks in his guilty ways.

²²The Lord said,
  "I will bring them back from Bashan,
  I will bring them back from the depths of the sea,
²³that you may bathe your feet in blood,
    that the tongues of your dogs may
      have their portion from the foe."

-e-

²⁴Thy solemn processions are seen, O God,
    the processions of my God, my King,
      into the sanctuary—
²⁵the singers in front, the minstrels last,
    between them maidens playing timbrels:
²⁶"Bless God in the great congregation,
    the Lord, O you who are of Israel's fountain!"
²⁷There is Benjamin, the least of them, in the lead,
    the princes of Judah in their throng,
      the princes of Zebulun, the princes of Naphtali.

-f-

²⁸Summon thy might, O God;
    show thy strength, O God, thou who hast wrought for
    us.
²⁹Because of thy temple at Jerusalem
    kings bear gifts to thee.
³⁰Rebuke the beasts that dwell among the reeds,
    the herd of bulls with the calves of the peoples.
 Trample under foot those who lust after tribute;
    scatter the peoples who delight in war.
³¹Let bronze be brought from Egypt;
    let Ethiopia hasten to stretch out her hands to God.

III

³²Sing to God, O kingdoms of the earth;
    sing praises to the Lord,   *Selah*
³³to him who rides in the heavens, the ancient heavens;
    lo, he sends forth his voice, his mighty voice.
³⁴Ascribe power to God,
    whose majesty is over Israel,
    and his power is in the skies.

[35]Terrible is God in his sanctuary,
the God of Israel,
he gives power and strength to his people.

Blessed be God!

(I) We approach Ps 68 as one would an ancient cathedral, perceiving the sweep of grandeur, the complexity of details, the time-worn pavement with its blurred memories, the ancient monuments partly neglected and partly effaced, repairs poorly executed, new additions where modernity and antiquity clash (Gaston Brillet and Louis Jacquet). Yet, the cathedral edifice of Ps 68 is no museum, but like the ancient cathedral, a popular place of worship. In fact, because of continuous use, Ps 68 is worse for wear and turns out to be one of the most textually corrupt of all psalms.

As we read and reread Ps 68, we visualize various marches or processions through Israel's history. In fact, the psalm begins with the "marching song" of Num 10:35 (slightly adapted for a hymn), when the ark and meeting tent were dismantled and the people broke camp, first at Sinai, later throughout the wilderness, on the long road to the Promised Land, eventually to the holy city of Jerusalem. This march of Israel through the wilderness is remembered principally through liturgical processions. We may even claim that liturgy gave the original event a place in Israel's history. Our primary source of information about Israel's movement out of Egypt and through the wilderness lies in the liturgy — just as eucharistic celebrations best preserve the memory of the Lord's Last Supper, his death and resurrection.

After Israel had settled in the land, Jerusalem became the goal of marches and pilgrimages. One of the key, theological insights of Ps 68 sees Jerusalem as the new Sinai. As Jerusalem took on the splendor of paradise (see Ps 46), journeys to the Holy City kept the people's vision always towards the future. Israel's golden age lies before them, not behind them in a mythical paradise of first creation. Likewise, the medieval cathedral was both the goal of pilgrimages but also the symbol of a goal beyond the bounds of this earthly life, in the heavenly kingdom with the glorified Christ.

We detect a number of other liturgical actions, elaborate and highly symbolical as one would expect in a cathedral, each recapturing an ancient memory and reliving it within a later age: vv. 1-6, the call to praise with strong Canaanite imagery; vv. 7-10, possibly a ritual with water and sacred bread, commemorating the manna; vv. 11-14, 15-16, 17-18, 19-20, 21-23, the approach towards the Jerusalem temple in which even foreigners join in bringing tribute; vv. 24-27, the procession into the sanctuary; vv. 28-31, petitions; vv. 32-35, conclusion of the ceremony. During this elaborate, full-bodied ritual, Israel's ancient struggles are re-lived: her defeats, renewals and transformations; even the violent moments of war, civil and international, where soldiers bathe their feet in blood as dogs lick it up (v. 23). In the ancient cathedral these latter moments are represented by the gargoyles.

Most of all, we have a sense of God, marching through the lives of our ancestors, moving through the blood of our own descendants, reaching out to fill the universe. We cannot forget God whose name rings out repeatedly: *'elohim*, 23x; *'adonai*, 6x; *'el*, 2x; *shaddai* or almighty in v. 14; *Yahweh*, v. 17; *Yah*, v. 4; *Yahweh 'adonai*, v. 20; *yahweh 'elohim*, v. 18. Even if Ps 68 is the most "elohistic" of any psalm in the second book of the psalter (see introduction to Pss 42-43), it still embraces a litany of Israel's history in addressing God. Ps 68 surrounds this intense presence of God with magnificent theophanies, equal to that given to Moses on Sinai, and now relived in the liturgical symbols of the Jerusalem temple/cathedral. Finally, while our attention is continually drawn to God, we realize that throughout the psalm God is attending to us, driving away our enemies in the opening line, giving us power and strength in the last line, in between caring for us as orphans, widows and prisoners, delighting in our singers, minstrels and youth.

The date of this national epic belongs to Israel's long history: a) an initial composition during the royalty of King Saul (1020-1000 B.C.) and possibly reflecting the ritual at a northern sanctuary at Mount Tabor (vv. 11-14). Here the northern tribes like Zebulun and Naphtali besides Benjamin, Saul's tribe (v. 27), remembered the Mosaic traditions and those of the settlement in the land; b) a serious revision, highlighting Jerusalem as the new Sinai (vv. 16 and 35) during the reign of David or Solomon; c) petitionary prayers were added during a time of crisis and its mastery, perhaps the royalty of Hezekiah (715-687 B.C.) after the Assyrian invasion, or during the early halcyon days of Josiah (640-609 B.C.).

(II) This processional hymn can be structurally divided: a) a double introduction, twice calling to praise (vv. 1 and 4) and twice providing motivation (vv. 2-3 and 5-6) like two mini-hymns.

b) the body of the psalm provides the major motivation:

vv. 7-10, Sinai and wilderness experience;	vv. 19-20, 21-23, victory
vv. 11-14, early settlement;	vv. 24-27, temple procession
vv. 15-16, 17-18, Jerusalem;	vv. 28-31, petitions

c) Solemn conclusion: vv. 32-35.

(III) Vv. 1-6, introduction. While the opening lines are drawn from Num 10:35, grammatical changes from the second to the third person in addressing God stress the contemporary moment of worship. In earlier days the ark was lifted up and carried forward, for guidance and protection (Judg 20:27; 2 Sam 6:11-12) and for victory (2 Sam 11:11); at this later age it is conducted in ritual procession, to symbolize and achieve *now* what happened in the past (Pss 24; 132). Immediately we are in the midst of a magnificent theophany in v. 2, reflecting the wonder of Sinai (Exod 19:16-20), prophetical visions (Isa 6:1-4), and imagery consistently found in the Scriptures (Pss 1:4; 37:20; Isa 29:5; etc.). V. 4, *who rides upon the clouds:* a common Canaanite way of referring to Baal and frequently attributed to Yahweh (Pss 18:10; 104:3; Deut 33:26); Yahweh became the exclusive provider of life and fertility.

Vv. 7-10, Sinai and wilderness days. The reference to *rain in abundance* combines the Lord's gift of manna with that of abundant rainfall of Canaan in the late autumnal period — each were given plentifully by the Lord for Israel's full life: *cf.*, Exod 16:4, "I will *rain* bread [or manna] from heaven for you"; also Ps 78:24-25.

Vv. 11-14, a section inspired by the song of Deborah (Judg 5) and the victories of Gideon (Judg 7-8). Deborah's or Barak's army assembled at the sanctuary of Tabor (Judg 4:6), a place responsible for the earliest origin of Ps 68. V. 13 is textually difficult; the metaphor of *wings of a dove* coalesces with a series of other references, comparing Israel to a dove: Ps 56, title; Ps 74:19; Hos 7:11; 11:11 — texts that may explain the symbolism of the dove in the baptismal account of Jesus (Matt 3:16; Luke 3:22) so that Jesus is the new glorious Israel. V. 14, *Almighty*, in Hebrew *shaddai*, one of the most ancient titles for God in the Bible (Gen 17:1; 28:3; 35:11; Exod 6:3), in the psalter only here and Ps 91:1; 31x in Job, part of its archaizing style.

Vv. 15-16, 17-18, center upon the new Sinai, Jerusalem, by no means the highest mountain in Israel (even the neighboring Mount of Olives reaches higher), yet the object of envy because God and the ark dwell here. *Mountains of Bashan,* the modern Golan Heights, always disputed territory between Israel and Damascus. V. 18, *leading captives ...and receiving gifts among men,* at first referred to the booty brought to Jerusalem after a victorious war, especially during the days of David; it may also carry memories of Deborah's and Barak's earlier victory in the period of the Judges (Judg 4-5). Perhaps because of a theological scruple that God does not need human gifts, it was changed to read, in Judaism, about Moses' ascent to Mt. Sinai to receive the gift of the Torah from God *for* men, *i.e.,* for Israel. This tradition is further adapted by Eph 4:8-11 to Christ who first went down in death before rising in glory to receive the Holy Spirit and thereby distributed the gifts of various ministries within the church.

Vv. 19-20, 21-23, victory! Many historical allusions converge here, even the story of Ahab and Jezebel and their tragic end. The dogs licked the blood from their multilated bodies (1 Kgs 21:19; 22:38; 2 Kgs 9:36).

Vv. 24-27. Solemn procession, led by the ark of the covenant.

Vv. 28-31. Petitions, possibly reflecting the preservation of Jerusalem from the Assyrian attack under King Hezekiah (see Ps 46). The attitude towards foreigners remains ambiguous, less complimentary than in Isa 2:4, closer to Ps 72:8-11.

Vv. 32-35. Glorious finale to the procession and hymn. V. 35, *Terrible is God in his sanctuary:* the phrase sounded magnificently though less correctly in the Vulgate: "Mirabilis Deus in sanctis suis — wonderful is God among his saints."

(IV) Ps 68 acquired a paramount place in the liturgy for Pentecost among Jews and later among Christians. The "church year" according to a very ancient tradition was numbered according to the Sundays after Pentecost, so that liturgically as in Ps 68 we relived the movement or "procession" of Jesus through the land of Palestine in each of the Sunday gospels between Pentecost and Advent. The feast itself of Pentecost commemorated Jesus as the new Moses, receiving the new law at the new Sinai-Jerusalem, and granting plentiful gifts, particularly of ministry, among the disciples. We, as disciples, are called upon to march ahead, reliving the ancient history, guided by our ark of the covenant, the gospels, to wage fierce battles for righteousness, personally and communally, and to experience the tremendous theophanies of God's presence in our midst.

Ps 68 has been put to good and bad use! It is frequently sung for the consecration of churches and altars. It has been seared in our memory by Savonarola and his monks who sang it as they were led to their fiery death, and by the Huguenots on the black night of their martyrdom. It was a favorite battle song of the Crusaders.

Psalm 69
To The Choirmaster: According To Lilies. A Psalm Of David.

¹Save me, O God!
    For the waters have come up to my neck.

²I sink in deep mire,
    where there is no foothold;
  I have come into deep waters,
    and the flood sweeps over me.
³I am weary with my crying;
    my throat is parched.
  My eyes grow dim
    with waiting for my God.
⁴More in number than the hairs of my head
    are those who hate me without cause;
  mighty are those who would destroy me,
    those who attack me with lies.
  What I did not steal
    must I now restore?

⁵O God, thou knowest my folly;
    the wrongs I have done are not hidden from thee.

⁷For it is for thy sake that I have borne reproach,
    that shame has covered my face.
⁸I have become a stranger to my brethren,
    an alien to my mother's sons.

⁹For zeal for thy house has consumed me,
    and the insults of those who insult thee have
      fallen on me.

²⁰Insults have broken my heart,
    so that I am in despair.
  I looked for pity, but there was none;
    and for comforters, but I found none.
²¹They gave me poison for food,
    and for my thirst they gave me vinegar to drink.

> ^{22}Let their own table before them become a snare;
>   let their sacrificial feasts be a trap.
> ^{23}Let their eyes be darkened, so that they cannot see;
>   and make their loins tremble continually.
> ^{24}Pour out thy indignation upon them,
>   and let thy burning anger overtake them.
> ^{25}May their camp be a desolation,
>   let no one dwell in their tents.

(I-III) Composed possibly by a very sick person, at least by someone severely hounded by persecutors, the psalm blends sorrow and compunction with vigor and decisiveness. The structure is clear enough in English translation:

v. 1a,	call for help	vv. 13-18,	prayer
vv. 1b-4,	lament	vv. 21-22,	lament
v. 5,	confession of guilt	vv. 22-28,	prayer and curse
v. 6,	prayer		against the enemy
vv. 7-12,	lament	vv. 30-36,	thanksgiving
			(vv. 35-36,
			addition)

The many parallels with the prophecy of Jeremiah link this psalm with disciples of the great prophet of Anathoth and manifests the impact of Jeremiah upon the private piety of postexilic Israel. We cite some notable examples:

vv. 1-4,	Jer 38, in the deep mire;	vv. 19-20,	Jer 18:23, God knows; Jer 23:9, broken heart
v. 3,	Jer 45:3, crying out		
v. 7a,	Jer 15:15; 20:8, shame	vv. 22-28,	Jer 18:21-22, revenge
v. 7b,	Jer 51:51, confusion	v. 35,	"cities of Judah," over 12 times
v. 8,	Jer 12:6, stranger to family		in Jeremiah.

(IV) Our comments under I-III have been limited so that we may discuss the New Testament application of Ps 69 and the problem in general of the "curse psalms."

Ps 69 turns out to be one of the most quoted psalms in the New Testament. As the following list manifests, the citations range over the entire psalm with the largest concentration from the psalmist's prayer for revenge against the enemy (vv. 22-28):

v. 4,	John 15:25, "They hated me without a cause," about the persecution of Jesus and his disciples;
v. 9,	John 2:17, "Zeal for thy house will consume me," for Jesus' cleansing the temple; Rom 15:3, "The reproaches of those who reproached thee fell on me" so that "we who are strong might bear with the failings of the weak";
v. 21,	within the Passion account, *cf.,* Matt 27:34;
vv. 22-24,	Rom 11:9-10, "Let their feast become a snare and a trap...their eyes be darkened so that they cannot see," about those in Israel who "were hardened" and "failed to obtain what was sought."
v. 24,	Rev 16:1, "Go and pour out on the earth the seven bowls of the wrath of God" in the final, eschatological conflict;
v. 25,	Acts 1:20, "Let his habitation become desolate and let there be no one to live in it," in view of Judas Iscariot's violent end and exclusion from the ranks of the twelve apostles.

As many of these citations will manifest upon closer study, the New Testament can seriously adapt the Old Testament passage to a new theology about Jesus and world redemption. Therefore, we do not prove the New by the Old but rather look to the Old in order to enrich our insights into the mystery of the New. The New, furthermore, offers its own intuitions into the theological implications of the Old. As an example, we turn to Ps 68:10 and John 2:17. John not only applies Ps 68:10 to Jesus' anger at the merchants in the temple but also makes a further, important observation. We read this explanation in John 2:21-22, "But he spoke of the temple of his body. When therefore he was raised from the dead, his disciples remembered that he had said this; and they believed the scripture and the word which Jesus had spoken." John, therefore, moves from Jesus' wrath against sin in the temple to the wrath of God against sin in the crucified body of Jesus.

	ZEAL	FOR YOUR HOUSE	CONSUMES ME
Psalm 69	hopes and ideals of the psalmist;	for the people Israel in their sins;	psalmist is object of persecution
John 2	Jesus' hopes and ideals;	for the Jerusalem temple;	Jesus' indignation against the merchants in the temple;
Cross	Jesus' hopes and ideals;	House is now the body of Jesus on the cross;	Jesus is consumed by death;
Today	Jesus' hopes and ideals;	House is the church, the body of the Lord;	Suffering members of the church.

This variation in the meaning of "House" from the people of Israel, to the Jerusalem temple, to Jesus' suffering body on the cross, to the suffering members of the church today, unites our prayer with a rich tradition, with major saints of the Old and New Testament, with the disciples of Jeremiah, with Jesus and his disciples, with the martyrs of our contemporary church.

The fact that the New Testament quotes several times from the prayer for revenge (vv. 22-28) shows that Christianity cannot disregard the "curse psalms" as beneath its elevated spirituality! The New Testament quotes without qualification. Nonetheless, the curse psalms are not easily understood. Here we propose a series of reasons for supporting these passages in the Bible as the inspired word of God today. No single reason is sufficient of itself. Even if the entire exposition leaves us at least partially unsatisfied, then we admit again that for something as negative and horrendous as violence, there will never be a satisfactory explanation. We begin with more factual data and conclude with the more convincing reasons.

1) Biblical exaggeration. Semitic people are eloquent. Both praises and curses are executed with elegance! Some vindictive phrases that strike us as grim, even ghastly, like "Happy shall he be who takes your little ones and dashes them against the rock" (Ps 137:9), belonged to "conventional lament motifs" of the Ancient Near East (Sabourin, 319). "Children" in this case stood for all the inhabitants, particularly the adults; "rock" meant the walls of the enemy city. The entire phrase prayed for the conquest and leveling of the enemy city (*cf.,* Isa 13:15-16; Jer 14:1).

2) Out of the liturgy of Israel there emerged the curse of the foreign countries that fought against God's people and eventually the prophetic oracles against the nations (Isa 13:23; Ezek 25:32; 38-39). Associated with Israel's wars of preservation would be the practice at times of the extermination warfare (Deut 20:4, 10-20). Just as Christianity has not yet thought through the theological implications of modern warfare, neither did Israel arrive at an adequate religious position on ancient warfare — despite scattered attempts by the prophets (*cf.,* Isa 2:1-4). It is also possible that the curse psalms represented a popular way of praying for protection against individual oppressors or a temple liturgy for blessing the army (see Pss 20 and 21). Finally, Israel possessed ceremonies of excommunication for serious offenses or for contagious diseases (Deut 17:12-13; 19:16-21; Num 5:11-31; Lev 13-14).

3) Different from our religious books, the Bible at times can simply be a record of what happened, without defending or excusing the action. The episode of Abraham in Egypt (Gen 12:10-20) or Judah "in the land of Canaan" (Gen 37) are not explicitly and directly condemned. Yet the larger context of the patriarchal stories would make these two incidents appear less than noble! Included in the record of what happened would be the people's exasperation under long oppression; curses would be almost like a valve to release pressure, a healthy way of controlling anger.

4) Biblical spirituality realistically admits that sin always brings sorrow, at least for the larger community. (The reverse is not always the case: sorrow does not necessarily mean personal sin — see Pss 7; 50:16-21). What the Bible adds to this law of human life is a disciplinary or purifying process in the suffering that follows sin (*cf.,* Jer 2:5, 18). Suffering not only trains us to be more careful in the future, but produces a strength of patience and endurance that comes in no other way (*cf.,* Ps 12). The curse psalms ask God to further this process of sin-suffering-purification in ourselves and in our enemies.

5) The Bible endorses a theology of union, not substitution, for the redemption of sin. The suffering of good people does not substitute for what evil people should endure nor by itself does it obtain pardon for them (*cf.,* Ps 51). Through a strong bond of love and life, good people bear the wickedness of the evil. Yet, this happens in the sense that each of us have our share of goodness and our share of evil. Each person bears something of the evil of every other person. According to this interpretation, salvation is granted more to the entire family of the elect than to individuals, one by one! We are saved as a family. *Cf.,* Isa 53:5, "He was wounded for our transgression, he was·bruised for our iniquities; upon him was the chastisement [literally, discipline] that made us whole. . .," a profound statement, verified in all great saints in the Old and New Testament, as in the case of Moses (Deut 1:37; 3:26) and of Jesus (Matt 8:17). In cursing the enemy we too suffer, because we belong at least to the same family of the human race.

6) Biblical anthropology did not make the theoretical distinction between sin, which we hate, and sinner whom we love. The Bible is more realistic. If sin exists, it exists in the sinner. This approach may seem cruel, when it curses the sinner. Yet, it also enabled the Bible to deal, perhaps more practically than happens at times in Christianity, with the seriousness of sin in the sinner.

7) The curse psalms are the prayer of people, so oppressed and even so dehumanized by their suffering that they are no longer able to pray. People in concentration camps, prisons

and ghetto slums can be turned into sub-human wrecks of humanity. Yet, if these people could pray, their only possible words would be: "God destroy the oppressor who has done this to my parents, my spouse, my children, my brothers and sisters." How else would the Nazi concentration camps have been liberated? We also hear an echo of the biblical question, "How long, O Lord?" (Pss 13:1-2; 35:17). These dehumanized people, however, cannot pray; they must be human for that act. Surely, there ought to be some place in biblical religion — in the Bible, in the synagogue and in the church — where their prayer — if they could say it — would be shouted to the world, not every day, nor on every page of the Bible, but somewhere some time.

8) No nation in recorded history has suffered more than Israel. The people, then, who composed the curse psalms against the enemy suffered the most themselves! Granted that the identity of "enemy" in the psalms is one of the most difficult questions to unravel, we must still recognize that wherever Israel was an enemy of God and failed in God's ideals of compassion and helpfulness, God attacked that enemy fiercely — to root out the evil, to purify the people, and to prepare a nation acceptable to the Lord. If we recite the curse psalms today, we are almost taking a vow to suffer. God will not let us at peace till we are fully purified ourselves.

Psalm 70

An individual lament, found earlier almost verbatim in Ps 40:13-17. Here in Ps 70, the divine name is *'elohim* rather than Yahweh, as to be expected in the Elohistic Psalter (Pss 42-89). While Ps 40 is disconnected and plagued with difficulties, Ps 70 is a lapidary piece, carefully cut and polished from start to finish.

Psalm 71

> ¹In thee, O Lord, do I take refuge;
> let me never be put to shame!

²In thy righteousness deliver me and rescue me;
  incline thy ear to me, and save me!
³Be thou to me a rock of refuge,
  a strong fortress, to save me,
    for thou art my rock and my fortress.

⁴Rescue me, O my God, from the hand of the wicked,
  from the grasp of the unjust and cruel man.
⁵For thou, O Lord, art my hope,
  my trust, O Lord, from my youth.
⁶Upon thee I have leaned from my birth;
  thou art he who took me from my mother's womb.
  My praise is continually of thee.

¹²O God, be not far from me;
  O my God, make haste to help me!
¹³May my accusers be put to shame and consumed;
  with scorn and disgrace may they be covered
  who seek my hurt.

¹⁷O God, from my youth thou hast taught me,
  and I still proclaim thy wondrous deeds.
¹⁸So even to old age and gray hairs,
  O God, do not forsake me,
 till I proclaim thy might
  to all the generations to come.
Thy power ¹⁹and thy righteousness, O God,
  reach the high heavens.

Thou who hast done great things,
  O God, who is like thee?

Each psalm, but especially Ps 71, needs to be understood according to its style and spirit of composition, and in this case that means by long reflective prayer on the psalm. Composed by an elderly person (vv. 9 and 18), consecrated to God from birth either as a levite or even a nazirite (Num 6:1-21), afflicted by new trials in advanced years (vv. 10-11, 13, 20), this person speaks with the language of the ancient psalms which have become part of bone and blood. In many ways Ps 71 is a filigree of other laments or songs of thanksgiving:

vv. 1-3,	Ps 31:1-3a	v. 13,	Ps 35:4, 26
vv. 5-6,	Ps 22:9-10	v. 18,	Ps 22:30-31
v. 12a,	Ps 22: 1, 11, 19	v. 19,	Ps 36:6
v. 12b,	Ps 38:22; 40:13		

Lines and phrases blend smoothly, and the same meditative tone continues in the modulation from confidence (vv. 1, 3, 5-6, 7-8, 14-15, 18b-19, 20-21), to prayer for help (vv. 2, 4, 9, 12, 18a), lament (vv. 10-11), prayer against the enemy (v. 13), praise (vv. 16, 17), and thanksgiving (vv. 22-24). The tone is so tranquil, even in speaking of the enemy, and the overall spirit so confident, that it is difficult to decide if the psalm is one of individual lament or of confidence. Because the psalmist, even in old age, and possibly in critical illness is hounded to the grave (v. 20) by whispers and inuendo, this very person who was once a source of strength and instruction to others, is now reaching out for consolation and assistance. We classify the psalm as an individual lament. Ps 71 is one of the very few psalms, written by an elderly person for the elderly. Yet, whatever our age, we all need this psalm so that we too will find our praise, our prayer, our confidence, *in thee, O Lord.* The final emphasis, again and again in Ps 71, lies in the Lord.

Psalm 72
A Psalm Of Solomon.

I

¹Give the king thy justice, O God,
   and thy righteousness to the royal son!
²May he judge thy people with righteousness,
   and thy poor with justice!
³Let the mountains bear prosperity for the people,
   and the hills, in righteousness!

II-a

⁴May he defend the cause of the poor of the people,
  give deliverance to the needy,
  and crush the oppressor!

⁵May he live while the sun endures,
  and as long as the moon, throughout all generations!
⁶May he be like rain that falls on the mown grass,
  like showers that water the earth!
⁷In his days may righteousness flourish,
  and peace abound, till the moon be no more!

-b-

⁸May he have dominion from sea to sea,
  and from the River to the ends of the earth!
⁹May his foes bow down before him,
  and his enemies lick the dust!
¹⁰May the kings of Tarshish and of the isles
  render him tribute,
  may the kings of Sheba and Seba bring gifts!
¹¹May all kings fall down before him,
  all nations serve him!

-c-

¹²For he delivers the needy when he calls,
  the poor and him who has no helper.
¹³He has pity on the weak and the needy,
  and saves the lives of the needy.
¹⁴From oppression and violence he redeems their life;
  and precious is their blood in his sight.

-d-

¹⁵Long may he live,
  may gold of Sheba be given to him!
 May prayer be made for him continually,
  and blessings invoked for him all the day!

III

¹⁶May there be abundance of grain in the land;
  on the tops of the mountains may it wave;
  may its fruit be like Lebanon;

and may men blossom forth from the cities
  like the grass of the field!
17 May his name endure for ever,
  his fame continue as long as the sun!
May men bless themselves by him,
  all nations call him blessed!

IV

18 Blessed be the Lord, the God of Israel,
  who alone does wondrous things.
19 Blessed be his glorious name for ever;
  may his glory fill the whole earth!
  Amen and Amen!

V

20 The prayers of David, the son of Jesse, are ended.

(I) Composed for a royal anniversary, most likely of the king's enthronement, this psalm communicates in elevated poetic form how God's hopes and promises for Israel were entrusted to the Davidic kings, who in fact were God's viceregent (or "lieutenant," in the literal meaning of that word, "holding the place of") — see Ps 2. The human person of the king, like the human words of Scripture, became the point of contact between Israel and God, the mediator and symbol of God's blessings and even of God's presence. Royalty was an ancient institution, locked into Near Eastern history, and yet it was able to address the future. Surprisingly enough, when the Davidic royalty collapsed in 587 B.C., the royal psalms did not fall into desuetude but were re-read as announcements of the future king and tended to express ever more clearly the purest hopes for the messianic age. When human institutions failed to fulfill their inherent promises, these promises could be faced ever more clearly as God's special, mysterious pledge, to be achieved ever more divinely and sublimely.

Ps 72 does not seem as ancient as Ps 2 or 110; it manifests contact with Isaiah (Isa 9:2-7; 11:1-9). For this reason it may have been composed for a festival, honoring Isaiah's favorite king, Hezekiah (715-687 B.C.). It is also likely that vv. 5

and 10 were added still later, after the exile and under the influence of Isa 60:6-10, when the former Davidic dynasty had been transformed into a messianic hope for future times.

Most of all, Ps 72 represents the biblical sense of *shalom* or peace, the fullest integration of life's blessings, be these physical, emotional or religious, reaching into economics and politics, throughout the Israelite kingdom and across the world — the fullest union of heaven and earth, God and the human family. Although this "international" and even "cosmic" feature was present from the beginning, due not only to Yahweh as the one God of the universe, but also to royal protocol across the ancient Near East, still its full meaning for the "messianic" age became apparent only after the exile when the Davidic dynasty had actually disappeared, due to its own serious mistakes and the mightier armies of the Babylonians and Persians. Yet, the ideal of an integral unity between heaven and earth remained; God's messianic kingdom was never to be an ethereal reality of "souls," but one that embraced and transfigured our human existence. The Bible is always calling us to wholeness, not to fragmented transcendence.

(II) The division of this royal psalm must take into consideration its place at the end of the Second Book of the Psalter (Pss 42-72). At present, vv. 18-19 form a closing doxology for Book Two; v. 20, *the prayers of David...are ended,* forms a conclusion to Books I and II, which began with the royal enthronement psalm (Ps 2) and which include the largest collection of Davidic psalms, fifty-five altogether. Originally, vv. 18-19 may have belonged to Ps 72 as a liturgical or community finale. The psalm can be subdivided:

vv. 1-3, Introduction, summarizing the blessings of Davidic royalty;
vv. 4-7, 8-11, 12-14, 15, Individual strophes in praise of the king;
vv. 16-17, Conclusion, summarizing the justice and fertility granted by God through the Davidic kings, linking up with the words in v. 1, *justice* and *royal son* or fertility.

vv. 18-19, Conclusion of Book Two of the Psalter (Pss 42-72);
v. 20, Conclusion of Books One and Two of the Psalter, the major
Davidic collection of psalms.

(III) Vv. 1-3, Introductory prayer and acclamation in
honor of the king, who is to achieve God's righteousness and
justice, a public fulfillment of God's promises, especially
among the poor, for that would then mean everywhere. For
the mountains [to] *bear prosperity* [*shalom*] indicates the
strength and abundance of all good things whereby an
integral and consistent good life surrounds everyone. The
phrase, *give the king justice*, probably refers to a ritual act,
either at the enthronement of the king or on its anniversary
celebration, when the tablets of the law are handed to the
king, to support him and to receive his obedience (Deut
17:18-20; 1 Sam 10:25 — A. A. Anderson). *Royal son* not
only indicates legitimacy in the Davidic family but also
fertility, a good sign for prosperity across the land.

Vv. 4-7, Fertility and Compassion. The key motif in this
stanza is the rich rainfall, that spreads life across the country
(*cf.,* Hos 6:3; Isa 45:8; 55:10-11). This life is to be shared
evenly and is frequently associated with good health and
care for the poor (2 Sam 23:1-17; Isa 11:1-9). Fertility and
parenthood always bring a new tenderness into people's
lives; the association of life with royalty emphasizes *the
cause of the poor* across the land.

Vv. 8-11, Power and Expansion. The psalm reflects the
ideal limits of the Davidic empire: from the borders of Egypt
north beyond Damascus to the Euphrates River, from the
Transjordan plains westward to the Mediterranean Sea
(Gen 15:18; Exod 23:31; Deut 1:7; 1 Kgs 4:21; Sir 44:21).
The references, moreover, to *sea, river* and *ends of the earth*
carry a strong mythological image of the raging oceans
which surround the earth and which have to be kept always
behind strong barriers, as we saw in Ps 46 or again in Ps
89:9-14. The king's victory is really God's achievement. V.
10 reflects another series of biblical references to David's or
Solomon's far flung trading empire, enhanced with time so
as to become symbolic in Isa 60:6-10 of an eschatological

domain: *Tarshish* in western Spain, colonized by the Phoenicians (Isa 23:1; 60:9); *the isles*, scattered over the Mediterranean, especially around Greece (Ps 97:1; Isa 11:11; 24:15); *Sheba*, in southern Arabia, modern Yemen (Gen 10:7, 28; Jer 6:20); *Seba*, probably modern Ethiopia, the home of the Queen who visited Solomon (1 Kgs 10; Gen 10:7; Isa 43:3).

Vv. 12-14. This time the poor are considered blood relatives of the king and he is obliged to come to their rescue out of affectionate loyalty; the Hebrew words for *redeem* (*ga'al*) and *blood* carry this connotation (*cf.,* Ps 19).

Vv. 15-17. The patriarchal blessings, especially to Abraham, are fulfilled through the king, through whom *people bless themselves* (v. 17), *cf.,* Gen 12:2-3; 22:18; 26:4.

(IV) The long history of the Davidic dynasty assures us that no hope or ideal is bestowed by God in vain. It will be fulfilled beyond our expectations, even if at times everything seems lost. From the very first we are given signals, that may seem too fantastic to be true; yet they sustain us over the long haul. The extended preparation is not meant to spiritualize the final fulfillment but to share the peace or prosperity with a family beyond our expectations. This sharing of God's gifts focuses upon fertility and life, tenderness and justice. These qualities interact with one another, blending in such a way as to produce the finest human virtues. As this psalm ultimately points to Jesus, we see how Jesus is born out of our human stock but he also brings it to a fulfillment of hopes beyond our human ability and dreams.